CHINA
AND HER
NEIGHBOURS

CHINA AND HER NEIGHBOURS

ASIAN DIPLOMACY FROM ANCIENT HISTORY TO THE PRESENT

MICHAEL TAI

ZED

Zed Books
Bloomsbury Publishing Plc
50 Bedford Square, London, WC1B 3DP, UK
1385 Broadway, New York, NY 10018, USA
29 Earlsfort Terrace, Dublin 2, Ireland

First published in Great Britain 2019
This edition published in Great Britain, 2021

Cover design: Alice Marwick
Cover image © Philadelphia History Museum at the Atwater Kent,
Courtesy of Historical Society of Pennsylvania Collection, Bridgeman Image

ISBN: HB: 978-1-7869-9776-0
PB: 978-1-7869-9777-7
ePDF: 978-1-7869-9780-7
eBook: 978-1-7869-9779-1

Printed and bound in Great Britain

To find out more about our authors and books visit
www.bloomsbury.com and sign up for our newsletters.

To my dad

CONTENTS

ACKNOWLEDGEMENTS

This book is the fruit of two years of research on the East and South China Seas at the University of Cambridge's Centre of Development Studies. The topic arose in consultation with Peter Nolan about the maritime disputes in the East and South China Seas. The aim at the outset was to understand the causes of the conflict for which it is necessary to study the history of the region. Conflicts arise where there is a lack of trust and the maritime disputes present a timely opportunity to explore the nature of China's relations with her maritime neighbours.

This book would not have been possible without generous funding from the Cambridge China Development Trust and the Cambridge Malaysian Education and Development Trust for which I am deeply grateful to Peter Nolan and Anil Seal. I am equally indebted to Chris Henson for his careful proof-reading and editorial suggestions. Writing a book involves a good deal of personal effort, but I gained courage and insights from friends and colleagues along the way. My sincere gratitude goes to Hong Hai, Ian Randall, Michael Quicke, James Houston, Jens Zimmerman, Simon Mitton, Walter van Herck, Helena Hurd and Pavel Suian. Last but not least, I remember the staff and students of St. Edmund's College which became my home during the writing of this book.

ACKNOWLEDGMENTS

CHAPTER 1

INTRODUCTION: CAN THE WORLD TRUST CHINA?

China's reemergence as a leading economy has prompted sharp debate about her role in the world. There are concerns and even anxiety in some quarters about her rise and what it could mean for the international order. Is China a responsible stakeholder? Will she foster peace and prosperity or pursue her own interests at others' expense? Is she a benign giant or a recalcitrant troublemaker? Humanity faces the threat of financial crisis, global warming and cataclysmic war which can only be countered through international collaboration. Cooperation requires trust, but on whose terms can China be trusted?

The history of bilateral relations is an important determinant of trust between states. History is memory. It is the record of past events and conduct, and former cooperative relations build trust whereas a history of aggression and treachery destroys it. Empathy is an equally important factor. It is the ability to put oneself in the other's shoes to see things from their perspective. We are more likely to trust those who show they understand us especially when demonstrated through deeds. Empathy requires an understanding of the other's history and culture, and has the potential to build trust even when there is none. Current opinions about China, however, are influenced by deeply rooted cultural and ideological biases. The 19th century French-Russian sociologist Jacques Novikov coined the term 'yellow peril' to embody a psycho-cultural perception of threat from the East. It expressed a vaguely ominous, existential fear of the vast, faceless, nameless horde of yellow people opposite the Western world which Kaiser Wilhelm II of Germany invoked to urge European empires to invade, conquer and colonize China.[1] How we construe ourselves and the world matters because our intuition shapes our fears, impressions and relationships.[2] Writing in the 1960s, sinologist Raymond Dawson confessed that for many in the West, China is 'mainly associated with such trivialities as pigtails, slant eyes, lanterns, laundries, pidgin English, chopsticks, and bird's nest soup'.[3] Although the 'whimsical notions of a quaint civilization in a setting which resembles the design on a willow-pattern plate' have since been updated by increased trade and travel, many racial and political stereotypes live on. John K. Fairbank warned early on that Chinese society is very different from America, and that US policymakers would fail unless they took the difference into account.[4] The greatest lesson of Vietnam, according to Robert McNamara, was to know one's enemy:[5]

What went wrong was a basic misunderstanding or misevaluation of the threat to our security represented by the North Vietnamese. It led President Eisenhower in 1954 to say that if Vietnam were lost, or if Laos and Vietnam were lost, the dominoes would fall. I am certain we exaggerated the threat. We didn't know our opposition. We didn't understand the Chinese; we didn't understand the Vietnamese, particularly the North Vietnamese. So the first lesson is know your opponents. I want to suggest to you that we don't know our potential opponents today.[6]

It is ill-advised to form opinions about a nation without reference to its history, and it would be a grave mistake to study China in a historical vacuum considering only the People's Republic of China today. Chinese leaders are acutely in tune with their country's long history which continues to shape their thinking in powerful ways, while Western policymakers remain narrowly focused on contemporary China with some still referring to it as 'communist China', a label infused with Cold War presuppositions. Although the country is ruled by the communist party, the pillars of communism such as state ownership of all property, a centrally planned economy and monopoly of political power by the working class, have long given way to private ownership, market economy and inclusive political representation; the party now represents the interest of every social class and counts tycoons among its members. Marxism and Leninism were not ends in themselves but means to achieve the fundamental goals of China's leaders, namely, freedom from foreign imperialism, unification of the nation, creation of effective political power, establishment of stability, and the building of prosperity and prestige. From Beijing's perspective, there are better ways to achieve well-being than by adopting Western policies which have produced much social, economic and political malaise around the world.[7] Asia is undergoing fundamental change, but no single conceptual model is sufficient to describe the evolving Asian system. There is growing interdependence and cooperation among state and non-state actors with China increasingly at the centre of this evolution but neither realist nor liberal international relations theory is able to capture the complexities of the region.[8] Instead a stronger grasp of the region's history is necessary to make sense of the shift.

The purpose of this book is to shed light on the political culture and foreign policy of the Chinese state by examining the history of her relations with her neighbours. Just as we judge a person by his deeds, so too can we understand a country by its history. China's relations with her maritime neighbours dates back more than two thousand years and provides rich material by which to discern her self-understanding and place in the world. Outside of narrow specialist circles, however, the history of the region is not widely known, even among East Asians. Each country's secondary school curriculum focuses on its own history and devotes little space to regional history and geography. Public opinion is shaped by news reports which convey a piecemeal and often skewed perspective. Anyone under 40 today was born after the Vietnam War, and among those who remember the conflict, few know why America intervened or what the French were doing in Indochina before that. What were China's relations with Vietnam at that time and how did the Chinese respond to French encroachment there? Why did Japan invade China in the 1930s even though she looked up to the latter for centuries as the fount of civilization? When and why did the Chinese migrate to Southeast Asia, and what did they encounter there? How were they received by the local population and their colonial rulers, and what role do the Chinese immigrant communities play today in China's relations with Southeast Asian states? And what is the history of the territorial claims in the East and South China Seas? The question of China's rise has attracted much attention since the reforms of 1978, and became particularly salient in the wake of the 2008 Global Financial Crisis. The resultant discourses convey many conflicting messages about China and her ambitions. This work takes a fresh look at the evolution of China's regional diplomatic and strategic thinking via the use of case studies related to maritime history. It begins with Japan and the Ryukyu Kingdom before moving to Vietnam, the Philippines and Malaysia. By telling the story of China's engagement with her maritime neighbours, the author hopes the reader will gain a deeper understanding of that nation.

CHAPTER 2

CHINA AND JAPAN

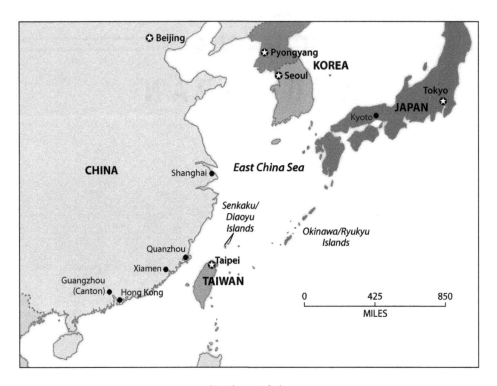

Northeast Asia

EARLY CONTACTS

On 12 April 1784, a farmer preparing an irrigation ditch on Shikano Island in Kyushu, Japan unearthed a large, stone box-like structure. It took two adults to lift the stone slab off the top and inside the box they found a gold seal. The five Chinese characters inscribed on the seal identified it as the seal of the King of Nu, a state of Wa (Japan) and a vassal of the Han Empire. The seal is believed to have been cast in China and bestowed by Emperor Guangwu 光武帝 (5 BC–57 AD) to an envoy bearing tribute from Japan in 57 AD. Made of 95 per cent pure gold, the seal consists of a 2.4 centimetre square base with a handle on top in the shape of a coiled serpent. Recorded in the *History of Later Han* 後漢書 (445 AD), it was the first mention of Japan in Chinese chronicles, but legends about Japan circulated long before.[1]

According to early Chinese legends, ancient Japan was an island of magic plants, animals and immortals.[2] It was a land of golden vegetables with mulberry trees rising a thousand metres from the sea. A 3,000-year-old divine beast resembling a horse with eight dragon wings lived on the island, and carried the Yellow Emperor (said to live circa 2,600 BC) on tours of his realm. Divine spirits protected the island making access hazardous: approaching ships faced opposing winds and currents, or the island itself would mysteriously sink into the ocean. Chinese legends place the first contact between China and Japan at 1,000 BC when a sage king ruled China. A messenger bearing a rare fragrant herb from Japan came to pay homage to the king, praising the host kingdom's prosperity and tranquility. But in truth, the Chinese knew very little about Japan, a land situated across the waters of the East China Sea; primitive navigational and shipbuilding technology made regular contact impossible, and knowledge about the other was mostly hearsay.

According to the History of the Later Han, the first Qin emperor, seeking immortality, sent the Taoist alchemist Xu Fu 徐福 in search of a life-saving plant on an island in the Eastern Sea 東海. After several years, Xu Fu came back empty handed. Fearing punishment, he claimed he was stopped on the way by the Sea God who demanded him to bring 'young boys, virgins and craftsmen of every kind' as gifts in exchange for the plant of longevity.[3] The emperor ordered the construction of a fleet of 60 ships to send Xu Fu off again in 219 BC with a crew of 5,000, and 3,000 each of boys and girls. Not surprisingly, he failed to return and is said to have settled instead on an island believed to be Japan. The farming techniques and many plants that Xu brought are believed to explain the abrupt end to Japan's 6,000-year Jōmon 繩文 hunter-gatherer culture and the rise of the agricultural economy of the Yayoi 弥生 period. The many temples in Japan honouring Xu Fu as the god of farming, god of medicine and god of silk lend credence to the Chinese accounts.

More reliable information about the Japanese came only in 57 AD when the Wa emissary arrived at the Han court and received the aforementioned gold seal. The Chinese records described the Wa people in great detail: they dwelled on a mountainous island southeast of Korea (most likely referring to Kyushu) and formed more than a hundred communities, some of which maintained diplomatic ties with the Han court through envoys and scribes. The Wa walked barefooted, ate with their hands from bamboo and wooden trays, and lived to over a hundred years. It was an egalitarian society with 'no distinction between father and son, men and women'.[4]

The Chinese did not set foot on Japanese soil until some two hundred years later when in 240 AD an envoy from the Wei court (220–265) arrived. From then on, there were regular exchanges of emissaries until the end of the Tang dynasty (618–907) which yielded a trove of information that revealed a colourful Japan with a rich history. Japan then appeared in successive Chinese dynastic records including the histories of the Wei 魏, the Liu-Song 劉宋, the Sui 隋, the Tang 唐, the Song 宋, the Yuan 元 and the Ming 明. The Chinese learned that the Japanese tattooed their bodies, dyed their teeth black and practised divination in a process similar to tortoise shell divination in China. Women outnumbered men and polygamy was common. Some men had four or five wives which did not seem to produce domestic strife; the women were faithful and trusting, and sat alongside men at social gatherings. The society had strict norms and punishment for offences was severe. For a misdemeanour, the offender could lose his wife and children and for grave offences, his entire family could be exterminated. Murderers, robbers and rapists were sentenced to death. Crime was low, and litigation rare.

Society was organized into clans which pooled resources to reclaim land, build irrigation, grow crops and construct stockades for protection. They formed regional groups which the Chinese called *guo* 国 or states, some thirty of which emerged as powerful contenders for hegemony, and sent messengers to gain Chinese recognition. Records show Nuguo 奴国, a state in northern Kyūshū, requesting the bestowal of titles and emblems such as gold seals and bronze mirrors which conferred rank in the imperial hierarchy. To handle such requests, the Chinese instituted an investiture system and gift exchanges which developed into the tribute system. Japan belonged to the family of tribute states, but as a distant island across the sea, it did not command the same attention as continental neighbours until the modern era.

TRIBUTE SYSTEM

The tribute system originated in the Western Zhou dynasty (1046–771 BC) and institutionalized relations between the Zhou king and his subjects. Relations were ranked according to geographic distance between king and subject. A subject belonged to one of five classes with respective rites to affirm subordination and obligations to the court. A sovereign-vassal relationship was established through titles and seals, and maintained by regularly exchange of gifts. The vassal obeyed the king in return for political and military support.[5] A paternalistic system requiring the king to give more than he received, it created a community of states which was an extension of the domestic political order and became the framework for China's foreign relations for centuries. It was based on the assumption of Chinese primacy even though the Chinese did not maintain a large army, and her neighbours were awed more by the force of her civilization than her military might. The size of the empire, coupled with a sophisticated government bureaucracy, infrastructure, art, literature, philosophy, medicine and culinary culture, earned wide admiration and respect. The more sinicized a state, the more it was considered civilized, and political association with China was seen as a source of legitimacy and prestige. The tribute system served as a trade and diplomatic network through which states interacted with each other often using Chinese writing and protocol. It comprised a core of sinicized states followed by more distant ones. The core states of Korea, Japan and Vietnam adopted the Chinese writing system, Confucianism and Buddhism, and Chinese-style bureaucracy and statutes.[6] Other tribute states included Formosa, Ryukyu, Annam, Cambodia, Siam, Champa, Samudra, Java, Pahang, Paihua, Palembang and Brunei.[7]

The tributary system was not a static framework centred on China but a delicate equilibrium, sensitive to the needs of all parties. Relations ranged from total subjugation to *de facto* equality, and member states were not passive subjects, but dynamic players of international politics, with each deciding the timing for establishing or ending ties with China. A vassal sought Chinese titles to enhance prestige at home and abroad, but sometimes chose to ignore Chinese policies, stopped bringing tribute and even clashed with the suzerain. The vassal was not a satellite and relations often descended into mere form.[8] The tribute system also sought to mollify, if not defuse, security threats, but the nomad tribes of the northern steppes who plundered Chinese towns and villages for grain, metals and textiles were a perennial danger. The Chinese sought to keep them at bay with trade, diplomacy, warfare and alliances.[9] Emperor Wu 漢武帝 (140–87 BC) befriended the Scythians (Yuezhi 月氏) in order to check the Xiongnu 匈奴.[10] Li Yuan 李渊, founder of the Tang dynasty, turned to the Eastern Turks for support against the Sui. The Tang court later allied with Uighurs to put down rebels and fend off the Tibetans.

Depending on the balance of power, nomads were peers and sometimes the stronger party in the alliance.[11] On the whole, the Chinese preferred to keep peace using a 'loose rein' or *jimi* 羈縻制 system of autonomous rule distinct from the tribute system.[12] The Chinese saw little gain in conquering nomad lands which were 'stony fields' with tribes resistant to Chinese culture. Nor were they keen to adopt them as vassals and bear the consequent obligations of a suzerain either.[13] Formidable cavalrymen, the nomads conquered huge swathes of northern China between the fourth and sixth centuries and succeeded in bringing the whole country under their rule during the Yuan (1279–1368) and the Qing (1644–1911) dynasties.

JAPAN IN THE TRIBUTE SYSTEM

Japanese emissaries came sporadically. After the first Wa mission in 57 AD, no emissaries came for the next fifty years. Between the first and ninth centuries, there were active periods as well as long dormant ones. No Wa visitors came during the second and early third centuries, but there were four missions (238, 243, 245, and 247) in a span of nine years. The erratic tempo suggests that the Japanese set their own agenda. In the seventh century, an important shift occurred; five Japanese ambassadors came from 600 to 614 but none requested Chinese titles. The once coveted honours lost value after Japan achieved political unity and no longer looked to Chinese institutions to confer legitimacy. Material and cultural interests often went hand in hand, and during the Sui and the Tang, Japanese diplomats used their offices to purchase precious wares while studying Chinese culture and institutions. After a lapse of twenty-three years from the first (630) mission to the Tang court, seven came from 653 to 701, a period when the Japanese imperial household went through six emperors and an empress in brisk succession. In the eighth century, missions averaged one every ten years, and in the ninth century, one every thirty years. The fluctuation in frequency reflected Japan's needs and sovereignty within the tribute system.

In addition to titles and wares, the Japanese sought talent, learning and craftsmanship. In 284, senior Wa officials travelled to Baekje (in Korea), a Chinese vassal, to hire the scholar Wang Ren 王仁 to tutor their crown prince.[14] Baekje sent Confucian scholars and specialists in medicine, divination, astronomy, calendrical science and music to serve the Wa court. Wa ambassadors recruited seamstresses, weavers, tanners and physicians, while blacksmiths, potters, saddlers, brocade weavers, painters, interpreters, irrigation engineers, sericulturists and carpenters came from the ranks of refugees. According to the *Shoku Nihongi* 続日本紀, an 8th century court-commissioned history, Yuan Jinqing 袁晉卿 went to Japan in 735 at the age of 18, and taught Chinese phonetics 唐音 at the Japanese court academy 大学寮.[15] Wa diplomats succeeded after repeated attempts to bring the renowned Buddhist monk Jianzhen 鑒真 to Japan in 754.[16]

RELATIONS WITH THE TANG

Ancient Japan was primitive compared to China, and the Tang referred to the Wa as 'eastern barbarians' 東夷. The Tang (618–907) was the most cosmopolitan dynasty in Chinese history, and saw the wide appropriation by Japan of Chinese ideas and institutions.[17] The assumption was that China had all that mattered, and Japan would only improve by learning from it. From 630 onward, Wa monks, students and officials, as many as six hundred at a time, travelled to the capital Chang'an 長安 to study Chinese technology, social system, history, philosophy, art and architecture. The Wa copied the Tang political system and bureaucracy, modelled Heian-kyō 平安京 (today's Kyōto), the Japanese capital (794–1868) after Chang'an (today's Xian), adopted Chinese writing, dress and culinary habits, and some even became scholar officials in China. The gifted Abe no Nakamaro 阿倍の仲麻呂 (698–770) travelled to China at the age of 19 and gained entry to the Taixue 太學 or Imperial Academy, the highest institution of learning at the time. He obtained the highest degree 進士 in the civil service examinations in 727 and was given senior positions in Chang'an and served as governor-general of An-nam 安南 (present day northern Vietnam), a Chinese province at the time. Among his friends were the poets Li Bai 李白 and Wang Wei 王維. After sixteen years in China, he asked to return home, but permission was not granted until 752. On the voyage home, he was shipwrecked off the An-nam coast and made his way back to the capital. Never able to return to Japan, Nakamaro lived 53 years in China, and became an icon of Sino-Japanese amity.[18]

In 663, however, Yamato Japan joined forces with Baekje against a combined Tang and Silla army on the Korean peninsula, which at the time was divided into three rival kingdoms – Baekje, Silla and Goguryeo. This was the first Sino-Japanese conflict in history. At the Battle of Baekgang 白江戰鬪, Japan suffered its greatest defeat in premodern history. In a naval engagement on the River Baek, the numerically superior Japanese lost 400 ships and 10,000 men. The fiasco stunned the Yamato court which did not attack Korea again for the next 900 years. The war was costly on several fronts. Fearing a Tang or Silla invasion in the wake of Baekgang debacle, the Yamato court built a huge network of shore fortifications which drained the imperial treasury. The campaign cost Japan a key ally, Baekje, as well as direct trade and access to Chinese technology and culture. Japan sought to rebuild ties with China and dispatched its first mission after 32 years in 702. As a change in name might help to mend fences and lend a fresh start, the emissaries, led by Awata no Mahito 粟田の真人, asked the empress Wu Zetian 武則天 (685–704) if their country could be called Japan日本 instead of Wa, the name given by the Chinese. They explained that Wa was no longer a minor entity, but a union of several states called the Yamato kingdom. The Tang empress agreed and peace reigned for nearly a millennium, with much progress made in culture, trade and diplomacy, until the last decades of the Tang when Chinese prestige suffered following the devastating An Lushan Rebellion (755–763). Spanning the reign of three emperors, the prolonged revolt by the Sogdian general An Lushan 安禄山 severely weakened the empire and led to the loss of most of central Asia. Japan continued to learn from China but with diminished esteem.

RELATIONS WITH THE SONG

Trade with Japan accelerated during the Northern Song (960–1127) with Chinese vessels calling at Japanese ports 106 times. The Chinese needed metals for reconstruction after the destruction of the last years of the Tang. In exchange for gold, metal ores, fans, screens and swords, the Chinese sold silk, porcelains, medicine and artwork to Japan. Song coins were exported in large quantities, which spurred the Japanese economy and remained in circulation for several centuries. The merchant vessels were mostly Chinese boats carrying crews of sixty to seventy men that sailed from ports on the lower Yangzi across the East China Sea to Chikanoshima, Hakata and Tsuruga.[19] Chinese records offer a glimpse of how the Japanese were treated under Chinese law. When a crew member of a Japanese ship, the Higō Tōtaro, struck dead a Chinese person, the court ordered him to be put in chains and sent home to be tried under the Japanese law. Japanese boats shipwrecked on the Chinese coast were given food, shelter and money until the crew and passengers could return home.[20]

The relative rank of states in the tribute hierarchy changed according to geopolitical realities but statecraft mattered. During the Northern Song, Japan related to China as equals but in 1127, the Chinese court sent gifts and a letter addressing the emperor as 'King of Japan' 日本王, implying that he was of lower rank than the Chinese emperor. Chief minister Taira no Kiyomori 平の清盛 took no offence and replied with gifts. By his composure, Kiyomori put relations on a new footing and won direct trade (instead of via Korea) privileges. The succeeding Kamakura regime (1185–1333) continued to enjoy direct trade but lost respect for the Chinese when the Song dynasty was destroyed by Mongols who established the Yuan dynasty in 1279.

RELATIONS WITH THE YUAN

The Mongols had heard that Japan was a land rich in gold, and the Mongol khan Khublai sent six missions to Japan demanding tribute but were rebuffed. Furious, he ordered the invasion of Japan. The amphibious campaigns which took place in 1274 and 1281 were complete disasters and produced a new Japanese self-understanding. The invaders outnumbered the defenders, but on both occasions typhoons destroyed the invading armadas and saved the day. For the Japanese, this had to be more than coincidence; the miraculous deliverance by *kamikaze* 神風, or divine wind, inspired belief that gods protected them, which gave birth to the idea that they are a special race. The self-confidence coincided with the rise of a warlord regime, or *bakufu* 幕府, at the expense of the imperial court. Despite tensions with the Mongols, trade continued and three years after the first invasion, Japan sent a large shipment of gold in exchange for iron and copper, while maritime customs bureaus 市舶司 were opened in the ports of Quanzhou and Ningbo to attend to Japanese merchants.[21] The defeats dealt a heavy blow to Khublai's prestige, and after his death in 1294, his successor abandoned the idea of conquering Japan and pursued active trade instead. Religious activity continued unabated and hundreds of Japanese monks visited China in the first half of the fourteenth century, but unlike those of the Tang period who came to learn Zen meditation and copy sutras, these were more keen on the arts and spent their time painting, trading poems with Chinese scholars, sculpting Buddha images and inscribing tombstones.

RELATIONS WITH THE MING

Zhu Yuanzhang 朱元璋 toppled the Mongols and founded the Ming in 1368 and sent emissaries to Japan demanding tribute. The shogun Ashikaga Yoshimitsu 足利義満 (1358–1408) accepted his demands and the lesser title of king 日本王 in order to secure trading privileges. Those who felt that Japan already equalled or surpassed China bitterly opposed subordination, but coffers depleted by decades of fighting badly needed replenishing and trade was the means to achieve that. In 1401, the shogun dispatched his first mission to the Ming court bearing gold, horses, swords and other gifts. Like Taira no Kiyomori, Ashikaga stabilized relations, and up to twenty trade missions led by venerable Zen monks were sent between 1401 and 1547.[22] The Chinese controlled trade volume using tallies 勘合 or trade permits and the second mission in 1403 returned with a trove of a hundred tallies. Literate Zen monks doubled as diplomats and helped merchants navigate local customs and bureaucracy, and thanks to improved shipbuilding techniques, not a single vessel was lost to the waves during the Ming, but harmonious ties were soon destroyed by a warlord called Toyotomi Hideyoshi.

TOYOTOMI HIDEYOSHI

Toyotomi Hideyoshi 豊臣秀吉 (1537–1598) stands out for his role in unifying Japan after a 136-year struggle for supremacy by daimyō 大名 feudal lords. The Sengoku period 戦国時代 (1467–1603) was marked by social upheaval, political intrigue and near-constant warfare. One of the most remarkable men in Japanese history, Hideyoshi was born a commoner in a farming area. His father, Yaemon, a peasant foot soldier, served the local warlord, Oda Nobuhida, until a battlefield injury sent him home where he died when Hideyoshi was seventeen. Portraits show Hideyoshi as a small and unattractive man with a thin and deeply lined face. His lord, Oda Nobunaga, called him the 'bald rat', but Hideyoshi claimed that his mother had a dream when she conceived him:

> That night, a ray of sun filled the room as if it were noon time. All were overcome with astonishment and fright and when the diviners had gathered, they interpreted the event saying: 'when he reaches the prime of life, his virtue will illumine the four seas, his authority will emanate to the myriad peoples'. [23]

Hideyoshi first served Matsushita Yukitsuna and later Oda Nobunaga, but rose to become the Imperial Regent 関白.[24] After defeating his rivals and bringing peace to the country, he launched invasions to conquer Korea and China. For the expedition of 1592, he mustered 158,000 seasoned troops, who quickly overwhelmed the Koreans. They landed in Pusan and captured Seoul, the capital, in three weeks. The Korean king fled and appealed to China for help. In a lightning campaign, Hideyoshi's men advanced to Pyongyang and reached the Yalu River (the border with China) within three months, but Korean militia fought back using guerrilla tactics, while the Korean navy disrupted Japanese supply lines. Ming Chinese troops intervened, and the war reached a stalemate. The first campaign lasted four years followed by fruitless negotiations. In 1597, Japan forces attacked a second time, and after initial victories were forced to withdraw to the southern coastal areas of the peninsula. Pursuing Ming and Korean troops were unable to dislodge the invaders, and fighting ground again to a halt. In Japan, Hideyoshi succumbed to illness and died on 18 September 1598. The war in Korea was called off and the peninsula abandoned; Hideyoshi's forces withdrew, and the succeeding Tokugawa regime closed the country to the outside world for the next two and a half centuries.

All parties to the conflict paid dearly. Total military and civilian casualties numbered an estimated 1 million, a staggering figure by medieval standards. The campaigns weakened the Toyotomi clan's power, and rekindled domestic power struggles. The losses incurred by Toyotomi's feudal lords in Korea shifted the balance of power in the favour of his rival Ieyasu Tokugawa 家康徳川. Ming China suffered heavy financial losses which weakened its position in Manchuria, allowing the Jurchen chieftain Nurhaci to expand his control and crush Ming forces in 1644, bringing an end to one of China's great dynasties. Korea suffered the most. The invasions proved more devastating than any other event in the nation's history and caused the Korean people almost unbelievable suffering. Few structures dated prior to 1592 can today be found anywhere south of Pyongyang, a mute testimonial to the savagery of the war. The countryside was badly scarred with farm acreage reduced to 66 per cent of prewar levels causing widespread famine, disease, and rebellion while some 60,000 Koreans were taken captive and sold as slaves abroad.[25]

Throughout the Tokugawa period (1603–1868), there were no state-to-state relations between Japan and China. Tokugawa Ieyasu 徳川家康, the warlord who founded the regime, sought rapprochement with Ming China shortly after the war in Korea, but failed to overcome Chinese mistrust. By the early 1620s, his successors had lost interest in restoring ties, and made no attempt to approach the Ming court until the final days of the Tokugawa era. Under the policy of *sakoku* 鎖国 or *kaikin* 海禁, the *bakufu* government banned overseas travel by its subjects from the mid-1630s to the late 1850s. During this period, the only contact between the two neighbours was through Chinese merchants calling at the port of Nagasaki and indirectly through exchanges with Korea and the Ryukyu Kingdom. In 1853, a squadron of American warships under the command of Commodore Matthew Perry sailed into Tokyo bay demanding diplomatic relations and the opening of ports to American trade. Unable to resist the Americans, the *bakufu* collapsed and was replaced by a new regime called the Meiji. From afar, the Japanese had followed the developing story of China's military defeats by technologically superior Western forces and sought to avoid a similar fate. In 1862, they sent a delegation to Shanghai to study trade and diplomacy. This was the first official meeting between Chinese and Japanese in several centuries. The Chinese did not agree to Japanese requests for trade ties and a consulate, but nine years later signed a treaty of amity, which by recognizing the equality of states, marked the beginning of the end of the hierarchical tribute system.[26]

Japan modernized swiftly through reforms during the Meiji period (1868–1912), transforming itself in less than fifty years into an industrial society with a modern military. In 1895 it defeated China in a war over Korea where Qing 清朝 forces were routed on land and at sea by a Japanese military trained in strategy and tactics by British, French and Prussian advisors. The Imperial Japanese Navy modelled itself after the British Royal Navy, while the Imperial Japanese Army adopted German military doctrine and organization. After six months of unbroken successes by the Japanese and the loss of the port of Weihaiwei on the Shandong peninsula, China sued for peace in February 1895 and paid reparations of 340 million taels of silver – the equivalent of 6.4 times the annual Japanese government revenue. By the Treaty of Shimonoseki in April, the Qing government recognized the 'full and complete independence and autonomy' of Korea and ceded the Liaodong Peninsula, Taiwan and the Pescadores Islands to Japan 'in perpetuity'. The cession of Taiwan to Japan was greeted with deep resentment by its Chinese inhabitants, who for two years waged a bitter guerrilla campaign against the occupiers and over 100,000 Japanese troops put down the resistance with much cruelty. Men, women, and children were ruthlessly slaughtered, and thousands of peasants who were driven from their homes continued to wage a vendetta war even after the main resistance had been crushed.[27] The uninhabited Diaoyu/Senkaku islands were not named in the treaty, but Japan annexed them all the same.

Defeat at the hands of an Asian state long considered subordinate in the Confucian sphere dealt a bitter psychological blow. Japan's victory made the island nation the premier power in Asia but its victory over Russia – the first by an Asian power over a European in the modern era – ten years later stunned the world and put it firmly in the ranks of the great powers. Aping the West, Japan set out to build its own colonial empire, and in 1931 seized Manchuria, a territory two and a half times larger than California and as big as Texas, Louisiana and Alabama combined, to establish a puppet state called Manchukuo. Japan portrayed it as a pan-Asian state comprising Japanese, Chinese, Koreans, Manchus and Mongols marking the birth of a New Order in East Asia 大東亞新秩序.[28] Rich in natural resources, it became with substantial Japanese investments an industrial powerhouse and was seen by the Japanese public as a lifeline essential to Japan's recovery from the Great Depression. The South Manchuria Railway Company, or *Mantetsu* 満鉄, formed to operate the Russian-built railway network, became a giant corporation owning factories, ports, mines, hotels and telephone lines and dominated the Manchurian economy. The powerful Kwantung Army, an army group of the Imperial Japanese Army, stationed in Manchuria, drafted over 10 million Chinese as slave labour and established a secret biological-chemical warfare unit, Unit 731, which tested bacteriological weapons on humans and conducted vivisection on live Chinese, Russian and Korean subjects.[29]

In July 1937, following a skirmish between Chinese and Japanese troops at the Marco Polo Bridge near Beijing, Japan launched a full-scale invasion of China. The war reflected differences in moral assumptions; while the Japanese saw their position in China as a matter of national destiny and economic need, the Chinese considered themselves victims of a long pattern of predation by foreign powers.[30] Advancing swiftly, the Imperial Japanese Army took the capital Nanjing on 13 December 1937 and proceeded to punish the city with six weeks of wanton slaughter. Japanese troops massacred 300,000 civilians and raped 80,000 women.[31] Militarily, Japan was better prepared for war than China and in the space of two years gained control of most of the ports, the majority of the main cities as far west as Hankou, and the larger part of the railways. Emperor Hirohito authorized the *sankō sakusen* 三光 作戦 'three alls' (kill all, burn all, loot all) policy, which caused death and suffering on a far larger scale than the unplanned atrocities at Nanjing.[32] Seeing it as Japan's 'divine right' to rule all Asia, Japanese nationalists and military leaders urged wider war, and on a December day in 1941, Japanese forces simultaneously attacked Pearl Harbor and invaded the Philippines and

Malaya.[33] Following a series of quick victories, Japan captured the Philippines, Malaya, Singapore and Indonesia and poised to invade Australia. By mid-1942, the Japanese held a vast area stretching from the Central Pacific to the Indian Ocean but lacked the resources to defend it and just five months after Pearl Harbor, the tide turned. Japan was simply not able to replenish its losses in men and *matériel* the way the US with its enormous industrial and training capacity could. The Allies gained the advantage and the war in China came to an abrupt end when Japan surrendered following the atomic bomb attacks on Hiroshima and Nagasaki and the Soviet advance into Manchuria in August 1945.

Japanese sentiments toward China in the postwar years were complex. There was a reluctance to face their guilt for the war and the atrocities committed in China, but there was also condescension toward China for its present backwardness for which Japan was much responsible, but admiration for its past cultural achievements to which Japan owed much. There was also eagerness for trade, and Japanese businesses established ties with China in the early 1950s despite an American trade embargo. The Japanese left was sympathetic towards Maoist China, and leading members of the Japan Socialist Party (JSP) visited Beijing while senior members of the Liberal Democrat Party (LDP) had links to Beijing which served as informal diplomatic channels.[34] Progressives and rightists in the LDP clashed over the interpretation of the history of Japan's invasion of Korea and China, but with the onset of the Cold War, thousands of leftists were purged from important institutions, and by the mid 1950s the Ministry of Education discouraged open criticism in school textbooks of Japan's role in the Pacific War. At stake was the larger question of Japan's identity and its relations with its neighbours, and when the Chinese and Koreans, beginning in 1982, protested against textbook revisions, conservatives saw the criticisms as interference in Japan's domestic affairs. But the majority of the LDP called for sensitivity; along with a measure of guilt, there was also a desire to avoid unnecessary friction at a critical juncture in China's transition to a market economy. An unstable China was bad for Japan and they felt that Japan had a role to play in helping China to develop.

After World War II, America became Japan's new object of reverence and the population grew enamoured with American pop culture. Japan rose from the ashes of war to become an industrial powerhouse even as China remained backward. In 1990, China's per capita GDP was a mere $343 compared to Japan's $25,140, and bicycles and portable radios were luxury items to many Chinese, while the Japanese holidayed in Australia or Hawaii. There was little to learn from China about modernity, but things soon changed; in 1978, the Chinese government turned from socialist crusade to market reforms, putting the country on the road to economic success. China overtook Japan in 2011 to become the world's second biggest economy, and in 2014 surpassed the US to become the world's largest economy in real terms (purchasing power parity terms). Although its per capita GDP remains a fraction of the American and Japanese ones, it has become a force to be reckoned with. In 2009, China became the biggest market for Japanese exports and soon overtook America as the most popular destination for Japanese students going abroad (21,126 chose to study in China compared to 19,568 in the US in 2012).[35]

SAN FRANCISCO SYSTEM

Japan's relations with China, however, remain hostage to the San Francisco System, which takes its name from two treaties signed in San Francisco on September 8, 1951, under which the terms for restoring Japanese independence were laid out. One was the multilateral *Treaty of Peace* between Japan and forty-eight nations; the other was the bilateral *US-Japan Security Treaty*, which encouraged and supported Japanese rearmament while allowing the stationing of American troops on Japanese soil. Importantly, neither the Beijing government (the People's Republic of China (PRC) on the mainland) nor the Taipei government (the Republic of China on Taiwan) were invited to the peace conference, despite the fact that China bore the brunt of Japanese aggression and occupation. The conference also excluded South and North Korea even, though the Korean people suffered grievously under Japanese colonial rule. The Soviet Union attended, but refused to sign the treaty because of the exclusion of the PRC and Washington's plans to integrate Japan into its Cold War strategic planning and security architecture.[36]

The San Francisco settlement laid the groundwork for an exclusionary system that detached Japan from its closest neighbours. After the conference, the United States warned the Japanese government that Congress would not ratify the peace treaty unless Japan signed a parallel treaty with Taipei, effectively recognizing that regime as the legitimate government of China. Even pro-American and anti-communist supporters in Japan balked at Washington's demands as the isolation of the PRC was unpopular in business circles. The indefinite presence of US bases in the country was worrisome, and Washington's plan to rearm Japan seemed impulsive and risked provoking a backlash at home and abroad. Left with no real choice, Tokyo agreed and peace and reconciliation with its most important neighbours were deferred. The Soviet Union and Japan established diplomatic ties in 1956, but have yet to sign a formal peace treaty. Japan and South Korea did not normalize relations until 1965, while diplomatic relations with the PRC were not restored until 1972, and both sides signed a formal peace treaty only in 1978. The long-term consequences of this estrangement between Japan on the one hand, and China, Korea and Russia on the other, are still being realized. Unlike postwar Germany, Japan was inhibited from reconciliation and reintegration with its Asian neighbours, and the wounds of imperialism were left unaddressed and largely unacknowledged in Japan. Instead of holding Japan accountable for its wartime misdeeds, the United States made Japan an ally against China. The Americans rehabilitated many of Japan's wartime military and civilian leaders, some of whom went on to hold high offices. Among them was Nobusuke Kishi, a member of the wartime cabinet and an A-class war criminal, who became prime minister in 1957. His grandson is current premier Shinzo Abe. In a speech in 1965, Kishi called for Japanese rearmament as 'a means of eradicating completely the consequences of Japan's defeat and the American occupation…[enabling] Japan finally to move out of the post-war era and for the Japanese people to regain their self-confidence and pride as Japanese'. Abe promised by his grandfather's grave that he would 'recover the true independence' of Japan, and few things are more emblematic of that mission than the Yasukuni Shrine.[37]

Consecrated in 1869, the Yasukuni Shrine in the heart of Tokyo, not far from the Imperial Palace, honours the souls of those who died 'protecting the emperor'. They are revered as deities 神 and include soldiers who fought in Taiwan, Korea, Manchuria, China and South-East Asia. The nearly two and a half million imperial protectors inscribed in Yasukuni's 'Book of Souls' 霊璽簿 are viewed as a divine shield. Whereas war cemeteries are places where dead soldiers are buried, Yasukini is a Shinto shrine where their souls are deified and worshipped. Names once enshrined cannot be removed, and in 1978, Yasukuni priests covertly installed fourteen political and military leaders, including General Hideki Tojo, the wartime prime minister. All had either been executed or died in prison, and honouring them is of no small political significance; the priests are unlikely to have acted on their own accord, and visits by nationalist politicians such as Shinzo Abe have increased since.

POLITICAL IDENTITY

Japan's political identity is inextricably linked to its alliance with the United States. The postwar government of Prime Minister Shigeru Yoshida devoted its resources to rebuilding its economy while relying on the US for security. Resisting American pressure to speed up rearmament, it spent less on guns and more on butter, and with access to US markets, Japan soon became an economic and technological powerhouse. In 1965, its GDP was estimated at $91 billion; fifteen years later, it had grown more than tenfold to $1.065 trillion and stood poised to overtake the US as the world's leading economy, but the bursting of the bubble in 1991 and the end of the Cold War raised questions about the Japanese economic model and the political order of the San Francisco System. Japan may need to craft a new political identity compatible with the rise of China, but no Japanese government can survive without Washington's consent.[38] Prime Minister Yukio Hatoyama, who sought to put relations with the US on a more equal footing, lasted barely nine months in office. Hatoyama, a PhD graduate from Stanford University, won a landslide victory in August 2009 and tried to set a new course for his country, arguing that the era of US-led globalization was coming to an end. He told Chinese premier Wen Jiabao that Japan had 'depended on the US too much' and wanted to forge closer ties with China. Japan's foreign policy would become less American-centric and more Asia-focused, he said. That did not go down well in Washington and for his audacity, he was snubbed by President Obama at the Nuclear Non-Proliferation summit in Washington in 2010.[39] The Americans wanted him out and after caving in to US pressure to retain the US marine corp base on Okinawa, he resigned. His party general secretary, Ichiro Ozawa, who also opposed the base, fell victim to a media campaign based on an old corruption charge, and was forced out too.[40]

Since the Meiji Period, Japan has striven to join the ranks of the West.[41] During the drive to modernize in the 19th century, it constructed a 'non-Asian' national identity 脱亜論 by imitating Western culture and institutions.[42] After the war, Japan faced its Asian neighbours not as a defeated nation but as a partner of the United States, an arrangement which perpetuated Japan's prewar stance of superiority *vis-à-vis* Asia.[43] Many Japanese believe they are a unique race, 日本人論, an ideology with roots in the *kokugaku* 国学 movement of the 18th century. Japan's remarkable Meiji modernization and economic development since 1945 inspired national self-confidence and until recently, the country was seen as the leading bird in the flying geese pattern of economic development in East Asia.[44] But with rising populism and America's retreat into protectionism, Japan may need to reexamine its priorities. Because Japan and China are deeply integrated into the East Asian supply chain, President Trump's trade war hurts them both and forces the Asian neighbours to cooperate. Japan's shrinking population means a dwindling domestic market which will make Japan more reliant on exports. China is already on track to overtake the US to become Japan's largest trade partner.[45] Her population is more than four times greater than the US population, and as incomes rise, she will become an even more important market for Japanese goods and services. The Chinese economy is growing three times faster the US economy[46] and Chinese per capita income increased tenfold from 1991 to 2017 while the US per capita income grew 50 per cent in that period.[47] China has 300 million middle-class consumers, almost as numerous as the entire population of the United States, and that number is expected to double in the next 10 to 15 years. The long-term trends are clear and despite the US-Japan security alliance, Japanese policymakers are not blind to the convergence of interests with China as the economic landscape shifts in her favour.

CHAPTER 3

THE RYUKYU KINGDOM

The Ryukyu Kingdom thrived as an independent kingdom until invaded by Japanese forces in 1609. The kingdom comprised a chain of islands stretching from the southern Japanese island of Kyūshū to the island of Taiwan. Although the Ryukyuans spoke a language akin to Japanese, they were of a different stock. Peaceful and welcoming, they were likely a mix of Malay, Mongol and Ainu stock with darker complexion, round eyes, and wavy hair.[1] Whereas the Japanese ate fish, the Ryukyuans consumed pork as their main source of protein, a dietary preference which became an object of derision by the Japanese. At first, the main island consisted of three rival principalities occupying the north, central and south – Hokuzan 北山, Chūzan 中山 and Nanzan 南山 – which vied for recognition by China, but were eventually united in 1429 by the king of Chūzan, Shō Hashi 尚巴志, who established his capital in Naha. The kingdom's location made it ideally suited for transit trade, and for nearly two centuries, it played a key role in maritime trade between China, Japan, Korea, Vietnam, Java, Luzon, Siam, Pattani, Malacca, Palembang, and Sumatra.[2] Goods traded included silver, swords, lacquerware and folding screens from Japan, medicinal herbs, minted coins, glazed ceramics, brocades and textiles from China, sappan wood, rhino horn, tin, sugar and iron from Southeast Asia, ivory from India and frankincense from Arabia.

Ryukyu's diplomatic ties with China began in 1372, when the Ming emperor Hong Wu 洪武帝 sent envoys to the Ryukyu king Satto 察度 (reigned from 1350–1395). Two years later, the king sent his younger brother Taiki 泰期 with gifts to accept Chinese suzerainty in return for trading privileges. The relationship which was political, cultural and economic in nature lasted five hundred years.[3] The Ming court allowed one mission every two years, each consisting of no more than three ships, and regulations specified the number of persons who could be sent and how many could travel beyond the port of entry Quanzhou 泉州 to the imperial capital. Over time, a permanent Ryukyuan settlement grew up in Quanzhou where the mission became acquainted with the daily life and the arts and crafts of the city. Returning home, they brought the artifacts, customs and beliefs of the Chinese, but also those of Arabs, Indians, Malays, Siamese and other merchants living in Quanzhou, and Chinese cultural influences entered the habits of the Ryukyuan gentry and commoners alike. In 1393, at the behest of the Ming government, a Chinese immigrant community of teachers, clerks, shipbuilders and craftsmen was established on Ryukyu to teach government administration and new methods of ship-building.[4] Children of the Ryukyuan élite were sent to study in China where they learned history, ethics and poetry at the capital for two to three years, funded by the Chinese. A community of Ryukyuan students grew up in Beijing that thrived for five hundred years. They built strong friendship bonds with Chinese students and those from other tributary states and took up high offices back home.

Confucianism, a pacifist philosophy, suited the gentle Ryukyuan temperament and the Ryukyuans quickly adopted the sage's teachings. For their diligent observance of Confucian ethics, etiquette and rituals, the Ming emperor commended them with the gift of a large signboard inscribed with the words 守禮之邦 or 'Land of Propriety', a term normally referring to China herself. The Ryukyuans displayed it on the gate to the royal palace where it proudly remained until destroyed by Allied naval bombardment in 1945.[5] Avid sinophiles, the Ryukyuans became purveyors of all things Chinese, and over the next centuries, Ryukyu prospered as an East Asian trading hub and merchants from as far as Burma, Siam, Sumatra, the Philippines, Ceylon and Bengal could be seen on the streets of Naha the capital.[6] The Ryukyuans themselves ventured abroad and mingled with Arabs, Armenians, Persians, Turks and Indians in Malacca and other Southeast Asian trading centres. The kingdom's success soon became the envy of many, including Satsuma.

Medieval Japan consisted of feudal domains called *han* 藩 under the lordship of a warlord regime called the Muromachi

shogunate 室町幕府 (1338–1573). The Satsuma domain 薩
摩藩, situated on the southern Japanese island of Kyushu,
was ruled by the Shimazu clan 島津氏. The Ryukyu kingdom
conducted trade with Satsuma and paid occasional tribute to
the Muromachi shogun. Over time, Satsuma came to depend
on Ryukyu for wares to trade with other parts of Japan and with
Korea. By the mid-16th century, the Japanese had heard about
and feared incursion by Europeans. The Portuguese conquest
of Malacca in 1511 and the ruthless conduct of European
merchants were by now well known throughout the region,
and the Japanese wanted an outpost to monitor the southern
approaches to their homeland. In 1592 the feudal lord Toyotomi
Hideyoshi ordered the Ryukyu king Shōnei 尚寧 (1564–1620)
to provide supplies for his invasion of Korea. He demanded
provisions to sustain 7,000 men for ten months, but the tiny
Ryukyu kingdom delivered only half the amount. On the pretext
of punishing the Ryukyuans for their 'disobedience', Hideyoshi
unleashed Satsuma samurais on the Ryukyus in February 1609.
The Ryukyuans were no match for the 3,000 seasoned Satsuma
warriors armed with muskets. A hundred captives, including
the king and senior officials, were carried off to Kagoshima, the
Satsuma capital, and presented with a document of surrender
in which Ryukyu professes to be a long-time vassal of Satsuma:

The islands of Ryukyu have from ancient times been
a feudal dependency of Satsuma; and we have for ages

observed the custom of sending thither, at stated times, junks bearing products of the islands, and we have always sent messengers to carry our congratulations to a new Prince of Satsuma on his accession.[7]

That no such tributary relationship existed prior to 1609 made the document a bitter pill for King Shōnei and his officials. The oath accused the king of neglecting his duty to Satsuma, and therefore deserved punishment. Fortunately, 'our merciful Prince [of Shimazu] has shown his loving kindness; and taking pity on master and servants whose country seemed all lost to them, gave them his leave to return to their homes; not only so, but also allowed themselves to govern some of their country's islands'. The Ryukyuans were ordered to swear allegiance to the Satsuma lord:

> If, peradventure, any man of Ryukyu, forgetful of this great-hearted deed, ever in times to come, plans a revolt against you, yea, if it were our Chieftain himself who should be drawn to join [in] revolt, yet we nevertheless obedient to the commands of our Great Lord, will never be false to our Oath by abetting a rebel, be he lord or churl.[8]

Tei Dō, commander of the defeated Ryukyuan forces refused to sign the oath and was promptly beheaded. Satsuma annexed five northern Ryukyu islands, and posted men in the capital

Naha to ensure obedience.[9] Trade with China and elsewhere would henceforth require Satsuma's permission. In 1613, the Satsuma daimyō, Iehisa 島津家久, prohibited Ryukyu from conducting relations with other countries and sent officers to monitor the movement of ships at Tomari port. Upon the death of King Shōnei in 1621, Iehisa decreed that no one could ascend the Ryukyu throne without Satsuma's blessing and he limited tribute missions to China to one every ten years.[10] A Japanization policy followed along with one of the longest deceptions in diplomatic history.

As Hideyoshi's invasion of Korea in 1592 and 1597 brought an end to direct trade with China, the Tokugawa shogun, who succeeded Hideyoshi in 1603, had no choice but to trade via Ryukyu and Satsuma. Because of Ryukyu's longstanding ties with China, Satsuma had to hide the fact that the islanders had fallen under Japanese control. In 1616, Satsuma reversed the Japanization policy, and ordered the Ryukyuans to preserve their identity. It restored some administrative control to the royal court, forbade Ryukyuans to adopt Japanese names, hairstyle or clothing and banned visits by Japanese from other domains but Japan continued to tighten its grip. In 1634 the kingdom became a Japanese feudal domain with the king reduced to a provincial governor. Two centuries later, as the East Asian power balance shifted in Japan's favour, Tokyo annexed the kingdom outright. For this, it needed an excuse which came in form of a shipwreck.

In 1871 a Ryukyuan ship ran aground off the southern tip of Taiwan and fifty-four of its crew were captured and beheaded by aborigines. Twelve survived and were rescued by Han Chinese who repatriated them via China. Tokyo demanded the Qing government punish the perpetrators, but the Chinese, seeking to dodge the issue, said the aborigines did not fall under their jurisdiction and unwittingly made what amounted to a renunciation of sovereignty over Taiwan. Ostensibly to punish the aborigines, the Japanese dispatched an expeditionary force in 1874 which killed thirty tribesmen and wounded a large number. Under a settlement brokered by the British that same year, Japanese forces withdrew after the Qing government agreed to pay an indemnity of 500,000 taels (about 18.7 tonnes) of silver. The expedition demonstrated that the Qing government did not have effective control over Taiwan, let alone the Ryukyus. Tokyo seized on ambiguous wording in the settlement (drafted by the British) to argue that the Qing government had no suzerainty claim over the Ryukyus. The settlement contained a line stating that 'Taiwan aborigines had gratuitously harmed Japanese subjects'.[11] Tokyo took the reference as proof of Chinese acknowledgement that the Ryukyus belonged to Japan. In 1879 Japan asked the British to arbitrate, and the British concluded that Japan had sovereignty over the Ryukyus. The Ryukyuan government pleaded with the Meiji government to keep the status quo but to no avail. In March, Meiji envoy Matsuda Michiyuki 松田道之 marched up to Shuri

Castle with 160 police officers and 400 armed soldiers to force King Shō Tai 尚泰王 to accept the annexation of his kingdom. The Chinese rejected the arbitration outcome, but could not prevent Japan from taking *de facto* control over the Ryukyus and carrying the king off to Japan. The Chinese protested, and the matter was put through another round of arbitration by US president Ulysses Grant during which the Meiji government offered to split the Ryukyus between Japan and China. The Qing government rejected the proposal but was too weak to stop Japan from annexing the kingdom. Tokyo renamed the islands 'Okinawa Prefecture.' The Japanese had exploited legal technicalities against a Qing government inexperienced in the system of international laws developed by the West. Rather than democratic constructs, the rules were wholly alien but the Chinese were obliged to comply nevertheless.

DISCRIMINATION ON THE MAINLAND

After annexation, broad-based education was introduced to implant Japanese language, values and identity as the Ryukyus had 'the same race, habits and language [as Japan], and [had] always been loyal to Satsuma'.[12] In reality, the Japanese did not accept the Ryukyuans as members of the same race. In the six decades between the abolition of the Ryukyu Kingdom and the outbreak of World War II, many Ryukyuans moved in search of employment to mainland Japan, particularly to Yokohama,

Kawasaki and the industrial areas of Kansai but because of real or imagined differences, they encountered mistreatment and felt as foreign as those who migrated to more distant places overseas.[13] Okinawan poet Yamanokuchi Baku (1903–1963), who spent most of his adult life on the mainland lamented: 'wherever I go, people stare at me strangely – as if I'm not even human'.[14] Speaking Japanese with an accent, Ryukyuan workers suffered at the hands of mainland employers who sometimes sought to exclude them altogether. Records from the 1920s and 1930s reveal a pattern of discrimination in employment contracts, housing, and even workplace safety measures. Factories recruited Koreans, Okinawans, and Burakumin, the outcast group at the bottom of the Japanese social order and assumed that Okinawans could be paid lower wages, put up with abusive working conditions, and did not require compensation for fires or accidents. They were housed separately and given cheaper meals than Japanese workers. Kinjō Tsuru, who worked in 1919 at a spinning factory on the mainland, recalled:

> My contract was for three years, but I ran away after working for only one … I couldn't stand it anymore, always being made fun of because I was from Okinawa. I was taunted especially by the woman of about fifty who was in charge of our rooms in the dormitory. Whenever she talked to me, she would yell out scornfully, 'Hey, you Ryukyu' or

'Listen here, Ryukyu'. I am no weakling though and I yelled back at her ...[15]

OKINAWAN MIGRATION OVERSEAS

The discrimination triggered the first wave of migration to Hawaii, Peru and Brazil in the 1900s. Life for these early migrants was harsh; many laboured under abusive conditions on sugar cane and coffee plantations in the middle of malaria-infested jungles. They faced discrimination from Japanese migrants who had arrived earlier, and who regarded the Ryukyuans as racially and culturally inferior. Conditions in the Ryukyus continued to deteriorate as the Japanese government exacted twice as much tax as it invested in the prefecture. In 1921, the price of sugar cane, the prefecture's main cash crop, plummeted, triggering a famine which forced more to leave. With immigration to the US being prohibited by the 1924 Immigration Act, many went to Central and South America and to Japan's expanding empire in Taiwan, Manchuria and the Pacific islands, where they endured extreme hardship for the sake of family members left behind. Remittances from the workers made up 66 per cent of Okinawa's income in 1929. Many disguised their accent and adopted Japanese names, but discrimination continued into the postwar years and signs barring them from taverns 居酒屋 and restaurants were common until the mid-1980s.[16]

AMERICA AND THE RYUKYU KINGDOM

The first contact with the Americans came in May 1853 when American warships under the command of Commodore Matthew Perry sailed into Naha. Sent by President Fillmore to open up Japan, Perry threatened to attack the city unless he were allowed to trade and provided land for a coaling station. He landed marines and demanded an audience with King Shōtai 尚泰. Before setting sail from the US, Perry wrote to the Secretary of the Navy proposing the occupation of the Ryukyu islands on the following grounds:

> Now, it strikes me, that the occupation of the principal ports of those islands for the accommodation of our ships of war, and for the safe resort of merchant vessels, of whatever nation, would be a measure not only justified by the strictest rules of moral law, but by what is also to be considered by the laws of stern necessity; and the argument may be further strengthened by the certain consequences of the amelioration of the conditions of the natives, although the vices attendant upon civilization may be entailed upon them.[17]

Perry sent an armed party to explore the interior of the island, brushing aside all protestations by Okinawan officials. The *New York Herald* of 3 January 1851 condescendingly described the Ryukyus as: 'a kingdom in themselves, yet a dependency of Japan. For gentle dignity of manners, superior advancement in the arts and general intelligence, the inhabitants of this group are by far the most interesting unenlightened nation in the Pacific Ocean'.[18] Perry's mission was to penetrate Japanese markets. American businessmen had brought pressure on Congress to send an expedition, and Perry's policy of coercion on the Ryukyuans was calculated to intimidate Japan. Previous missions to open up trade with Japan had failed, and Perry determined that the US government must never again be 'exposed to indignities'. A decision was made to override all Ryukyuan objections to the establishment of a supply base on shore. Chief interpreter S. Wells Williams, a lay-missionary who had spent twenty years in China, observed:

> It was a struggle between weakness and right, and power and wrong, for a more high-handed piece of aggression has not been committed by anyone. I was ashamed at having been a party to such a procedure, and pitied these poor defenseless islanders who could only say 'no'...[19]

Perry demanded to see the king, who was still a boy. The Ryukyuan officials made clear that he was not welcome at the palace but Perry proceeded to the castle in a sedan chair carried by four Chinese coolies followed by armed marines and a marching band. The party of some two hundred men stood at the palace gates refusing to leave until they opened and the Americans marched in to the tune of *Hail Columbia!*:

> *Immortal patriots, rise once more,*
> *Defend your rights, defend your shore!*
> *Let no rude foe, with impious hand,*
> *Let no rude foe, with impious hand,*
> *Invade the shrine where sacred lies*
> *Of toil and blood, the well-earned prize,*
> *While off'ring peace, sincere and just,*
> *In Heaven's we place a manly trust,*
> *That truth and justice will prevail,*
> *And every scheme of bondage fail.*

The fleet sailed a few days later for Tokyo where they threatened the use of force on the capital unless the Japanese opened up ports to trade. This was not the last the Ryukyuans saw of the Americans; they returned in 1945.

TYPHOON OF STEEL

The Battle of Okinawa between March and September 1945 was among the bloodiest battles of World War II.[20] Dubbed the 'typhoon of steel' 鉄の雨, it saw American and Japanese forces engage in a ferocious all-out confrontation. The battle pitted 540,000 American troops supported by naval and air power against 110,000 Japanese defenders who had no air or naval support but had built strong defenses across the island. Caught in between were half a million civilians. Okinawa's importance as the last line of defence between Allied forces and the Japanese mainland meant that resistance would be stiff. The Japanese deployed more suicide bombers and boats than in any other battle in the Pacific War to stall the enemy's advance, but also to inflict maximum casualties and deter an Allied invasion of the mainland. Okinawa was a pawn to be sacrificed and little effort was made to protect the civilian population. Regarding Okinawans lesser than Japanese (unable to become 'perfect' Japanese), the military sacrificed them to achieve military objectives.[21] They suffered abuse, deprivation and even killing at the hands of Japanese soldiers.[22]

Okinawa was the only Japanese territory on which a ground battle was fought between American and Japanese forces during the Pacific War. That battle lasted from 26 March to 23 June 1945 and took the lives of more than a quarter of the local population. Civilian deaths (130,000–140,000) outnumbered military deaths by almost two to one. American casualties included 14,000 dead with many more wounded. The damage was so severe that the survivors were left with no means of livelihood: homes, land, tools and food were gone. Nearly all were detained in camps, many for up to two years, and when released, they found their communities had been destroyed. Residents of Yomitan Village reported:

As far as we could see, there were American military facilities, and there was no longer a trace of the village that we knew before the war. Trees were cut down; stone walls and hedges had been taken away; pampas grass and weeds were growing everywhere; wild birds from the mountains were nesting and mongooses were roaming in the midst of what used to be our village; it was sheer desolation. We could even see the bones of goats, horses, and cows lying on the ground.[23]

One family recalled its homecoming:

Though permitted to go home from the Oura Camp in Kushi Village [now a part of Nago City], we could not go straight back to our home village, so we stayed in a place called Furijima for several days. From there looking at our village, everything looked white like snow. We discovered that the village had been turned into an airfield. Every house had been burned down, and the fertile farms were buried under the runway.[24]

Civilians were relocated to areas designated by the military without regard for agriculture, fishing and the integrity of the community, and many were forced to resettle to outer islands or mainland Japan. In 1954, the US Civil Administration Ryukyu Islands (USCAR) announced the 'Yaeyama Development Plan' to resettle 16,000 Okinawans overseas. The military ruled Okinawa until its return to Japan by the 1971 Okinawa Reversion Agreement, but despite being politically marginalized by Tokyo, Okinawa remains the keystone of the US-Japan military alliance and carries a disproportionate share of American military installations in Japan; it comprises 0.6 per cent of Japanese territory but it hosts 74 per cent of US bases in the country.[25] Nuclear weapons were secretly deployed on the island before its reversion and massive stockpiles of Agent Orange where buried there after the Vietnam War.[26] More than 20 per cent of the land on the main island is occupied by bases, including Kadena Air Base, the largest and most active US air force base in the Far East, and the Futenma Marine Corp Air Station situated in the middle of an urban area close to schools and homes. Residents have pleaded for the marine base to be shut down but to no avail. Since the end of World War II, there have been many incidents involving US personnel. Protected by the Status of Forces Agreement (SOFA), they enjoy immunity from local laws, and have over the years committed crimes ranging from drunk driving to assault and rape. In 1995, three American soldiers kidnapped and raped a 12-year-old schoolgirl. The incident sparked outrage and came to symbolize Okinawa as a victim of Japanese and American violence and hegemony.[27] In their history, the Okinawans encountered Chinese, Japanese and Americans. Regrettably, they enjoyed genuine sovereignty and peace only with the first.

CHAPTER 4

VIETNAM

Southeast Asia

According to Vietnamese folklore, the first Vietnamese king, De Minh, was descended from a divine Chinese ruler. De Minh's grandson Lac Long Quan is said to have married a Chinese immortal called Au Co who bore him a hundred sons. The couple later separated; Au Co took fifty of the sons and settled up in the highlands, while Lac Long Quan remained with the other sons in the valley. Lac Long Quan's eldest son, Hung Vong, became the founder of the first Vietnamese dynasty, the Hung Bang, which is said to have ruled from 2,879 BC to 258 BC. This remarkable legend proclaimed that these early Vietnamese kings originated from a Chinese mother. Linguistic research, however, suggests the Vietnamese are a Malayo-Polynesian people who came from Indonesia. These people called themselves the Lac and their kingdom Van Lang 文朗 or 'the Land of the Tattooed Men'. The Lac were distinct among the many peoples whom the Chinese generally called the Yue 越 (or 'Viet' in Vietnamese) living to the south of the Yangzi River between the first millennium BC and the first millennium AD. They included the early inhabitants of what are now the southern Chinese provinces such as Guangdong, Guangxi and Fujian and were sinicized as the Chinese empire expanded southward. Blood ties, real or mythical, and dynastic imperialism animated repeated attempts to absorb the Lac too, but they held on to a separate identity.

In 258 BC, Van Lang was conquered by a neighbouring warlord who united it with his domain and called the new state Au Lac. Au Lac was in turn annexed in 207 BC by the Chinese military governor, Zhao Tuo 赵佗 (Trieu Da in Vietnamese), and became a part of Nam Viet 南越国 or Southern Viet, a province comprising most of present day Guangdong and northern Vietnam. When the ruling Chinese Qin dynasty collapsed the following year (206 BC), Zhao Tuo declared himself king of Nam Viet.[1] Seeking to build an independent kingdom, Zhao Tuo purged all officials loyal to the Qin emperor, adopted Viet customs and created a self-consciously non-Chinese state by ruling through local nobles and chieftains. About a hundred years later, however, Nam Viet was reconquered by the great Chinese emperor Han Wudi 汉武帝 in 111 BC and became again a Chinese province for the next thousand years.

A THOUSAND-YEAR RULE

A thousand-year rule of one state by another is extremely rare. At first, Chinese control was fairly loose.[2] The Chinese introduced new tools, skills and animals such as the water buffalo which greatly improved agriculture.[3] Chinese governors ruled through local feudal lords as Zhao Tuo had done. However, they also tried to assimilate their Lac subjects through intermarriage and the introduction of Chinese culture. To better exploit the local resources such as minerals and timber, Chinese governors later brought in Han administrators to run the province directly. This angered the local feudal lords and in 39 AD, the Trung sisters overthrew the governor and made themselves the new rulers but the regime lasted only three brief years before the Chinese reestablished themselves.

The native Vietnamese were not alone in wanting independence. Because of the province's rich resources and great distance from the Chinese court, Chinese governors themselves, like Zhao Tuo before them, were tempted to secede. As the Han court weakened in the third century, the governor Shi Xie 士燮 broke away. Shi Xie benefited from the influx of scholars and mandarins fleeing the disorder accompanying the fall of the Han dynasty.[4] Many came as single men, and took local wives for themselves. Over time, the intermarriages diluted their Chinese-ness and created a Sino-Vietnamese élite that became more and more Vietnamese and less and less Chinese.[5] Vietnam was the only one of China's neighbours to experience centuries of Chinese rule. For the Chinese, Vietnam (under the provincial name of Jiaozhi 交趾) was as much a part of China as Guangdong and Guangxi. The province consisted of the Red River basin, only a fraction the size of modern day Vietnam. None of China's neighbours experienced as much

inter-racial mixing as the Vietnamese. Schooled in the Confucian Classics, the Sino-Viet élite embraced Chinese culture, yet
remained deeply committed to a Vietnamese identity. From this
élite emerged Ly Bon who led a great rebellion that drove the
Chinese out in 542. Like the Trung sisters five centuries earlier,
however, he was defeated by Chinese armies three years later.
Over the next five centuries, the Sino-Vietnamese upper class,
organized repeated uprisings, but it was not until the decline
of the Tang dynasty (618–907) that victory became possible.
Under the leadership of Ngo Quyen, the Vietnamese routed a
Chinese fleet and gained independence in 939.

INDEPENDENCE AND CHINESE INVASIONS

Vietnam in 939 was in a sorry state. Ravaged by decades of war,
the country faced internal instability and the threat of reconquest by China. It acknowledged Chinese suzerainty and sent
tribute missions every three years in return for military protection and self-rule. In the first seventy years of independence, the
country went through three dynasties, each founded by an able
leader, only to be followed by weak successors. It was the fourth
dynasty, the Ly 李, that brought stability and lasting change.
Ironically, the Ly, who ruled for 215 years (1009–1224), were
ethnic Chinese originating from Fujian Province. The Ly court
adopted the Chinese civil service examinations and during the
first half of the dynasty, replaced feudal lords with mandarins

trained in the Confucian tradition. Political stability paved the way for economic prosperity. The Ly built roads, dykes, canals and a postal system, and although vigilant against the Chinese, the Ly themselves were patrons of Chinese art and literature – a sign of the primacy of Chinese culture in that part of the world.

Greater economic progress was hindered by constant wars to fend off Chinese attempts to regain Vietnam. In 1057, the Vietnamese fought a Song army and defeated it after a four-year struggle. As battle raged in the north, Champa, an Indianized client state of Cambodia, invaded Vietnam from the south. In a bitter contest, the southern provinces were lost and recovered multiple times. Champa and Cambodia (the Khmer Empire) attacked again in 1128, 1132 and 1138 and invaded another five times between 1138 and 1216. Like previous dynasties, the Ly lacked able leaders in its later years, and the last Ly emperor, a psychopath, was forced to abdicate in favour of his seven-year-old daughter. The dynasty was brought to an end by civil wars which produced Vietnam's second great dynasty, the Tran 陳 (1225–1400), a royal house lasting almost two centuries.

The Tran continued the policies which made Vietnam strong during the Ly dynasty, but like the Ly, faced the constant threat of invasion, this time by the Mongol armies of Kublai Khan who had conquered China by 1271. The Mongols invaded in 1257, but were decimated by tropical heat and disease. They tried again in 1284 with a bigger force of 500,000 men, but succumbed again to malaria. A third invasion three years later also ended in defeat. Before they could recover from the Mongol scourge, war broke out again with Champa. The endless campaigns exhausted the nation and produced deep economic and social crises. By the end of the fourteenth century, there was widespread famine and revolts, and in 1400, Ho Qui Ly, the regent to the four-year-old king, usurped the throne and massacred the Tran house.[6] Ho, who traced his roots to China's Zhejiang province, founded a new dynasty, but abdicated two years later in favour of his son.

The Tran was a tributary of China and when the Ming emperor Yong Le 永樂 learned of Ho's treachery, he sent a punitive expedition in 1406. Father and son were captured and brought before the emperor in Nanjing but the Ming army stayed and Vietnam (then called Annam 安南) became once more the Chinese province of Jiaozhi 交趾. The Ming exploited the country's resources and suppressed Vietnamese culture.[7] Vietnamese books were burned and schools taught only in Chinese, while women donned Chinese dress and men wore their hair long *à la chinoise*. The sinicization policies only made the Vietnamese more defiant and in 1418, Le Loi, a wealthy landowner, led a ten-year uprising which expelled the Chinese. Le established the next great dynasty, indeed Vietnam's longest-ruling house, the Later Le (1428–1787). To acquire new land for their people, the Le rulers fought a long series of campaigns against their southern neighbour Champa. These were genocidal wars burning huge swaths of land and they slaughtered 60,000 inhabitants when they seized the capital Vijaya in 1471. The southward expansion, or Nam Tien 南遷, absorbed most of Champa turning the country into Vietnam's 13th province by the end of the 15th century.[8] Vietnamese peasants and soldiers settled in the newly conquered areas, pushing the borders all the way to the Mekong delta. Only some 160,000 Chams survive today.[9]

THE TAY SON UPRISING

Around 1620 war broke out again, this time between two rival clans; the Trinh in the North and the Nguyen in the South. With occasional pauses, the Trinh fought for over fifty years to gain control of the South, but gave up after the last campaign in 1673. Both sides pledged loyalty to the powerless Le court at Hue, but maintained separate governments for the next hundred years. In 1772, an uprising led by three able brothers broke out against both ruling houses. The Tay Son brothers (named after their native village 西山) led a broad-based revolt drawing from peasant and merchant classes seeking social and political reform, and succeeded in overthrowing the southern regime in 1777. Preaching the equality of the rich and the poor, they redistributed food and money to the peasants and burned government tax registers. The people greeted them as 'virtuous and charitable thieves'.[10] They were brilliant soldiers and led an army of peasants, craftsmen, Chams, Chinese and even some scholars which swept through villages smashing the old political system. The entire Nguyen household was killed except for Nguyen Anh, a 15 year-old nephew of the king, and after conquering the South, the Tay Son turned their attention to the North. It took another ten years of fighting to overcome the Trinh. During this time, however, Nguyen Anh, aided by Cambodian mercenaries and Chinese pirates, recaptured Saigon, but lost it again in 1783. The Tay Son abolished the Le dynasty in 1787. The following year, China, taking advantage of the civil war, invaded, but was repulsed. As the Tay Son were busy fighting the Chinese, Nguyen Anh regained with French help the entire South. He went on to take Hue and Hanoi and declared himself emperor in1802. Reigning as Emperor Gia Long 嘉隆, he founded the last dynasty, the Nguyen 阮朝 and renamed his kingdom Vietnam.

FRENCH RULE

French involvement in Vietnam can be traced to a Jesuit scholar named Alexandre de Rhodes (1591–1660) from Avignon. Jesuit missionaries expelled from Japan by Lord Toyotomi Hideyoshi were allowed to enter Vietnam in 1615. They established themselves at Hoi An 會安 (formerly called Faifo), a Portuguese trading junction fifteen miles south of Danang. The city soon became a mission post where Portuguese, Spanish and Italian missionaries mingled with French Jesuits. De Rhodes is said to have learned Vietnamese in six months, and completed the romanization of the Vietnamese language, which until then had been written using Chinese characters. Despite the civil war between the North and the South, Rhodes made it to Hanoi in 1627. There he won many converts, but was soon expelled by the Trinh regime wary of foreign influence. The state saw Christianity as a threat to the traditional Confucian order and French missionary activity was closely associated with trade right from the outset. Because Pope Alexander VII had strained relations with France he showed little enthusiasm for mission work in Indochina. Rhodes tried to enlist the support of merchants by touting the riches waiting to be found in Indochina. In a book published in Paris in 1653, he claimed, among other things, that the country produced so much silk that the material was used in making fishing lines and sailing chords.

Missionary activity became increasingly risky as the state cracked down on the missionaries and their Vietnamese converts. Trade too made little headway as the majority of the population consisted of peasants too poor to buy French goods. In 1767, French general Count Charles Hector d'Estaing proposed dispatching a force of 3,000 troops to capture Tourane (Danang), but the French, after the loss of their possessions in India to the British, lacked the resources for such an expedition. French fortunes took a turn toward the end of the 18th century when another cleric Bishop Pigneau de Béhaine (1741–1799) involved himself in the Vietnamese civil war. Pigneau had befriended the young Nguyen Anh when the latter sought refuge in his seminary in the southern coastal town of Ha Tien. The bishop at first appealed to Paris to help Nguyen Anh, but the court of Louis XVI, in the throes of the French Revolution, could offer none. Not to be deterred, Pigneau privately recruited sailors, soldiers and officers from the French navy and colonies for Nguyen Anh's army. With French arms and mercenaries, Nguyen Ahn wrested control of the country from the Tay Son in 1802 after a prolonged struggle.[11]

Nguyen Anh, now the Gia Long emperor, was indebted to individual Frenchmen for his success and kept some as advisers in his court, but he was a Confucianist at heart. Although he saw the power of Western science, he retained key Confucian institutions such as the civil service examination. Like his predecessors, he regarded Christianity and the French as a threat to the Vietnamese way of life. For his successor, he appointed Minh Mang, the eldest son of his first concubine. Minh Mang was known for his anti-Western sentiments, and rejected French proposals for diplomatic and trade relations. His successor, Thieu Tri, was equally cautious about the French and their missionary project. By the middle of the 19th century, Catholic converts had grown to an estimated 300,000. Franco-Vietnamese relations deteriorated, and in April 1847, two French warships sent to secure the release of two French missionaries in Danang, were attacked by Vietnamese corvettes. The French returned fire, sinking the Vietnamese vessels, and they bombarded the harbour, killing hundreds of civilians within a few hours. In 1856, the French attacked Danang again, when the emperor Tu Duc ordered two French priests to be executed. By this time, France under Napoleon III was ready to join other European powers in the scramble for colonies. In the 1850s, French industrial capitalists coveting a larger share of overseas markets joined missionaries in calling for military action. On 31 August 1858, fourteen French warships with 2,500 men on board, including the Jesuit Monsignor Pellerin, sailed into the port of Danang and captured the city the next day. But the French met stiff resistance beyond the city and tropical disease soon claimed more lives than actual combat. The setback sowed doubts in Paris about the colonial enterprise, but the French pressed on, and twenty-five years later, completed the conquest of Vietnam, when the court at Hue capitulated and signed a treaty giving the French control over the whole country.[12]

Vietnamese citizens defied the French right from the start. Passive resistance by Vietnamese civil servants bogged down the colonial government. The French themselves had no understanding of how to run the colony, which soon became a steady drain on the French treasury. Paul Doumer, a new governor determined to stem the losses, took charge in 1897. Doumer brought in thousands of bureaucrats from France, and kept the Vietnamese in minor positions where they received a fraction of the wages of even low-grade French officers. Seeing the country as a market for French goods and a source of valuable raw materials, he built roads, railways, bridges and harbours, but showed no interest in developing local industry; rice, coal, rare minerals and rubber were exported without processing. Little of the profit was reinvested, and whatever progress made benefited only French businesses and a small class of Vietnamese large landowners created by the French. Colonial Vietnam profited neither the French state nor the French people back home. The treasury in Paris never recovered the vast sums spent over forty years to pacify Vietnam, and ordinary Frenchmen continued to pay the same price for rice and rubber products as consumers in countries without colonial rice and rubber industries. Industry in France too was robbed of customers by the anti-development policies. Without industrialization, there was no Vietnamese middle class, and peasants, who made up 90 per cent of the population, could simply not afford French goods. The Indochina market for French merchandize consisted of the mere 6,000 or so large-scale indigenous land-owners and French residents.[13]

Not surprisingly, the Vietnamese gained nothing under colonial rule. For the majority, life was harder in 1930 than a century before. Doumer levied onerous taxes to finance the construction of roads and railways, which were mostly under-utilized.[14] Even though rice acreage quadrupled between 1880 and 1930, the average peasant's rice consumption decreased. Great parcels of land opened up by irrigation were not distributed to needy peasants but auctioned off to Vietnamese collaborators and French speculators. The policy created a new class of large landowners who taxed tenant farmers as much as 60 per cent of their harvest, leaving barely enough for the farmer's family. Small land-owning farmers fared only slightly better; their rice fetched less than 15 per cent of the price at the Saigon export market, the difference accruing to Chinese middlemen and French exporters. To balance the colony's finances, Doumer levied taxes on opium, wine and salt, and made salt production a state monopoly which curtailed supply and led to a tenfold price increase. The government conscripted corvée labour for public works projects while healthcare was grossly deficient with two doctors for every 100,000 people, compared to 25 in the Philippines, and 76 in Japan.[15]

SINO-VIET RELATIONS DURING THE COLONIAL PERIOD

Vietnam's relations with China improved thanks to the French. After centuries of mistrust, adversity drew the two neighbours together. Facing a common enemy, they became natural allies. The Chinese frustrated French ambitions in northern Vietnam (which the French called 'Tonkin'), but suffered a major naval defeat at Fuzhou in 1884 which forced it to relinquish suzerainty over Vietnam. Nevertheless, the Vietnamese continued to watch developments in China closely. Many Vietnamese intellectuals were trained in the Confucian tradition and were literate in classical Chinese. Patriots such as Phan Boi Chau 潘佩珠 and Phan Chu Trinh 潘周楨 sought the advice of Chinese reformists such as Kang Youwei 康有為 and Liang Qichao 梁啟超, and Phan Boi Chau modelled his own revolutionary party, the Vietnamese Restoration League, after Sun Yat-sen's Kuomintang. However, Vietnamese born after 1900 were educated in French and did not share the same regard for Confucian values, which led to a decline in Vietnamese intellectual esteem for China, a trend exacerbated by the latter's own incapacity to resist European imperialism. Like the Chinese, the Vietnamese began looking to the West for political ideas. Mirroring the debates in China, Vietnamese intellectuals pondered the question of which theories best suited Vietnam. Marx was little known outside the West, but the Russian Revolution impressed the Chinese and Vietnamese, who began to study his ideas. The Vietnamese Revolutionary Youth League, the first Marxist group in French Indochina, was formed in 1925, just four years behind the Chinese Communist Party (CCP), and the destinies of both parties were closely linked from the outset. They found immediate appeal among radical intellectuals, and to escape the French police, the Youth League set its headquarters in Guangzhou (Canton) where some of its members also joined the CCP.[16]

The Vietnamese, however, were guided by the Moscow-based Communist International (Comintern), and promising league members were sent to train in Russia. After Chiang Kai-shek's crackdown on the communists in Guangzhou in

1927, the Youth League became even more dependent on Moscow. To stay out of Chiang's reach, the league moved its headquarters to Hong Kong. Under constant pressure from Chiang and the Kuomintang (KMT), the CCP's position grew increasingly precarious. Then, in 1941, Hitler invaded the Soviet Union, and Russia suddenly found herself fighting for her own very survival, and had little interest left for the Vietnamese cause. This brought the Chinese and Vietnamese back into direct contact, mainly through Ho Chi Minh.

HO CHI MINH

Ho Chi Minh (1890–1969) epitomized the fraternal link between China and Vietnam in their struggle against the West. Ho was a cosmopolitan nationalist with a deep understanding of China, Vietnam and the West. The son of an accomplished Confucian scholar, Ho mastered classical Chinese at an early age, and wrote Chinese poetry, but at his father's behest, attended a French school. At twenty-two, he left Vietnam as a galley hand on a French ship and travelled widely, including the US and England. In France (1919–1923), he grew interested in politics, and became a founding member of the French Communist Party. After years overseas, Ho spoke fluent French, English, Russian, Cantonese and Mandarin in addition to his native Vietnamese.[17] On state visits abroad, he often spoke without interpreters.

In 1923, Ho enrolled at the Communist University of the Toilers of the East (KUTV), an élite college in Moscow for communist cadres from the colonial world. The school's alumni included Liu Shaoqi, Deng Xiaoping, Chiang Ching-kuo and Mahabendra Nath Roy. He returned to Guangzhou in 1924, when he gave lectures at the Whampoa Military Academy to young Vietnamese who would later become the backbone of the communist movement in Vietnam. In Guangzhou, Ho met and married Zeng Xueming (Tăng Tuyết Minh) 曾雪明, a young Chinese Catholic woman. She was 21 and he was 36. When his comrades objected, he said: 'I will marry her despite your disapproval because I need a woman to teach me the language and keep house'. The following year, Chiang Kai-shek launched a brutal anti-communist purge, and Ho fled to Moscow. He faced constant danger, and the couple never saw each other again.[18] Ho served as adviser to Chinese communist forces and had frequent contact with top CCP leaders. He worked tirelessly for the cause, and by the outbreak of World War II, had built the Vietnamese communists into a disciplined force.

WORLD WAR II

The Japanese invaded China from the north in July 1937, and captured the capital Nanjing within a few months. Japanese troops advanced into the southern provinces Guandong and Guangxi in November 1939, and Chiang Kai-shek's beleaguered forces there depended on the French railway to bring in supplies from the port of Haiphong. The Japanese moved swiftly to sever this vital lifeline, and to use Vietnam as a staging area for the invasion of Southeast Asia. By the summer of 1940, Paris had fallen, and French colonies came under the control of the French Vichy government of Marshal Philippe Pétain. As an ally of Germany, Japan now enjoyed Berlin's support through the Vichy government. On September 22, France signed an accord allowing Tokyo to station 6,000 troops in Indochina. Within hours, Japanese troops under the command of General Akihito Nakamura, crossed the border and by October, over 10,000 had poured in. The French colonial government remained in place, but only as long as it suited the Japanese high command.[19]

To fight the French and the Japanese, Ho formed the *Viet Nam Doc Lap Dong Minh* (or Viet Minh 越盟), the League for the Independence of Vietnam in 1941. Ho sought Kuomintang support and got none, but Zhang Fakui, the Kuomintang commander in south China, allowed the Viet Minh to operate freely in his area. Aid from the Chinese communists was modest since they were absorbed in their own struggle against the Kuomintang and the Japanese. Meanwhile, material assistance from Moscow had all but dried up. As Vietnam's conditions were similar to China's, Ho abandoned the Soviet model of workers' revolution in favour of Maoist peasant revolution. From the Chinese, Ho Chi Minh and Vo Nguyen Giap learned to wage a 'people's war'. Giap spent a good part of 1942 in Yan'an studying Mao's strategy for political and guerrilla warfare, which he skilfully applied against the French. With Japan's sudden surrender in August 1945, the Viet Minh launched a general uprising, and gained control of most of the country within two weeks. On 2 September 1945, Ho declared independence and established the Democratic Republic of Vietnam (DRV) with its seat of government in Hanoi. At the Potsdam Conference a few months earlier, however, the Allied leaders had decided to hand Indochina back to the French. With British and American help, the French returned in force, but the Viet Minh remained determined to eject them.

THE TIGER AND THE ELEPHANT

Against the French, the Vietnamese adopted Mao's strategy of 'surrounding the cities from the countryside' by mobilizing the peasants.[20] The Viet Minh 'would crouch in the jungle like a tiger and come out of its lair at night to tear the French elephant to pieces'.[21] At first, the Viet Minh could only mount small-scale guerrilla attacks but the balance shifted decisively once the Chinese Communist Party came to power in 1949. The Chinese stepped up aid to the Viet Minh, trained Vietnamese commanders, reorganized defences and strengthened their economic base. They taught the Vietnamese how to mobilize the peasantry through land reform, and overall, transferred a significant amount of knowledge and experience. Moscow and Beijing agreed to a division of labour, whereby Stalin supported communist parties in Eastern Europe, while Mao backed communist movements in Southeast Asia. During this period, the Chinese and Vietnamese enjoyed a close, productive relationship. Mao was eager to export his model of revolution, and Ho was ready to learn but it was not a simple teacher-student relationship; Ho was his own man and set his own agenda, even when it contradicted the Chinese.

DIEN BIEN PHU

With Chinese aid, the Viet Minh took the offensive, and pushed the French out of all key positions along the Chinese border by late 1950. Both Truman and Eisenhower considered Indochina vital to American interests, and Washington bore 80 per cent of the cost of the war. Yet the French were losing. Heavy and ill-suited to the jungles and swamps of Indochina, the equipment supplied by the Americans kept French troops tied to the roads. By 1953, the Viet Minh controlled most of the North, and great swaths of the Center and South. The French fielded half a million men in Indochina, an advantage of two to one, but suffered heavy casualties in jungle fighting. In February 1954, the Viet Minh surrounded a strong French garrison in Dien Bien Phu, deep in the hills of northwestern Vietnam close to the Laotian border. Viet Minh forces were led by Vo Nguyen Giap, a former school teacher with a keen interest in military history and strategy, and who closely studied Sunzi and Napoleon. Supplies came from China 200 miles away, transported by 75,000 men and women on foot and on bicycle. The French garrison was deployed in a basin ('la cuvette') surrounded by mountain peaks. In one of the most extraordinary feats of military history, the Viet Minh hauled heavy artillery supplied by the Chinese through difficult terrain up the rear slopes of the mountains surrounding the French positions, then dug tunnels through the mountains, and placed the guns overlooking the French. Hidden in well-camouflaged caves, the artillery was virtually invisible to French spotters.

Numbering 49,000 men by early March, the Viet Minh shelled the French before launching their first infantry attack on 13 March 1954. Fierce fighting ensued. The French garrison, made up of crack paratroopers and foreign legionnaires combined with Moroccan, Algerian and Indochinese units, repulsed repeated Viet Minh assaults on their positions. They were resupplied by air, but as key positions were overrun, the garrison perimeter shrank and resupply became impossible. Viet Minh anti-aircraft fire crippled French air support, while artillery pounded the garrison day and night. Distraught at his inability to bring effective counterfire to bear on the Viet Minh guns despite his contempt for his adversary, the French artillery commander, Colonel Charles Piroth, killed himself in his bunker with a hand grenade.[22] As the situation grew desperate, the French asked Washington for help. A plan called 'Operation Vulture' was mooted to use American B-29 bombers from the Philippines to drop four nuclear weapons.[23] President Eisenhower, however, ruled out American intervention unless other allies joined in. Left to its fate, the garrison fell on 6 May after a two-month siege. The French put 16,000 men into Dien Bien Phu, or a tenth of the total French force in Indochina. The defeat dealt a serious blow to French prestige and showed that the Vietnamese were capable of defeating a European army in a pitched battle. The Indochina war had cost the French 92,000 dead, 114,000 wounded and 28,000 captured. Public opinion polls in February 1954 showed only 7 per cent of the French people wanted to continue the fight. The French government resigned, and the new leftwing prime minister, Pierre Mendès France, ordered French withdrawal from Indochina, marking the end of the French colonial empire in the East.

THE GENEVA ACCORD

Less than three months later, a ceasefire agreement was reached at the Geneva Conference attended by the United States, Soviet Union, China, France and Great Britain but disagreement between China and Vietnam led to mistrust. Ho was eager to reunite his country, but the Chinese feared that a military drive to capture the South would provoke American intervention. China had just fought a bitter campaign against the US-led forces on the Korean peninsula (1950–1953), one which spent valuable resources and took a toll on the Chinese economy. She was not keen to fight another war and preferred to stabilize the situation in Indochina and focus on her own development. The Russians concurred, and together with the Chinese, persuaded Ho Chi Minh to stop at the 17th parallel arguing that if Ho waited two years, he could easily win in the national elections and reunify the country without firing a single shot. Otherwise, the Americans might intervene, they cautioned. The best strategy according to Sunzi, the 6th century BC strategist, was to win without a fight if possible.

To implement the ceasefire, the country was divided at the 17th parallel into two military zones; the French would withdraw to the South while the Viet Minh retreated to the North. The accord called for national elections within two years, but the United States did not sign the accord, and following the French withdrawal, stepped in to prop up the South with massive military and economic aid.[24] The Ngo Dinh Diem regime in Saigon refused to hold elections, and the country remained divided. The Vietnamese subsequently accused the Chinese of betraying them at this important juncture, and of preferring a divided Vietnam. The Chinese denied the charge, saying that China, being so much stronger, had no reason to fear a reunified Vietnam. They said they no more wished for a divided Vietnam than for a partitioned Korea. To show empathy and fraternity, Mao openly condemned dynastic China's transgressions against Vietnam, and Zhou Enlai laid a wreath at Hanoi's Nhi Chinh Temple to commemorate the revolt against Chinese rule in 39 AD.[25] Beijing continued to send substantial levels of men and material to help Vietnam reconstruct and face the unfolding struggle against America. By 1961, China provided over $600 million of aid to Vietnam, far exceeding the amount of support from the Soviet Union. Beijing also assured Hanoi that it was ready to give still more aid if the US attacked North Vietnam.[26]

As prospects for peaceful reunification faded, Hanoi took up arms once again. Whereas Kruschchev was reluctant to confront Washington, Mao was more ready. Developments inside China also influenced foreign policy. Beijing's simultaneous programme of collectivization and industrial development failed, resulting in famine exacerbated by bad weather in which millions died. The Chinese Communist Party called a halt to the Great Leap Forward (1958–1961), as the initiative was called, laying the blame squarely on Mao. Despite his mistakes, however, Mao enjoyed huge popularity among the masses, and he staged a comeback in 1967 through the Cultural Revolution, a programme of intense class struggle. The radical tone of domestic politics spilled over into foreign policy.

THE SECOND INDOCHINA WAR

Beijing at first advised Hanoi to bide its time, but the North Vietnamese leadership decided in May 1959 to resume armed struggle in the South. At about the same time, Sino-Soviet relations soured, and whereas Moscow held back, Beijing said that 'on questions of such an important struggle of principle, we cannot act as onlookers or follow a middle course'.[27] The Sino-Soviet split undermined the world socialist movement and the anti-colonial struggle. Hanoi refrained from openly taking sides, despite pro-Soviet and pro-Chinese camps within party ranks. Although it was sympathetic to Vietnamese aspiration for reunification, Beijing did not wish to be drawn into an unnecessary confrontation any more so than the US. Hanoi was certain, however, that China would intervene (as they had done in Korea) if the Americans were to invade the North. In 1964, as Washington stepped up military involvement in Vietnam, Chinese foreign minister Chen Yi assured Hanoi that 'China and the DRV are friends and neighbors like lips and teeth. The Chinese people cannot be expected to look on with folded arms in the face of any aggression against the DRV'.

Then in October 1964, Krushschev was ousted and replaced by Leonid Brezhnev who was keen to support socialist movements around the world. When President Johnson started bombing the North, Brezhnev quickly offered support to Hanoi and called for an air corridor and the use of airfields in China to supply Vietnam. The proposal was a clever ploy to put Beijing on the spot and undercut her claim that she alone was willing to come to the aid of Third World friends. At the same time, it put pressure on China to live up to its promises to aid Vietnam. For Moscow, an escalation in Vietnam that drew the US and China, its two enemies, into war would benefit the Soviet Union. The CCP was split over how to respond. President Liu Shaoqi and CCP General Secretary Deng Xiaoping saw the United States as the main threat and advocated a temporary rapprochement with Moscow to resist the Americans whereas Chairman Mao and Minster of Defense Lin Biao saw the Soviet Union as the principal enemy. Nevertheless, both factions wanted to support Hanoi; they only disagreed over the extent of assistance to give. They wanted to help the Vietnamese win without provoking an open clash with the United States. They sent anti-aircraft brigades and hundreds of thousands of troops to help in construction and repair work but turned down requests for fighter pilots. According to Chinese sources, Beijing supplied more than 320,000 troops and large amounts of equipment including aircraft. Chinese support averaged $200 million a year.[28]

The Diem regime in Saigon grew increasingly repressive and refused to hold the elections promised in Geneva. In 1963, Diem and his brother Ngo Dinh Nhu were toppled in a *coup d'état* approved by Washington. American involvement in Vietnam increased steadily, spurred on by Cold War tensions and the domino theory that if Vietnam fell, other Southeast Asian states would follow suit. Acting at first as advisers, American troops soon engaged directly in combat. Following President Lyndon Johnson's election victory in 1964, troop numbers rose from 3,500 to 543,000 men by 1968. Rather than merely guarding key installations, General William Westmoreland sent his troops on merciless 'search-and-destroy' missions across the South.[29] The enemy was the guerrilla force known as the Vietcong 越共 (a contraction of Viet Nam Cong San or Vietnamese Communists), officially called the National Liberation Front of South Vietnam. This was a South Vietnamese movement distinct from the North Vietnamese, although they shared a common ideology and goal of national liberation. The conflict was fought with extreme ferocity and destructiveness. After taking office, Johnson ordered an air war against the North and in a sustained campaign codenamed 'Rolling Thunder', American aircraft dropped 643,000 tons of bombs compared to 503,000 tons in the Pacific theatre during World War II.[30]

By 1967, it was clear to US Central Intelligence Agency (CIA) analysts that enemy troop numbers reported by Westmoreland were grossly understated. Military officials, together with elements of the CIA leadership, were worried that the truth about enemy strength would undermine public confidence in the war's 'progress', intensify anti-war sentiments and exacerbate Johnson's domestic political woes. To prevent this, military intelligence set an artificial ceiling above which enemy strength was not allowed to climb. It would take the Tet Offensive of January 1968, a bold, coordinated and suicidal attack by Vietcong and North Vietnamese forces against Saigon, Hue and every provincial capital in South Vietnam, to stun the Americans and reveal the scale of the intelligence deception. Fifteen thousand American G.I.s died that year – the bloodiest year for the Americans – and it marked a turning point.[31]

According to a Gallup poll, American public support for the war fell to 26 per cent after the Tet Offensive. At this point, the conflict had already claimed 30,000 American lives, and America's political leadership wanted a way out of Vietnam, but Richard Nixon, reckoning that peace would hurt his chances of becoming president, sabotaged Johnson's 1968 peace initiative.[32] Nixon was elected president the next year, and fighting raged for another six years, during which he ordered the bombing of Hanoi and Haiphong, and secretly expanded the air campaign into neighbouring Laos and Cambodia.[33] Popular opposition to the war reached new heights with the publication of the Pentagon Papers in 1971.

DANIEL ELLESBERG AND
THE PENTAGON PAPERS

Educated at Harvard (graduated *summa cum laude*) and Cambridge, Daniel Ellesberg served for three years in the US Marine Corp before earning a PhD in economics from Harvard and working as an analyst for the RAND Corporation and the Pentagon. After two years in South Vietnam, he returned to RAND and contributed to a top secret study of the conduct of the Vietnam War of the period from 1945 to 1967. Commissioned by Defense Secretary Robert McNamara, the study completed in 1969 showed that the administrations of Harry S. Truman, Dwight D. Eisenhower, John F. Kennedy and Lyndon B. Johnson all misled the public about the degree of US involvement in Vietnam, from Truman's decision to extend military aid to France during its campaign against the Viet Minh to Johnson's plans to escalate the war as early as 1964 while claiming the opposite during that year's presidential election. It revealed that the real objective of the war was to contain China rather than secure an independent non-communist South Vietnam as Johnson had avowed. Comparing China to Nazi Germany and Imperial Japan, McNamara accused the Chinese of conspiring against the US:

China – like Germany in 1917, like Germany in the West and Japan in the East in the late 30's, and like the USSR in 1947 – looms as a major power threatening to undercut our importance and effectiveness in the world and, more remotely but more menacingly, to organize all of Asia against us.[34]

Classified documents revealed the true nature of the war:

It was no more a 'civil war' after 1955 or 1960 than it had been during the US-supported French attempt at colonial reconquest. A war in which one side was entirely equipped and paid by a foreign power – which dictated the nature of the local regime in its own interest – was not a civil war. To say that we had 'interfered' in what is 'really a civil war', as most American academic writers and even liberal critics of the war do to this day, simply screened a more painful reality and was as much a myth as the earlier official one of 'aggression from the North'. In terms of the UN Charter and of our own avowed ideals, it was a war of foreign aggression, American aggression.[35]

To expose the duplicity, Ellesberg leaked the Pentagon Papers, as the study came to be called, to the *New York Times*.

DISCORD OVER CAMBODIA

From 1965 onward, Hanoi started to rely more on Moscow while Beijing voiced reservations about Hanoi's war strategy. Vietnamese leaders were divided: Le Duan and Le Duc favoured closer links with Moscow while Vo Nguyen Giap, Truong Chinh and Pham Van Dong were less keen. Hanoi shifted toward Moscow after the death of Ho Chi Minh in 1969, and tensions soon arose with Beijing over events in Cambodia. In March 1970, a US-backed *coup d'état* overthrew Prince Norodom Sihanouk and brought a pro-Western government into power. Both Beijing and Hanoi favoured Cambodian neutrality, but

Vietnam and Cambodia were traditional enemies who fought bitterly over territory in the past. Beijing and Hanoi tried to maintain a delicate balance in Cambodia, but things unravelled with the rise of Pol Pot.[36]

Pol Pot (1925–1988) was of mixed Sino-Khmer descent and came from a moderately wealthy family of rice farmers. Schooled in a Buddhist monastery and later in a Catholic high school, he went on to study radio electronics in Paris where he became a Marxist. He returned to Cambodia in 1953 after failing his exams three years in a row but rose to become the head of the Khmer Rouge and the prime minister of Democratic Kampuchea (DK). During his term as premier (1976–1979), the Khmer Rouge forced urban dwellers to the countryside to work on collective farms and construction projects. About a quarter of the country's 8 million people died from harsh work conditions and malnutrition. Chinese officials disapproved of the policy, but the Khmer leadership did as it pleased. Pol Pot's relationship with Beijing was marked by mutual suspicion and held together by convenience rather than ideology. The Chinese were caught in a bind; they feared Pol Pot's murderous behaviour would draw them into direct confrontation with Vietnam and yet could not allow Vietnam to gain hegemony over Indochina. In the end, Pol Pot destroyed his own economy, embarrassed China, and provoked war with Vietnam.[37]

Sihanouk had allowed the Vietcong and North Vietnamese free passage along Cambodia's eastern borders and prevented

South Vietnamese and American troops from pursuing them into Cambodia. When the new regime of General Lon Nol demanded the withdrawal of North Vietnamese and Vietcong troops from Cambodia, Hanoi decided it was time to act. At a meeting in Beijing, Vietnamese premier Pham Van Dong proposed a united front against Lon Nol, but Beijing hesitated because of it had begun to align with Washington against the Soviet Union. Meanwhile, Pol Pot wrested power from the pro-Hanoi faction within the main Cambodian communist party – the Kampuchean People's Revolutionary Party (KPRP) later called the Kampuchean Communist Party (KCP). Hanoi saw Pol Pot as Beijing's tool while he, like any Khmer, distrusted the Vietnamese. Nonetheless, a coalition of revolutionary groups in Laos, Cambodia and South Vietnam took shape, but cooperation was difficult. Just as the Vietnamese disliked Chinese advisers, the Khmers resented Vietnamese advisers and ethnic friction was common.

Relations between Beijing and Hanoi continued to worsen. The peace talks in Paris coincided with rapprochement between Beijing and Washington, which fuelled suspicion in Hanoi about Beijing's intentions. Warming Sino-American ties made Washington more ready to compromise in Indochina, but to Hanoi it meant that the US could now take a tougher negotiating stance without fear of objection by Beijing. China had previously advised Vietnam to fight a protracted war, but in 1971 Beijing endorsed a DRV peace plan. Hanoi was pleased but was shocked shortly after by news of President Nixon's visit China. The Vietnamese immediately suspected Beijing and Washington of cutting deals behind their back detrimental to Vietnamese interests. The timing of Nixon's visit invited more suspicion: it took place in February 1972 just before a planned Easter offensive by which Hanoi hoped to strengthen its hand at the peace talks. To Hanoi, the Nixon visit was no less than a stab in the back.

POST VIETNAM WAR

The main source of tension was the conduct of the war and divergent perspectives about the broader context of global geopolitics. China saw the world in terms of two hegemonic powers — the United States and the Soviet Union, whereas Vietnam was focused on her struggle for liberation and leaned toward whomever offered the strongest support. Hanoi suspected Beijing of wanting to keep Vietnam divided in order to dominate Southeast Asia, even while Hanoi herself moved to gain advantage over her traditional rival Cambodia. The Chinese complained bitterly that the Vietnamese lacked gratitude for China's steadfast support in Vietnam's successive struggles against the Japanese, the French, and the Americans. Meanwhile, tensions flared over the fate of Vietnam's ethnic Chinese and competing territorial claims in the South China Sea.

After the fall of the Saigon regime in 1975, the Hanoi government seized several large ethnic Chinese-owned businesses, and in February 1978 started to expel ethnic Chinese, some of whom had been in Vietnam for generations. This sparked a refugee crisis as thousands fled across the border into China. The first to leave were those from the North; some reported losing their jobs or were forced to adopt Vietnamese citizenship (many ethnic Chinese carried Republic of China passports).[38] While Beijing encouraged overseas Chinese 華僑 to adopt local citizenship, many Southeast Asian states distrusted the loyalty of their Chinese subjects or envied their business success. Accusing Hanoi of reneging on a promise to allow gradual naturalization, Beijing cancelled numerous aid projects. Hanoi denied that the nationalization of private enterprise was racially motivated, insisting that it was merely doing what all socialist states, including the PRC, do. By July 1978, the refugee flood reached 140,000 but plans for a consulate in Ho Chi Minh City to process departure collapsed while ships sent to evacuate the Chinese were not allowed to dock. High-level talks to deal with the exodus ended in acrimony.

In December 1973, Hanoi informed Beijing that it planned to prospect for oil in the Gulf of Tonkin, and proposed negotiations to settle potential territorial disputes. China agreed but only after seizing several islands in the Paracels previously occupied by the Saigon regime. In the first round, Hanoi proposed using a 1887 Sino-French treaty as the basis for drawing maritime boundaries. The Chinese rejected the idea as it would mean giving Vietnam two-thirds of the Gulf of Tonkin. The talks failed and tensions mounted in the border areas followed by armed clashes. This time Beijing proposed talks but Hanoi declined preferring to let provincial authorities work things out, which was, of course, impossible. Shortly after the end of the Vietnam War in 1975, Vietnamese troops seized six islands in the Spratlys previously occupied by the Saigon regime. Beijing offered negotiations but Hanoi declined. Then in 1977, a Vietnamese newspaper published a map showing both the Spratlys and the Paracels as Vietnamese territory. The Chinese reacted angrily, citing a letter to Zhou Enlai from Pham Van Dong, one of Ho Chi Minh's closest lieutenants, acknowledging Chinese sovereignty over the two archipelagos in 1958.

INVASION OF CAMBODIA

Driven by age-old Khmer-Viet animosity and suspicions that Hanoi was seeking to dominate Indochina, the Khmer Rouge attacked Vietnamese villages along the Vietnamese-Cambodian border causing significant civilian casualties. After several months of border skirmishes involving ever larger numbers of troops, Hanoi launched a full-scale invasion to remove the Pol Pot regime. With material support from the Soviet Union, Vietnam attacked with 150,000 troops in December 1978. No match for the Vietnamese, the Khmer Rouge were swiftly routed. The Khmer Rouge leadership fled to Thailand, and a new pro-Vietnamese government formed under the leadership of Heng Samrin. Despite their murderous record, however, the Khmer Rouge managed to win support at the United Nations, which promptly called for the withdrawal of foreign troops from Cambodia. The Association of Southeast Asian Nations (ASEAN) too condemned the invasion, seeing it as aggression aimed at establishing Vietnamese hegemony over Indochina. Vietnam became isolated from the international community depriving it of desperately needed external aid to rebuild after decades of war. To push back against what he saw as Vietnamese territorial ambition, Deng Xiaoping ordered a punitive campaign against Vietnam in February 1979 which captured several border towns although raw Chinese recruits suffered heavy casualties against seasoned Vietnamese troops defending home ground. Declaring their mission accomplished, the Chinese withdrew after 27 days. In the aftermath, Vietnam suffered a good ten years of isolation, during which it relied heavily on the Soviet Union for raw materials and grain imports. But as the long Afghan campaign and the arms race drained Soviet resources, Moscow began cutting aid to Vietnam.[39] The beleaguered Vietnamese leadership seeing that isolation was too high a price to pay for occupying Cambodia, ordered a complete withdrawal in 1989.[40] Concurrent with the Soviet occupation of Afghanistan, the Cambodian occupation cost Vietnam 45,000 casualties. To reengage with the international community, Hanoi undertook economic reforms and restored ties with Beijing. In November 1994, President Jiang Zemin visited Hanoi to discuss principles for bilateral relations.[41]

The centrally-planned Vietnamese economy suffered acute shortages and when Moscow abruptly terminated aid worth billions of rubles and trade plummeted, the Vietnamese Communist Party decided to follow China's footsteps. Mindful of Hanoi's wariness, Beijing vowed to abide by the Five Principles of Peaceful Coexistence, and when the Soviet Union collapsed, Deng Xiaoping declined leadership of the international communist movement.[42] In the first decade after normalization of ties in 1991, trade grew 83 fold from $32.23 million in to $2.66 billion, easily surpassing targets set by both sides. By 2000, Chinese investments totaled $180 million while grants and interest-free loans amounted to a further $45 million.[43] A treaty defining land borders was signed in 1999, followed the next year by a treaty on maritime borders in the Gulf of Tonkin. President Tran Duc Luong's state visit to China in 2000 marked an important step in Sino-Viet reconciliation. Both countries are party to the China-ASEAN Free Trade Agreement and as regional economic integration gathers pace, bilateral trade is expected to grow further. Up to 80 per cent of engineering, procurement and construction projects are awarded to Chinese contractors. Disputes over the Paracel and Spratly Islands remain a thorn in the side, however. In their long history, Vietnam and China have been close allies as well as bitter foes. Sino-Vietnamese relations have returned to their usual pattern of skillful balance, and every Vietnamese leader must resist China and get along with it at the same time. Even as both sides continue to share fraternal links through common ideology, pro- and anti-Chinese factions vie for influence over the future of the nation.

While Sino-Vietnamese relations are marked by wars and great power politics, China's relations with other Southeast Asian states present a different picture. Rather than mandarins and soldiers, the main actors were merchants, artisans and labourers who crossed the South China Sea as early as the first century AD. At first transient and mostly men, they brought wares, tools and skills which transformed the local economy. They bore no arms, and over time, intermarried and produced a community of mixed heritage, but faced new challenges once the Europeans arrived. Who built Manila and how did the Spaniards and Filipinos regard the Chinese in their midst? How did Spanish colonial policies differ from French ones? We turn to these questions in the next chapter.

CHAPTER 5

THE PHILIPPINES

The Philippine archipelago comprises over 7,000 islands, but up to the end of the 19th century less than a thousand were inhabited. Before the advent of the Spaniards, the Philippines was not a unified polity. It was made of several small kingdoms with few extant historical record. The Laguna Copper Plate dated 900 AD is the earliest known written document found in the Philippines. Unlike Vietnam or Japan, there is no record of war with China. Sino-Philippine relations began not with state-to-state diplomatic exchanges, but with the activities of merchants, artisans and labourers who crossed the South China Sea to make a living. It is the story of Chinese immigrants and their interaction, first with the natives and then with the Spaniards, Americans and Japanese. Intermarriage between Chinese men and native women produced a community of mestizos who played an important part in the formation of the Filipino national identity, and who became the vanguard of the Philippine struggle for independence. This chapter traces the long history of Chinese involvement in Philippine society and its implication for Sino-Philippine relations today.

THE CHINESE IN THE PHILIPPINES

The Chinese arrived in the Philippines at least five centuries before Magellan set foot on the islands in 1521. Direct contact between China and the Philippines began at least as early as the Song period (960–1279).[1] Starting in the 9th century, Chinese merchants travelled to the Philippines to trade with Arabs barred from entering China. Thirteenth-century Chinese historian Ma Duanlin 馬端臨 wrote that merchants from the Philippines brought their wares to Guangzhou and Quanzhou in 982.[2] According to Chinese chronicles, Luzon produced gold, which became the source of its prosperity. A Spanish document of 1586 noted that the Filipinos were 'keen traders and have traded with China for many years, and before the advent of the Spaniards they sailed to the Moluccas, Malacca, Aceh, Borneo and other kingdoms'. Chinese geographers Zhao Rugua 赵汝适 (1209–1214) and Wang Dayuan 汪大渊 (1311–1350) noted that the pre-hispanic Filipinos were scrupulously honest. Commerce was carried out through barter, although commodities were priced in gold or metal gongs.[3] Chinese markets sprang up in coastal areas during the Song and in the hinterland during the Ming.[4] Admiral Zheng He's fleet visited the archipelago thrice between 1405 and 1417 and a high-ranking mandarin, Ko Ch'a Lao 許柴佬, was posted to Luzon.[5]

The arrival of the Spaniards in the 1560s brought new opportunities. Fujian merchants saw that they could ship goods from China to Manila for markets in Mexico, then part of the Spanish empire. Unlike the Portuguese, the Spaniards had no trading stations in China and could not transport goods from China in their own vessels. They relied on Chinese vessels from Quanzhou and Xiamen to bring silk, cotton cloth, ceramics, ironware, sugar, and other luxury goods to Manila to be transshipped to Mexico on the Manila galleons. On their return to Manila, the galleons carried Mexican silver to pay for the Chinese wares, and Chinese and Spanish middlemen made huge fortunes from this arrangement.[6] Founded by the Spaniards in 1571, Manila became the single largest foreign port for Chinese goods for the next two centuries as silver from the Mexico flowed into China via the galleon trade. The Spaniards began very quickly to rely on the Chinese to supply the colony with all kinds of goods and services. From China came not only silk and costly wares, but also cattle, horses, foodstuffs, metals, fruits and even ink and paper. From physicians, barbers, porters, tailors and shoemakers to metal-workers, silversmiths, sculptors, locksmiths, painters, masons and weavers, the Chinese provided efficient and inexpensive services in the sectors shunned by the Spanish colonists. Frugal, industrious and astute, they became the backbone of the economy.[7] The local population was sparse and the conquistadors relied on the Chinese as brokers, craftsmen and labourers to build the infrastructure, and by 1590, Manila's 7,000 Chinese were indispensable to the prosperity of the city. Like many immigrant populations, they came from poor peasant families and focused on making a living, and although they took Filipina wives, they remained attached to their homeland and showed little interest in local politics.[8] Anthropologist David P. Barrows (1873–1954) observed:

> Of all the Eastern races only one has been a constant and important factor in the life of the islands. This is the Chinese. The Chinese are without question the most remarkable colonizers in the world. They readily marry with every race. The children that follow such union are not only numerous but healthy and intelligent. The coasts of China teem with overcrowding populations. Emigration to almost any land means improvement of the Chinese of poor birth. These qualities and conditions, with their keen sense for trade and their indifference to physical hardship and danger, make the Chinese almost a dominant factor whenever political barriers have not been raised against their entry.[9]

This hardy people monopolized the retail trade and acted as *compradores* taking Chinese imports to the villages in exchange for local products for the Spanish community. But as they became more numerous than the Spaniards, they became perceived as a threat. By 1603, barely 32 years after the founding of Manila, the Chinese in Luzon numbered an estimated 20,000 compared to 1,000 Spaniards.[10] The Spanish attitude toward the Chinese was informed by their experience with the Moors and the Jews in Spain. Like the Chinese, they were economically necessary and yet culturally difficult to assimilate, and the Spanish tried to hispanize, segregate and even expel them from the Iberian peninsula. The Spaniards applied the same methods on the Chinese, and within a few years, relations became hostile. They called the Chinese 'sangley',[11] which soon became a term of derogation, taxed them more heavily than the natives (called *indíos* by the Spanish), imposed arbitrary levies and forced them to row galleys.[12] The Chinese rebelled, but usually ended up worse off. In 1603, Manila's entire Chinese community of 20,000 was massacred and in another uprising in 1639, 20,000 of an estimated 30,000 Chinese residents died. The Spaniards then tried to keep the Chinese population at 6,000, but never succeeded because they simply could not manage without their services.[13]

CHINESE MESTIZOS

The Chinese, mainly from Fujian and Guangdong, intermarried with Filipina women long before the Spanish arrived, and while there were marriages between Spaniards and Filipinas (called *indías* by the Spaniards), the majority of mestizos were children of *sino-india* marriages. The Chinese had an incentive to convert to Catholicism in order to remain in the colony, and the Church welcomed the Chinese mestizos since they usually became faithful converts. Even if a Chinese man already had a wife in China and eventually returned to her in his old age, he left behind mestizo children who were brought up by their devout indía mother. The mestizos moved freely, traded easily, and created their own subculture. 'More active and enterprising, more prudent and pioneering, more oriented to trade and commerce than the indíos', they became the most dynamic segment of society.[14] By the mid-eighteenth century, Chinese mestizos represented 5 per cent of the local population, but comprised a much larger proportion of Manila's inhabitants.[15] They enjoyed certain legal and political rights and favourable social status as the Spanish needed them to keep the capital functioning. They played a pivotal role in forming the Filipino middle class and Filipino nationality, and became the driving force of the 1898 revolution. Still, they were no match for the Chinese when it came to commerce, but obtained an unusual opportunity in the mid-18th century when the Spanish again tried to break Chinese dominance by expelling non-Christian Chinese. Governor Don Pedro Manuel de Arandía (1754–1759) ordered the unconverted Chinese of Manila to be expelled and Christian Chinese left behind to till the land. He tried to displace them with a company run by Spaniards, but the firm went out of business within a year. The Chinese expulsion order allowed mestizos to penetrate markets previously controlled by Chinese and to become the new provisioners. In the capital, they shared economic power with the Chinese as exporters-importers, wholesalers, retailers and artisans, and took over the retail business in the provinces. To circumvent Arandía's expulsion order, many Chinese converted and took *india* wives. By making religion the criterion for expulsion, Arandía inadvertently spurred the growth of the mestizo community, and by the mid-19th century, there were 240,000 Chinese mestizos compared to 10,000 Spanish mestizos. In the second half of the century, they became so numerous and influential that the term mestizo usually referred to them. In his report to London in 1861, the British vice-consul noted:

> The Iloilo mestizos, especially those of Chinese origin, are a remarkable commercial, industrial and speculative race, increasing yearly in social and political importance, and though not so fully pronounced as the Chinese of the persevering and commercial qualities necessary for a continued success under the pressure of great competition, are not without prevision, energy and enterprise sufficient to warrant expectation of a considerable development of cultivation from their operations.[16]

The Chinese mestizos flourished as entrepreneurs for a whole century and emerged as the middle class. From the 1850s, however, Chinese migrants returned in large numbers and their competitiveness forced the mestizos into sectors barred to the Chinese. Many mestizos moved into the provinces, shifting successfully to the professions, landholding, and cultivation of export crops, and became the new landowning class.[17] By the late 1860s, wealthy mestizos could enter prestigious local universities, and later send their children to school in France, England, Austria and Germany. The English traveller and diplomat W.G. Palgrave observed: 'Intellectually, they are generally superior to the unmixed around them. Their members, taken in comparison to the entire population is not great but their wealth and influence go far to make up for this deficiency'.[18]

NATIONALISM

As the mestizos became wealthier, they grew more independent-minded and less compliant. The Spaniards felt threatened by the mestizos who had 'no sympathy for Spain' and 'would be difficult to subdue'. As early as 1827, Spanish official Manuel Bernaldez Pizarro warned that indío and mestizo clerics had 'dangerous tendencies to revolution'. The Spaniards feared an indío revolution led by mestizos and concluded that 'race hatred between the Chinese mestizos and the natives' had to be fostered and the two classes 'separated at sword point'.[19] But it was difficult to separate them because the mestizos identified with the indíos culturally and socially, and with shared grievances, they formed political alliances. The severe punishments meted out to indíos and mestizos bridged the gulf that had separated them. Unlike the Spanish mestizos who identified with the Spaniards, the Chinese mestizo identified with the indíos, and by the last quarter of the 19th century, Chinese mestizo and indíos saw themselves as Filipino, a term previously reserved for Spaniards born in the Philippines. This sense of Filipino nationality first appeared in the writings of two Chinese mestizos – Pedro Paterno and Gregorio Sancianco. Paterno's poems, *Sampaguita* (1880) and his novel *Ninay* (1885) defined the Filipino national feeling, while Sancionco's *El Progresso de Filipinas* (The Progress of the Philippines) described the economic and political problems of the archipelago and denounced the tribute tax from which Spaniards and Spanish mestizos were exempted but which also discriminated between indíos and mestizos. He called for the Philippines to be made a province of Spain and its inhabitants given the same rights as Iberian Spaniards.[20] The ideas of Paterno and Sancianco were carried forward by José Rizal, a writer descended from a long line of mestizos and mestizas.[21] Paterno, Sancianco and Rizal articulated a growing Filipino national consciousness which gave birth to revolution.

SPANISH RULE

Nearly four centuries of Spanish rule were marked by brutality, ineptitude and racism. Mining and agriculture were left undeveloped, and the few thousand Spaniards became rich on graft and taxation. Under the *encomienda* system, the natives were apportioned among the Spaniards and treated like slaves. Whatever benefits the Spaniards brought were incidental as the system was designed to nurture graft and racism and win converts for the Catholic Church. Dominicans, Augustinians and Franciscans, who came to preach, soon controlled nearly half a million acres of the choicest land in the northern islands and prime property in the heart of Manila. They rented out the land to the natives on a share-cropping basis and used them as forced labour to build roads, churches and monasteries. The Spaniards belittled pre-Spanish Filipino culture and regarded the native as 'a machine that walks, eats, sleeps and exists' and 'an incomplete whole, a confusion of sentiments, instincts, desires, energies, passions, colors that crowd each other without forming any single particular one'. The Filipino was 'a motley mixture of different contradictory conditions and qualities…impossible to expose to curiosity and philosophical studies'.[22] The Spaniards used social stratification to keep people in place, and an 1837 legislation decreed that only Spaniards were allowed to wear ties whereas indíos and mestizos were to wear their shirts loose without any neck ornaments. The *Barong Tagalog*, the Philippine national dress, evolved from this proscription. Racial prejudice set the Filipino apart from the Spaniard, but it also fostered among the former a sense of common identity. Through their writings and speeches, Filipino intellectuals brought attention to the ills of the colonial government and the hated friars.

SECULARIZATION

Inherently religious, the natives converted easily to the Catholic faith but their religious devotion became a source of friction when many of the educated Filipinos wanted to become priests but were barred by Spaniards who feared that ordination would lead to social emancipation.[23] One Spanish critic saw a native priest as 'a caricature of the priest, a caricature of the indío, a caricature of the Spaniard, a caricature of the mestizo, a caricature of everybody. He is a patchwork of many things and is nothing'. This racism inspired an uprising in 1841. In response to the discrimination, Apolinario de la Cruz, a devout Catholic Filipino, formed his own religious order, the *Cofradía de San José*, which gained many followers in his home province. To give the Church a taste of its own medicine, the *Cofadria* refused to admit Spaniards and Spanish mestizos without de la Cruz's permission. At its peak, the fraternity boasted 4,500 to 5,000 members, and de la Cruz applied for his order to be recognized by the Church. When the Spanish sent troops to suppress de la Cruz and his followers, they fought back but were defeated. De la Cruz was captured, tried, and sentenced to death by musketry, his body dismembered, and his head hung in a cage on a pole in front of his parents' house in Lucban.[24]

More trouble was on the way. Many parishes were led by Spanish friars instead of priests, but churches came under the supervision of bishops and conflict arose when the bishops wanted to inspect the parishes run by the friars. The friars resigned in protest and the archbishop, Monsignor Pedro Pelaez, a Philippine-born prelate, expedited the ordination of Filipino priests to fill the vacancies much to the ire of the friars who regarded Filipinos unfit for the priesthood because of their brown skin and supposed lack of training and experience. The archbishop died in an earthquake in 1863. but the priests including three Filipinos – Fathers Mariano Gomez, José Burgos and Jacinta Zamora – carried on the struggle. Then, without explanation, the authorities withdrew certain privileges from Filipino soldiers and labourers at Fort San Felipe in Cavite, such as the exemption from tribute and corvée labour. When the men were told the news, they mutinied. The mutiny on the night of 20 January 1872 failed and the authorities executed Fathers Gomez, Burgos and Zamora, whom they blamed for the unrest. From then on, the Spanish government assumed that Filipinos were conspiring to overthrow Spanish rule.

JOSÉ RIZAL

Perhaps the greatest Filipino national hero, Jose Rizal (1861–1896) was born in Laguna Province as one of eleven children. His ancestor Lam Co, a Chinese merchant from Fujian province, emigrated to the Philippines in the 17th century to escape famine, plague and the Manchu invasion. He settled as a farmer and converted to Catholicism, changing his name to

Domingo Mercado in order to avoid discrimination. Rizal's mother came from an affluent Chinese mestizo family and taught her son to read and write by the age of 5. At 21, Rizal went to study medicine at the Universidad Central de Madrid, but also attended classes in Paris and Heidelberg. A polymath skilled in both the sciences and the arts, he wrote poems, essays and novels during his time in Europe, where he resided between 1882 and 1892. Two of his most famous novels, *Noli Me Tángere* (The Social Cancer) and *El Filibusterismo* (The Reign of Greed), unmasked the brutality and corruption of Spanish rule and inspired Filipino nationalism. Conversant in Spanish, English, French, German, Chinese and Arabic, he became the leader of the Propaganda Movement – an information campaign to garner support among Iberian Spaniards for the integration of the Philippines as a province of Spain, representation in the Spanish parliament, the replacement of Spanish friars by Filipino priests, and equality of Filipinos and Spaniards before the law. Rizal returned to the Philippines in 1892 and founded a non-violent-reform society called the Liga Filipina, a crime for which he was deported to Mindanao for four years. In 1896 the Katipunan, a Filipino nationalist secret society, revolted and although he had no part in the insurrection, Rizal was arrested, tried, found guilty by the military and publicly executed by a firing squad in Manila's Luneta Park. His martyrdom convinced Filipinos that there was no alternative to independence from Spain.

REVOLUTION

As a result of similarities in socio-political conditions between France and the Philippines, the Filipinos drew inspiration from the French Revolution of 1789. In both countries, the upper classes enjoyed power and privilege while the lower classes shouldered the tax burden. The Church, which possessed huge landholdings, controlled education and levied its own taxes, was a virtual state within a state.[25] At first, the Filipino middle class sought reform rather than independence and formed the Propaganda Movement whose members included Chinese mestizos who had studied in Europe, such as Marcelo H. Del Pilar, José Rizal, Graciano López Jaena. Their writings found sympathy among some Spaniards, but were largely ignored by the government in Madrid. Matters came to a head when the authorities arrested and executed the 'filibusterers' in Manila. The Revolution of 1896 was due to a large extent to the political awakening of the mestizos as they identified increasingly with the indíos. Spanish writer Enrique Polo de Lar warned in the late 1880s that:

The Filipino mestizo is a breed of all components; he is the herald of restlessness, the adviser of disturbances, and the adversary in obeying colonial laws. All officials must keep guard of them very specially so that with everybody's watchfulness, they will not mix with the ordinary masses.[26]

When the revolution broke out, mestizos participated not as mestizos, but as Filipinos, and comprised leaders of the Katipunan, such as Emilio Aguinaldo and Apolinario Mabini, as well as a large part of the rank and file.

THE KATIPUNAN

Founded in 1892 by Andrés Bonifacio (1863–1897), the Katipunan was a secret society which sought the overthrow of Spanish rule through armed struggle. Its discovery by the authorities in 1896 led to the outbreak of the Philippine Revolution. Bonifacio grew up in the slums of Tondo, and when his parents died, he left school to become the bread winner but remained an avid reader. While not strictly a religious movement, the Katipunan embodied Christian social and political ideals and its creed, *The Duties of the Sons of the People*,[27] included injunctions to love God with all your heart, to share your means with the poor, to die for the freedom of your country, and to believe that the will of the people is also the will of God.[28] By 1896, it boasted an estimated 100,000 members comprising mainly workers and peasants as the urban middle class continued to seek reform rather than revolution. Despite its numbers, the organization lacked the means to revolt and fighting broke out only when the Spaniards discovered its existence and moved to crush it. Hostilities began around Manila on 25 August 1896 and spread to the provinces. Against a superior force, they chose the only strategy possible – guerrilla war. Armed with about one rifle for every ten men, the rebels suffered heavy casualties, but also scored some surprising victories. When Governor-General Basilio Augustin offered amnesty for those who surrendered, some Katipuñeros laid down their arms only to be arrested and tortured for information. Hundreds were incarcerated and suspects in the provinces were brought to Manila to face 'just punishment'. Heads of families were shipped off to the Caroline Islands or penal colonies in Africa, while wealthy families were extorted to secure the release of loved ones. Divided into two rival factions, the rebels suffered serial defeats and retreated northward to Biak-na-bato where Aguinaldo proclaimed a republic in July 1897. In August, Aguinaldo, who had become the undisputed leader of the revolution, agreed to go into exile in exchange for 800,000 pesos to be paid in three instalments. The rebels saw this as a chance to live to fight another day. They were given a first instalment of 400,000 pesos and safe passage to Hong Kong, but never saw the rest of the money. Just as the settlement took effect, an American naval squadron appeared off Manila Bay.

THE BATTLE OF MANILA BAY

Halfway around the world, Spain was fighting another war in another colony. Like the Filipinos, the Cubans were fighting to for independence. The Cuban rebels enjoyed wide American public support because of American business interests on the island, but also due to newspaper coverage of Spanish abuses against the Cubans. Following an unexplained explosion on board the USS Maine, a US warship sent to evacuate US citizens in Havana, the US Congress declared war on Spain on 25 April 1898. US warships sank the Spanish warships in the port of Santiago de Cuba, while America troops landed and routed the Spaniards. On 1 May, before the Spaniards in Manila received notice of the US declaration of war against Spain, US warships sailed from Hong Kong and destroyed the Spanish squadron anchored in Manila Bay. Not having enough time to mobilize sufficient troops to capture Manila, the Americans urged Aguinaldo to return to the Philippines to renew the struggle against the Spaniards, assuring him that the United States had no interest in keeping the Philippines once it was liberated. Taking the Americans at their word, Aguinaldo, allied with the United States, returned to the Philippines and resumed fighting. By June, the rebels had gained control of nearly all of the Philippines with the exception of Manila and Aguinaldo declared independence on 12 June, but neither Spain nor the United States acknowledged his declaration.

THE SIEGE OF MANILA

American reinforcements arrived on 30 June followed by a second and a third contingent on 17 and 31 July. Now confident of dislodging the Spaniards from the city, American commander Commodore George Dewey began talks with Spanish Governor-General Basilio Augustin to persuade him to surrender without a fight. When Madrid learned of Augustin's plan to surrender, it immediately replaced him with General Fermin Jaudenes. Jaudenes too concluded that he faced certain defeat against the combined American and Filipino forces. To save face (and to satisfy the Spanish code of honour), he proposed a mock battle after which he would surrender but on the condition that the rebels not be allowed to take part in liberating the city. Dewey held back the Filipinos while the battle was enacted and duly 'captured' Manila in August. Filipino troops were barred from entering the city and as a settlement was being negotiated, President William McKinley dispatched another 10,000 troops. Filipino leaders were excluded from the peace talks.[29]

Two months later, on 10 December, Madrid and Washington concluded a treaty in Paris ending the Spanish-American War and Spanish rule in the Philippines. The Spaniards, who had lost virtually all territory, negotiated empty-handed with the Americans. Spain ceded the Philippines to the United States in exchange for $20 million as payment for 'Spanish infrastructure'. Filipino diplomat Felipe Agoncillo travelled to Washington to secure recognition of Philippine independence, but was snubbed by McKinley. He then hurried to the Paris talks to submit a memorandum, but was again ignored.[30] Agoncillo then hastened back to Washington to appeal to the US Senate not to ratify the treaty, contending that:

> If the Spaniards have not been able to transfer to the Americans the rights which they did not possess; if the latter have not militarily conquered positions in the Philippines; if the occupation of Manila was a resultant fact prepared by the Filipinos; if the international officials and representatives of the Republic of the United States of America offered to recognize the independence and sovereignty of the Philippines, solicited and accepted their alliance, how can they now constitute themselves as arbiters of the control, administration and future government of the Philippine Islands?

Brushing aside his plea, the senate approved the treaty on 6 February, 1899[31] dispelling all doubts of American duplicity.[32] The stage was now set for another war, but it would not be a war between two sovereign states; it would be simply the US enforcing its 'sovereignty' in the Philippines against an internal 'insurrection'.[33] There was an uneasy peace around Manila with the Americans controlling the city and the Filipinos surrounding them. Once the Spanish laid down their arms, Dewy treated Aguinaldo with contempt. The Filipinos saw they had been cheated. The US came to the Philippines not as a friend, but as an enemy masked as a friend.[34] Tensions ran high, and on 4 February, a US Army private fired the first shot at a Filipino soldier; the Filipinos returned fire. To defuse the situation, Aguinaldo told General Elwell Otis, the US commander, that the shooting had been against his orders but Otis insisted that 'The fighting, having begun, must go on to the grim end'.[35]

CHINESE MESTIZOS IN THE PHILIPPINE-AMERICAN WAR

As the war against Spain turned into the war against the United States, the Chinese mestizos continued to lead as US Army archivists. Captain John Taylor noted:

Natives who have led during the past few years of revolt have probably been almost all partly Chinese...Chinese mestizos, the descendant of Chinese, in many cases educated in Spain and other parts of Europe, are the leaders in the islands in wealth and intelligence. They are the men who were chiefly instrumental in overthrowing the power of Spain, and they are the men who, with the loudest voices, arrogate to themselves the right of speaking for the people of the archipelago. It is not always easy to identify them; they ... prefer to call themselves Filipinos ... but out of the 164 men who were sufficiently important to require separate index cards in classifying the papers of the insurrection in the Philippines against the United States, 27 seem undoubtedly to be of Chinese descent, and a more careful investigation will increase the number. Aguinaldo is one of the 27, and so are 2 of the members of his cabinet, 9 of his generals (one of them a pure blooded Chinese), 1 of 2 heads of his cabinet or council of government, and his principal financial agents.[36]

JOSÉ IGNACIO PAUA

Among the most resourceful leaders of the revolution was a migrant from Fujian called Liu Hengfu 刘亨赙, better known by his Spanish name José Ignacio Paua (1872–1926). From a destitute family, Paua left China at the age of 18 to work for a blacksmith in the Chinese quarter of Binondo, Manila. A quick learner, he soon opened his own hardware shop and ventured into the salt business. Once the revolution began, the revolutionaries desperately needed arms. Paua applied his knowledge of metallurgy to the repair of cannons and other weaponry and raised 400,000 pesos from the Chinese for the revolution. With the help of other Chinese blacksmiths, he built a munitions factory. Paua's knowledge of firearms and his sympathy for the Filipino cause impressed Aguinaldo. He distinguished himself fighting alongside his men and rose to become full general. Filipino leader Teodoro Gonzales recalled:

It was a strange sight in camp to see him — a dashing officer in a colonel's uniform but wearing a pigtail. His soldiers were Filipinos, all veteran fighters; yet they were devoted to him and were proud to serve under his battle standard, notwithstanding the fact that he was a Chinaman.[37]

On 12 June 1898, the day Aguinaldo proclaimed independence, Paua cut off his queue. When his comrades teased him about it, Paua declared: 'Now that you are free from your foreign master, I too am freed from my queue' – a symbol of subjection to the Manchus who ruled China. Other Chinese revolutionaries included Francisco Osorio, Mariano Limjap, Telesforo Chuidian and Roman Ongpin. Osorio, son of a wealthy family, was captured and executed; Limjap and Chuidian took up key positions in the government of the newly declared republic, while businessman and philanthropist Ongpin gave financial support. On the whole, however, the Chinese refrained from open commitment to either side. From bitter experience, the Chinese had learned that they would pay a heavy price if they backed the wrong side. During the British occupation of Manila (1762–1764), they supported the British, only to be left to the tender mercies of the Spaniards when the British withdrew.[38] As a small community, they could only endure the hardships and wait out the war. They were easy targets for the revolutionaries who robbed, destroyed or confiscated their properties, and even those who fled to the provinces were not safe from extortion, despite Aguinaldo's orders to spare them.[39]

AMERICAN CONDUCT

Many Filipinos saw the United States as a virtuous nation, one that had fought not only to win its own independence but also to help the Cubans win theirs. They looked upon the Americans as an altruistic ally, but soon discovered that they were just as brutal and racist as the Spaniards. To deprive the Filipino fighters of support from the general population, the Americans established 'zones of protection', where civilians were forced into concentration camps called *reconcentrados*, which a camp commandant dubbed 'suburbs of hell'. Between January and April 1902, 8,350 of approximately 298,000 prisoners died, with some camps reporting mortality rates as high as 20 per cent. One camp, two miles by one mile in area, was 'home' to 8,000 Filipinos.[40] As for the rules of engagement, the *Philadelphia Ledger* reported:

> Our soldiers…have taken prisoner people who held up their hands and peacefully surrendered, and an hour later, without an atom of evidence to show that they were even *insurrectos*, stood them on a bridge and shot them down one by one, to drop into the water below and float down as an example to those who found their bullet riddled corpses.[41]

…The present war is no bloodless, opera bouffe engagement; our men have been relentless, have killed to exterminate men, women, children, prisoners and captives, active insurgents and suspected people from lads of ten up, the idea prevailing that the Filipino as such was little better than a dog….[42]

The 'water cure' was applied, during which a man is made to lie on his back, and water forced through his mouth with a funnel until his stomach is near bursting. The water is then disgorged by sitting on his stomach and the process repeated. In an indignant speech to veterans and journalists on Memorial Day 1902, however, President Theodore Roosevelt defended the US Army against charges of cruelty by portraying the conflict as one fought between the forces of civilization and savagery. He dismissed the Filipinos as 'Chinese half-breeds', and insisted that 'this is the most glorious war in our nation's history'.[43] The war claimed an estimated 250,000 Filipino lives out of a population of 8 million.[44] Mark Twain wrote in dismay:

We have robbed a trusting friend of his land and his liberty; we have invited clean young men to shoulder a discredited musket and do bandit's work under a flag which bandits have been accustomed to fear, not to follow; we have debauched America's honor and blackened her face before the world.[45]

ANNEXATION OF THE PHILIPPINES

Theodore Roosevelt was a staunch defender of the colonial enterprise. Speaking in Chicago on 10 April 1899 as Assistant Secretary of the Navy (The Strenuous Life speech), he justified the new American possession as a valuable strategic strongpoint, as an inspiring commitment to 'the cause of civilization' and as a contribution to 'the great work of uplifting mankind' pioneered by British empire builders. He saw it as an extension of American westward expansion, and believed that Filipinos were inferior and ought to be treated as Native Americans had been. Allowing self-government under Aguinaldo 'would be like granting self-government to an Apache reservation under some chief'. He accused his critics of giving aid and comfort 'to a syndicate of corrupt Chinese half-breeds and ferocious Tagal bandits'. At the end of the war, Roosevelt said that Americans had now to turn to 'the task of working for the actual betterment, moral, industrial, social and political, of the Filipinos'. Only with instruction could these dependent peoples escape the tendency to swing between 'despotism and anarchy' and become ready for independence at some distant date.[46] His predecessor, President William McKinley, shared his ideas and wrote about how he prayed and received divine guidance about the future of the Philippines:

And one night late it came to me this way – I don't know how it was, but it came: (1) That we could not give them back to Spain – that would be cowardly and dishonorable; (2) that we could not turn them over to France or Germany – our commercial rivals in the Orient – that would be bad business and discreditable; (3) that we could not leave them to themselves – they were unfit for self-government – and they would soon have anarchy and misrule over there worse than Spain's was; and (4) that there was nothing left for us to do but to take them all, and to educate the Filipinos, and uplift and civilize and Christianize them, and by God's grace do the very best we could by them, as our fellow men for whom Christ also died. And then I went to bed and went to sleep and slept soundly.

Tricked and outgunned, the revolution failed. Aguinaldo was captured on 23 March 1901, and on 1 April forced to pledge allegiance to the US government. On 19 April he called on his followers to lay down arms but some continued the fight. The capture of General Vincente Lukbán and the surrender of General Miguel Malvar the following year dealt the revolution a fatal blow. The war officially ended on 2 July, 1902, but Katipunan veterans under the maverick General Macario Sakay continued the struggle for several more years. The economy was in tatters; farm production was disrupted and commodity exports came to a standstill. Guerrillas roamed the countryside and an outbreak of rinderpest wiped out 90 per cent of the carabaos (water buffaloes used as draft animals) resulting in a

75 per cent drop in rice production while locusts threatened to consume the remaining crop. It was not until 1909, seven years later, when the US Congress opened up free trade between the two countries, that agriculture revived.[47]

THE CHINESE UNDER AMERICAN RULE

Most of the 40,000 Chinese did not take part in the revolution, but once in charge, the Americans restricted Chinese immigration and applied the same anti-Chinese immigration policies in place in the United States to the Philippines. The Chinese exclusion laws remained in place until 1940 when a new act allowed an annual quota of 500 new immigrants.[48] By cutting off the supply of skilled artisans, the exclusionary policies affected the livelihood of Chinese labour contractors, *cabecilla* (head merchants) and innkeepers, and led to their decline in sectors such as building and construction, machine tools, repair shops and carpentry. Some turned to commodity (especially rice) speculation, while others tendered for contracts to supply goods and services to the new government. During the Hispanic era, the authorities farmed out opium contracts, gambling licences and tax collection to the Chinese. General Otis suspended tax farming, depriving the Chinese of an important source of livelihood and many struggled to make a living in the first decade of American rule. The Coastwise Shipping Act of 1923 barred foreign-owned firms, including Chinese ones, from the coastal shipping business. This legislation was followed by other filipinization laws which shut the Chinese out of the transportation and haulage business. They were not able to compete in the commodity export sector dominated by Western firms but made inroads into the domestic market.[49] During the two golden decades (1909–1929) before the Great Depression, they regained their position in the retail trade and by 1922 controlled 70 to 80 per cent of the sector. The codification of tax and company laws brought an end to the arbitrary levies of the Spanish era and opened up new opportunities.[50] They financed the production of rice and controlled its milling and distribution. They went into banking which touched virtually every business sector and extended over the entire country. Because of their sojourning mindset, the Chinese usually preferred not to invest in land and factories, but poured in some 200 million pesos by the 1930s into retail and wholesale merchandizing, real estate, banking, tobacco, liquor, soaps and candles, and owned no fewer than 10,000 companies of all sizes.[51]

Traditionally, the Chinese lacked a national consciousness as their sentimental links with their homeland rested on family, region and culture rather than politics but that changed in the first half of the 20th century. The Chinese Revolution of 1911 followed by the military campaign 北伐 to unify China in the 1920s and Japanese invasion in the 1930s stirred up patriotic feelings among the Chinese overseas.[52] In the Philippines, the Chinese pledged support to the KMT government in Nanjing and urged General Chiang Kai-shek to repel the Japanese invaders. They organized endless fund raising campaigns and by 1939, had donated 12 million pesos to the war effort, while young men, including high school students, volunteered for the frontline as soldiers, drivers and pilots. They boycotted Japanese goods, even when it meant hurting their own profits, and as the Chinese controlled the distribution channels, it led to a 50 per cent drop in Japanese imports between 1931 and 1933. The Japanese residents in the Philippines responded by building their own retail networks, and the number of Japanese stores rose to 775 (versus 13,818 Chinese stores) by 1935. Although smaller in scale, Japanese businesses began to wrest a market share from the Chinese, even as Filipinos sought to break the Chinese and Japanese grip on certain sectors. Then war broke out.

THE JAPANESE OCCUPATION

On 8 December 1941, just hours after the surprise attack on Pearl Harbor, Japanese troops from Taiwan waded ashore on the beaches of Luzon. The invasion force advanced swiftly and captured Manila on 2 January 1942. Under orders from President Franklin Roosevelt, General Douglas MacArthur, commander of the Philippine Army, fled to Australia on 12 March 1942 to escape capture. The rout was complete with the surrender of US-Philippine forces in the Bataan Peninsula in April and Corregidor in May. The day after taking Manila, Japanese commander General Masaharu Homma, announced the 'emancipation of the Filipinos from the oppressive domination of the United States'. Filipinos were now free to build a 'Philippines for the Filipinos' within the Greater East Asia Co-Prosperity Sphere 大東亞共榮圈, he declared. The government, renamed the Central Administrative Organization, operated under the guidance of Japanese advisers. For the next three years, the Philippines suffered the rigours of war. The Japanese occupation force showed a wanton disregard for human life and thousands were imprisoned or executed. Houses with unregistered radios were raided, and their occupants imprisoned and tortured in the dungeons of Fort Santiago. The water cure practised by the Americans made a comeback. Prisoners were strung up by their hands and beaten with lumber or pressed with red-hot iron or electric wire. In the early days of the occupation, Japanese soldiers raped women at will. Sentries on street corners slapped men, women and even children for failing to bow to them. Girls were abducted and forced into sexual slavery in military 'comfort stations', even as education was revamped to instil loyalty to Japan. The economy was geared toward the needs of the war effort and horses, cars, trucks and other means of transportation were commandeered. Rice production dropped and the limited quantities produced were diverted to feed troops. Food and medicine were scarce, and thousands died of malnutrition, malaria, tuberculosis, and other diseases. On the streets could be seen sick and starving men, women and children, often with tropical ulcers covered with flies. Between 500,000 to 1 million Filipinos lost their lives during the occupation. The ways of the Japanese turned everyone against them, and many fled to the mountains to join the resistance.[53]

The Japanese military targeted the Chinese. When they entered Manila, soldiers ignoring the rules of diplomatic immunity, arrested and shot the Chinese consul general Dr. Clarence Kwangson Young 楊光洼 and his staff in the back of their heads.[54] Anti-Japanese community leaders were rounded up and executed and large Chinese businesses were taken over or ordered to close. In the Greater East Asia Co-Prosperity Sphere, an economic master plan, the Chinese were to leave the retail sector and become farmers while others were sent to work as 'volunteers' on army projects. Chinese schools were shuttered and an association formed to control the Chinese and extract contributions.[55] To avoid falling into the hands of the dreaded military police, the *Kenpetai* 憲兵隊, some chose to collaborate only to be assassinated by resistance fighters. Both the Kuomintang (KMT) and the Chinese Communist Party (CCP) organized rival guerrilla units. Communist fighters comprised mainly working class men, many of whom were single and free of family encumbrances. Some, such as Xu Jingcheng 許敬誠 and Li Yongxiao 李永孝, had fled KMT persecution in China and brought valuable experience in underground work and guerrilla tactics[56] and the Filipino *Hukbalahap*, or People's Army, against the Japanese took the communist *huazhi* 华支 fighters into their ranks to learn their skills.[57] Emerging from a single organization before the war, the communists showed greater unity and better coordination than the KMT groups, which were often plagued by internal rivalry.[58] The tide of war turned eventually as US marines landed on Leyte on 22 October 1944 and closed in on Manila in February 1945. A 17,000-strong Japanese garrison defended the city against 35,000 US troops. The Americans subjected the city to intense bombardment, and in the month-long Battle of Manila, an estimated 240,000 of the city's inhabitants perished along with 16,000 Japanese soldiers. American casualties were unusually low – some 1,000 killed and 5,600 wounded. The fiercest urban fighting in the Pacific War, the battle saw the complete destruction of the great city with its rich architectural heritage dating back to the 16th century.

POSTWAR INTEGRATION

An estimated 10,000 Chinese died during the three and half year occupation, but the trauma brought no fundamental change to the community.[59] Their economic and social structure remained intact as did the old ideological differences and personal rivalries. In the immediate postwar years, the assassination of collaborators and political rivals continued. The KMT-sponsored

Federation of Filipino-Chinese Chambers of Commerce and Industry (commonly called 'the Federation') rose in 1954 to challenge the older General Chamber of Commerce and Industry (or 'the General Chamber') and become the leading voice of the community. Filipino attitudes toward the Chinese too remained unchanged; when several hundred Chinese took part in a mass rally on 23 September 1945 to denounce senatorial candidate Manuel Roxas as a wartime collaborator and demanded the removal of legislators who passed anti-Chinese laws, their voices were dismissed as 'unwarranted interference in the internal affairs of the Philippines'.[60] The Manila *Daily News* editorialized:

> We protest vigorously against the challenging attitude of these Chinese, who have no right in this country to meddle in our political affairs. They have thus become undesirable aliens. Under our laws, they can be seized and deported as unwanted aliens. We ask the president of the Commonwealth to take immediate action to have these Chinese rounded up and shipped back to their own country.[61]

The *Manila Post* chimed in with:

> The Chinese can advance no justification for butting into the Philippine collaborationist question, or into any of our domestic affairs for that matter. In passing judgment on our Congress, the Chinese have stepped over the heads of the

Filipino people who had elected their leaders to Congress, the Filipino people who are the only legitimate critics of the officials they have willed into office.[62]

As a tiny (0.6 per cent of the population in 1947), but economically potent minority, the Chinese had always contended with hostile host governments – first the Spaniards, then the Americans and then the Filipinos.[63] As elsewhere in Southeast Asia, their economic clout did not always translate into political influence. Instead they often became an easy target for politicians. In legal limbo, they were vulnerable to prosecution by their home government as well as host governments. To prevent smuggling, piracy and insurrection, the Song, the Ming and the Qing dynasties adopted a closed door policy which banned trade and overseas travel. Those who ventured abroad broke the law and could expect no succor from the motherland, and it was not until 1894 when the prohibition was lifted that they could return home safely.[64] Chinese leaders later appealed to the Qing government to open a consulate in Manila to protect its subjects from unfair taxation and arbitrary policies. The Qing government set up a consulate in 1897, and seven years later, the Chinese Chamber of Commerce was formed to represent Chinese interests, but because of strong kinship ties to the homeland, the Chinese remained ambivalent about their host country and showed little interest in taking up Filipino citizenship. Attitudes changed only after the mass naturalization of

1975 and the filipinization of Chinese schools since 1977.

Education had always played a crucial role in maintaining emotional and cultural links with China, and once the war was over, the Chinese schools reopened. Outside the purview of the ministry of education, these independent schools employed textbooks and teachers from Taiwan while students pledged allegiance to Taiwan and its president Chiang Kai-shek. For the parents, Chinese-style education was sacrosanct and they resisted attempts to filipinize their schools through the scaling back of the use of Chinese and the adoption of the Philippine curriculum. But mindful of anti-Chinese sentiments, younger leaders cautioned against 'Chinese-ness'.[65] The Chinese were at a crossroads and had no choice but to integrate.

The filipinization of schools reduced fluency in Chinese, and many students could barely converse with their parents without reaching out for English or Filipino expressions. Even the élite Chiang Kai-shek College, once a bastion of Chinese education, found it necessary to conduct periodic 'Speak Chinese' campaigns on campus. Mass naturalization gave momentum to integration and the end of martial law in 1986 opened the way for greater political participation and more and more Chinese chose to run for office on a Filipino rather than Chinese platform.[66]

CHINA POLICY

Although granted independence by the US in 1946, the Philippines has rarely enjoyed true sovereignty. Despite signs of greater promise than its Southeast Asian neighbours in the postwar period, corruption coupled with entrenched foreign and domestic interests stymied economic development and perpetuated a yawning gap between the rich and the poor. In 2017, the country's per capita GDP of $3,000 ranked 126th, placing it below countries such as Bhutan, Bolivia and Indonesia. Until 1992, the Philippines hosted America's two largest overseas military installations (the sprawling 262-square mile Subic Bay naval base located in Zamabales was nearly as large as Singapore) in a 'partnership'. In the words of Philippine statesman Claro Recto (1890–1960),

> A bankrupt administration must necessarily have a foreign policy of mendicancy; and it is inevitable that it should invite foreign intervention to do what it cannot do for itself. When a government cannot count on the united support of its own people, then it must unavoidably have recourse to the support of a foreign power; and because beggars cannot be choosers, we can be safely ignored, taken for granted, dictated to, and made to wait at the door, hat in hand, to go on in only when invited.[67]

Centuries of Spanish and American rule colonized not only the land but also the mind. Filipinos orient themselves toward the West and understand more about what it means to be

134

American than to be Malaysian, Indonesian or Chinese. Even when Americans disagreed among themselves over foreign policy, Manila voted consistently with the US in the United Nations. Following Washington's lead, Manila maintained diplomatic ties with Taipei after 1946 and switched recognition to Beijing in 1975 after President Richard Nixon's historic visit to China. Due to the country's long relations with the US, Philippine policymakers were slow to discern historical trends and Manila aligned itself with Washington, until Rodrigo Duterte became president in 2016 and struck a new path. The first president from the southern island of Mindanao, he studied law and politics, and served as public prosecutor and then as mayor of Davao City for 22 years where he was credited for cutting crime. There are 2 million ethnic Chinese in the Philippines and Duterte, whose grandfather hailed from Xiamen, estimates that a quarter of the Filipino nation is of Chinese descent to one degree or another. He adopted a non-confrontational approach in the South China Sea, and entered into agreements with Beijing to jointly explore oil and build badly-needed infrastructure in the archipelago. Duterte's foreign policy is guided by his reading of global trends coupled with an aversion to American hegemony. The antipathy stems from American conduct on Philippine soil, while his pivot to China is informed by centuries of contact across the South China Sea. In the words of foreign secretary Perfecto Yasay, the Philippines cannot 'forever be the little brown brothers of America'.[68]

CHAPTER 6

MALAYSIA

EARLY CONTACTS WITH CHINA

The Malay peninsula lies at the southern tip of the Indochina peninsula. About the size of England or New York state, it has a range of mountains that run down its spine, and is covered with dense tropical forest. Situated at the crossroads between the civilizations of China and India, it was only a matter of time before it was visited by Indian and Chinese traders. The earliest known Chinese contact with the Malays took place at around 300 BC; the visitors brought iron tools, which enabled the local inhabitants to emerge from the Stone Age.[1] Indian traders sought gold and tin, while the Chinese brought pottery.[2] There is also evidence of trade between the Mediterranean and China; fragments of Greek vases of the fourth and fifth century BC have been found in Malaya. Trade with Mediterranean Europe continued to grow in the first two centuries AD as silk reached Rome by caravan routes through Persia and Central Asia, and as Roman ships sailed from India through the Straits of Malacca to China.[3]

At first, most of the trade between China and India passed through the powerful Indianized kingdom of Funan on the

Indochinese peninsula. Following Funan's decline in the 6th century AD, the all-sea route via the Straits of Malacca became more popular, creating the opportunity for the rise of ports on the Sumatran and Java coasts. This led to the emergence of states in the hinterland of these ports, such as Srivijaya and Sailendra. The earliest reference to Srivijaya is found in the diary of a Chinese monk, Yijing 義淨, who visited the kingdom in 671 AD after a journey by sea of 22 days from Guangzhou.[4] Centred in Palembang in southern Sumatra, Srivijaya became the first kingdom to dominate most of the Malay archipelago, and became the Southeast Asian hegemon between the 7th and 11th century. Its main foreign interest was the lucrative trade with China which lasted from the Tang to the Song dynasty. Srivijaya was an important centre for the spread of Buddhism from the 8th to the 12th century, but was eclipsed by the rise of two powerful rivals, Singhasari and Majapahit based on Java, and ceased to exist in the 13th century. The control of the Malayan side of the Straits was lost to Siam, while the Sumatran side fell under the sway of the Singhasari. For a thousand years, the Malays derived their cultural and religious influence from India, but they now began to receive the new religion and culture of Islam. Islam created a fresh unity of ideas among the Malay states on both sides of the straits, and paved the way for a Malay successor to the power of Srivijaya, the Malacca Sultanate.

THE MALACCA SULTANATE

Malacca is situated at the estuary of the Malacca River. Its earliest inhabitants were a small population of Orang Laut of Proto-Malay race who built a primitive village to carry out fishing and piracy. Then in around 1400, came an influx of Malay chiefs escaping the destruction of Tumasik (modern day Singapore) by the Siamese. Among them was a Malay chief named Parameswara, who turned the settlement into a bustling entrepôt. Chinese records give the earliest accounts of Malacca's rise as a trading power. The best known of these are the writings of Ma Huan 馬歡 and Fei Xin 費信, and the Ming official history,[5] which give a chronological account of Sino-Malacca relations during the 15th century.[6] Strategically situated at the narrowest part of the Straits of Malacca, the port became prosperous through trade between East and West. Ships from India and China brought goods to Malacca where they discharged their cargo to be carried forward by ships from the other side. In this way, Malacca became the main point of exchange for goods from the West and India, on the one hand, and from China, the East Indies and Indochina, on the other. In his landmark *Suma Oriental que trata do Mar Roxo até aos Chins* (Summary of the East, from the Red Sea up to the Chinese), Portuguese apothecary Tomé Pires noted that 'Malacca is of such importance and profit that it seems to me that it has no equal in the world ... It is a city made for merchandize fitter than any other in the world ... .' Duarte Barbosa, his contemporary, concurred: 'Malacca is the richest seaport with the greatest number of wholesale merchants and abundance of shipping that can be found in the whole world'.[7]

Malacca, however, was from the beginning a vassal of Siam (Thailand) to which it sent an annual tribute of 40 taels of gold.[8] The port city sought protection from China against Siam, and in 1403, the Ming emperor Yong Le 永樂 sent an envoy Yin Qing 尹慶 bearing gifts of silk brocade. Two years later, in 1405, Parameswara sent a return mission to China, during which the emperor endorsed Parameswara as king of Malacca, and gave him a written commission, a seal, a suit of silk clothes and a yellow umbrella.[9] In 1408, the Chinese Muslim admiral Zheng He visited Malacca and reaffirm the state's sovereignty. The fishing village had become a vibrant centre of commerce with tin as its chief export while Chinese porcelain, beads and silk were imported. Parameswara returned Zheng He's visit in 1411 with a retinue of 450 including his wife, son, and ministers who were warmly received by the emperor. Parameswara's successors kept up the relations with gift exchanges and visits to pay homage. The first three rulers personally led missions to the Ming court,[10] and ties with China were cemented by the marriage of Sultan Mansur Shah (r. 1459–1477) to Princess Hang Lipo 漢麗寶 of the Ming imperial household. According to the *Sejarah Melayu* or Malay Annals, Hang Lipo came with an entourage of 500 who settled in an area called Bukit China or Chinese Hill. Evidence of this Chinese settlement are the 12,000 Chinese graves on the hill, the earliest dating back to 1622. After 1430, the Ming rulers adopted a close door policy, whereby travel overseas was restricted and trade confined to Canton. By this time, however, the sultanate had become a power in its own right, whose splendour, power and dominion were celebrated in the *Sejarah Melayu*. The sultanate reached the height of its prosperity in second half of the 15th century, and by the beginning of the 16th century, extended its power over both sides of the straits up to southern Siam and the east coast of Sumatra.

Malacca's rise owed much to the advent of Islam. Islam originated in the Arabian Peninsula at the beginning of the 7th century, and by the end of the century, Muslim rulers controlled Egypt, Syria and Persia and the medieval trade routes passing through Alexandria and Damascus. Muslims conquered huge swaths of the west coast of India including Gujerat, whose merchants, together with Persians and Arabs, soon dominated the trade of the Arabian Sea and rounded Kanyakumari, the southern tip of the Indian peninsula, striking out into South-east Asia. When Marco Polo passed through the Straits of Malacca in 1292 on his way back to Venice, he saw many Muslims among the coastal population of Sumatra. Malacca was brought into contact with Sumatran ports by the pepper trade and the need to import rice for its growing population. This brought an influx of Gujerati merchants from Sumatra who converted the Malay chiefs, and intermarriage between the ruling houses of Sumatra and Malacca boosted the prestige of the new religion. The growing importance of Malacca then attracted more merchants from India who intermarried with the local population, accelerating the spread of Islam. Trade with India was dominated by Muslim traders and the conversion of Malacca's rulers further integrated the port into the Muslim trading network. That Muslim monopoly, however, was soon challenged by the Portuguese with their heavily armed yet nimble vessels.

THE PORTUGUESE

Since Roman times, overland trade routes between the Mediterranean and China traverse Persia and the steppes of Central Asia. But the journey was treacherous. During the last part of the 12th century, the Mongols under the leadership of Genghis Khan conquered the lands stretching from northern China all the way to the Black Sea in southern Russia. By 1260, his grandson, Kublai Khan, had subdued the whole of China. Under his rule, peaceful conditions prevailed across Eurasia and trade was encouraged. The Mongols improved communications by building roads and post-houses, and for a century after 1260, it was easier to travel than at any time before. In the second half of the 14th century, however, conditions changed. In 1368 the Mongols were driven out of China, and in Central Asia, they converted to Islam and became hostile to Christians. Then in 1453, the Ottoman Turks captured Constantinople, capital of the Eastern Roman Empire closing the land route to China. The eastern Mediterranean, long the preserve of Italian merchants, was menaced by Turkish sea power, and a new route to the East had to be found. Portugal, a small and poor country, on the edge of the Iberian Peninsula, rose to the challenge.

Muslim Moors from north Africa had invaded Iberia in 711 and conquered most of the peninsula after seven years of fighting. The Portuguese fought back and freed themselves after a long struggle, but religious zeal and national expansion led them to pursue their adversaries into north Africa. They had heard about the legendary Christian kingdom of Prester John and sought to find and ally with him to overthrow Muslim power in North Africa. The Portuguese Prince Henry the Navigator (1394–1460) led the drive to develop ship-building technology. Progress was slow at first, but in 1488 Bartholomew Diaz rounded the Cape of Good Hope, and ten years later, Vasco da Gama made the first voyage round Africa to reach Calicut on the southwestern coast of India, in present day Kerala. Goods from the East were carried by Arab or Indian ships to the head of the Red Sea and the Persian Gulf, whence they were conveyed overland by caravan to ports on the eastern Mediterranean. It was clear that if the trade could be diverted by sea around the Cape of Good Hope,

Portugal would break the Muslim domination of trade from the Far East. The Portuguese saw all Muslims they encountered as hated 'Moors', and waged war against them as part of a national crusade. It was not long before they set their sights on Malacca.

On the strategic value of the city, Portuguese writer Duarte Barbosa wrote: 'Whoever is Lord in Malacca has his hand on the throat of Venice'.[11] In 1511, Afonso d'Albuquerque set sail for Malacca from Goa with a large fleet. With superior firepower, the Portuguese quickly overcame the Malay defenders. They captured the city by concentrating on it an intensity of firepower unseen before in the region.[12] The ruler, Sultan Mahmud, fled to Johor from whence he made several vain attempts to regain Malacca. With the capture of Malacca and other ports in the Indian Ocean, the Portuguese now enjoyed a virtual monopoly over the spice trade, which consisted of pepper and cinnamon at first and other products later. The use of violence by the Portuguese in the region was justified on business and religious grounds as British historian Brian Harrison observed:

The peculiar combination of commercial war and religious crusade that the Portuguese introduced was something with which the region had not been confronted before. For Portugal, the advance to the East was not simply an invasion along the main highway of Asian trade but also a great forward flanking movement in the holy war between Christianity and Islam. Her commercial aims, and the means of achieving them – deeds of violence against Moslems, or the plunder of Moslem shipping – were therefore conveniently sanctified.[13]

It was not until a whole century later that the Dutch, British and French were able to challenge the Portuguese monopoly and naval supremacy. The fall of Malacca forced a dispersion of the trade to other centres such as Patani, Johor, Pahang, Aceh and Banten. The growth in trade between 1500 and 1630 enabled these states to flourish in the interval between the fall of Malacca in 1511 and the rise of Dutch Batavia (present day Jakarta).[14] The loss of commerce and revenue to the Malay rulers seriously crippled their power and hold over their vassals.[15] With the force of superior arms, the Europeans exacted various treaties from weaker states, leading to the decline and fragmentation of the Malay world.

THE DUTCH

Portuguese power declined toward the end of the 16th century. Portugal simply did not have the manpower to hold and administer a vast empire stretching from Brazil to Macao. Tomé Pires observed: 'Great affairs cannot be managed by few people'. In the 16th century, Portugal only had a population of about a million people. Tropical disease and warfare took a heavy toll of its bravest sons while official corruption, a greedy policy, and the hatred by the native peoples for the vicious tactics of the Portuguese hastened the end. It was remarkable that the Portuguese held out as long as they did in Malacca.[16] Failing to keep pace with naval architecture, their ships were soon outclassed by Dutch and English vessels. In 1595, the Dutch sent their first expedition to the East Indies, and within six years, 65 ships organized by merchants in Amsterdam, Rotterdam, Middleburg and other Dutch ports followed suit. The Dutch succeeded in establishing a base for the spice trade in the port of Bantam in Java.[17] Determined to oust the Portuguese, they formed the *Vereenigde Oostindische Compagne* (VOC) in 1602, commonly referred to as the Dutch East India Company, a publicly listed joint-stock company, but one backed by the power of the state. At about the same time, the English too turned their gaze to the East Indies. The merchants of London asked Queen Elizabeth for a charter to protect them from competition, and on 31 December 1600 the English East India Company was formed with a monopoly of all English trade with the regions east of the Cape of Good Hope, although it could not count on the power of the state to the same degree as the VOC.

In 1641, the Dutch, allied with the Malays, captured Malacca. They took it in order to control all the approaches to the East Indies, not to make it a rival to Batavia, the centre of Dutch commerce in the East Indies. The trade of Malacca declined under the Dutch as it no longer lay on the direct sailing route from Europe to the East Indies, and as its harbour silted up, making it inaccessible to larger ships. Trying to monopolize the cotton trade between India to the East Indies, the Dutch forced ships passing through the straits to pay customs or a toll at Malacca. The policies were unsuccessful, and Malacca seldom generated enough revenue to meet its expenses, and had to be subsidized by Batavia. Malacca retained its importance as a port of call but was no longer the great entrepôt, and by 1726, the population dwindled to no more than 300 families. After 1730, the fortunes of the Dutch East India Company started to decline due, among other factors, to corruption, high mortality rate among employees and an unsustainable dividend policy which distributed dividends in excess of profits. Gradually, the Dutch abandoned their possessions – one group of islands after another. Taking advantage of this, the English East India Company built up a flourishing smuggling trade in the archipelago. The occupation of Penang by the British in 1786 dealt a fatal blow to Malacca, and by 1795, all that was left of the Dutch East Indian Empire was Java, the Moluccas, Malacca and a few forts elsewhere. In 1795 the British captured Malacca and the Moluccas. That same year, a commission appointed by the Dutch government reported that the VOC was bankrupt, and in 1798, the Dutch government annulled the company's charter and took over the administration of what was left of its possessions.[18]

THE BRITISH

British presence in Malaya began with the establishment of three settlements along the Straits of Malacca, which the British called the 'Straits Settlements'. The first settlement was founded by a British naval officer named Francis Light, who arrived in Penang in 1786 when there were only a handful of Malays living on the island covered with thick jungle. By clearing the jungle and making it safe from pirates, Light turned the island and its harbour into a commercial haven which attracted both European and Asian settlers. Next came the establishment of Singapore at the southern tip of the peninsula by another British officer Stamford Raffles. Raffles signed an agreement with the local sultan that gave Britain the right to establish a trading post in Singapore in 1819. Lastly, the British took possession of Malacca through a treaty with the Dutch in 1824 which marked out two colonial zones. The Anglo-Dutch Treaty of 1824 divided the Malay archipelago into a British zone in the north and a Dutch zone in the south. The British zone consisted of the Malay peninsula (territory to the north of Straits of Malacca), while the Dutch zone consisted of Sumatra, Java and other islands to the south of the straits. The British swapped the settlement of Bencoolen on Sumatra for the Dutch colony of Malacca and were promised undisputed control of Singapore. The Straits Settlements were largely populated by Chinese, with a tiny but important European minority. In 1832, their capital was moved from Penang to Singapore. The scattered nature of the three settlements made it difficult and expensive to administer after the English East India Company lost its monopoly in 1813.[19] Through successive treaties with the rulers on the Malay peninsula, however, the British gradually turned all the Malay states into protectorates, which together with the Straits Settlements came to be called 'British Malaya'.

THE CHINESE

China's relations with Malaya consisted not so much of state-to-state ties but of Chinese migrants and their dealings with the host country. Who were the Chinese who left their homeland for Malaya? What motivated them to go? How were they greeted by the native population and the European colonial rulers? What role did they play in the social, economic and political development of the host country? And finally, what influence, if any, do they have in the Sino-Malaysian relations of the 21st century? (From this point onward, it would be helpful to note that 'Malaysia' refers to the new state created in 1963 by the expansion of the Federation of Malaya to include Singapore and the Bornean states of Sabah, Sarawak.[20] The Federation of Malaya itself was formed in 1957.)

The earliest Chinese settlement in Malaya can be traced to the Malacca Sultanate in the 15th century. The thriving entrepôt for the exchange of products from China, India, and the islands of Southeast Asia attracted Chinese traders, some of whom remained to run their businesses. This small but growing Chinese community played an important role in the foreign trade of the sultanate. The leader of the Chinese community was appointed one of four port officials or *shahbandars* to help administer the affairs of foreigners.[21] The Chinese *shahbandar* controlled the commercial activities of the Chinese residents, regulated their behaviour, and acted as agent of the government in dealing with the Chinese population. The first Chinese came mostly from the city of Zhangzhou 漳州 in southern Fujian Province but were transient and did not put down roots. By the time the Dutch arrived in 1641, there were only 300 to 400 Chinese living in Malacca.[22] Their numbers increased to 2,161 by 1750, and ten years later, fell to 1,390 out of a total local population of 7,216.[23] Meanwhile, across the straits, the Chinese had become indispensable as tax collectors and middlemen to the Dutch on the island of Java as Stamford Raffles noted:

In all their eastern settlements, the favorite policy of the Dutch seems to be to depress the native inhabitants and give encouragement to the Chinese, who, generally speaking, are only itinerants and not children of the soil, and who follow the almost universal practice of remitting the fruits of their industry to China, instead of spending them where they were acquired. The Chinese, in all ages equally supple, venal, and crafty, failed not, at a very early period, to recommend themselves to the speculating Hollanders. They have, almost from the first, been their agents; and in the island of Java, in particular, they obtained from them the entire monopoly of the revenue farms and government contracts.[24]

Tax farming was a common practice in Egypt, Rome, Greece, and Great Britain where tax farmers bid for the rights to collect taxes, and were responsible for any shortfall in revenue.

Chinese immigration to Malacca picked up at the end of the 18th century just as the British started to arrive in the region. There was a constant influx of Chinese artisans and cultivators, mostly men who came but returned to China once they had made some money. A British medical doctor observed that 'The Chinese are the most enterprising, the most opulent, the most industrious and the most determined in pursuit of wealth'.[25] The majority were impoverished migrants from southern China, who borrowed the cost of their passage from the captains of junks. The captains sold their services to richer residents for a term of years till the debt was paid. The migrants then hoped to make enough money in a few years to return to the homeland. There were few Chinese women, for the poor labourers could not afford to bring their wives, and the Chinese authorities forbade female emigration. Most returned to China but some stayed on. Those who remained married Malay women and produced a community of 'Babas', who spoke Malay but carried on the Chinese way of life, modified by Malay and other local practices as Scottish physician and colonial administrator John Crawfurd (1783–1868) wrote:[26]

> Many of the Chinese returned to their own country, and the first intention of every emigrant is probably to do so, but circumstances detain a number of them on the islands, who, intermarrying with natives of the country, generate a race inferior in energy and spirit to the original settler, but speaking the language, wearing the garb, professing the religion, and affecting the manners of the parent country.[27]

The Chinese tended to live in urban areas. Some were forced by circumstances to cultivate land or work in the tin mines, but those who could get together enough capital became shopkeepers, the dream of every coolie and servant. Some fell victim to vices of gambling and opium-smoking, but in a lifetime, the penniless migrant often became a rich *towkay* or business owner.[28] There are few Chinese records of the period as the Chinese migrants were mostly men with little schooling, whose main concern was to earn enough to retire to China. Colonial administrators, however, left a rich literature about the Chinese. Of the population of Penang, Francis Light reported:

> The Chinese constituted the most valuable part of the inhabitants. They are men, women, and children, above

3,000; they possess the different trades of carpenters, masons, and smiths, are traders, shopkeepers and planters. They employ small vessels and prows and send adventurers to the surrounding countries. They are the only people of the East from whom a revenue can be raised without expense and extraordinary efforts of Government ...

The Malays ... form another considerable part of our inhabitants. They are for the most part indigent, ignorant of arts, manufactures, or trade; they are employed in cutting down wood, at which they are both expert and laborious, and in cultivating paddy. They may be divided into two orders, the one husbandmen, who are quiet and inoffensive, and easily ruled. They are capable of no great exertions, but content themselves with planting paddy, sugar-cane and a few fruit trees, the cultivation of which does not require much labour. The other order is employed in navigating prows. They are, in general, almost without exception, a bad description of people, addicted to smoking opium, gaming and other vices; to rob and assassinate is only shameful when they fail of success ... .[29]

The Chinese formed trading companies based on kinship ties linking Malacca with other Southeast Asian and Chinese ports to create a trading network that dominated Sino-Southeast Asian trade. The entry of the Europeans weakened the position of the Chinese traders, but they were able to maintain their dominant position throughout the 16th and 17th centuries because the Europeans were still restricted by the Chinese authorities from trading directly with China. The British penetration into Southeast Asia at the end of the 18th century, however, greatly altered the pattern of trade as new ports and British free trade policy expanded trade volume and intensified competition. British political domination privileged the British and European trading houses, but the Chinese adapted to the new situation by integrating themselves into local and international distribution channels. They took up the comprador role between European businesses and the local economy, and soon European manufactured products could not be effectively distributed without Chinese middlemen.[30] Welshman John Davis who lived in the archipelago for twenty years recorded in 1834:

[The Chinese] are keen, enterprising traders, extremely expert in their dealings, and understand the nature of trade of those countries in which they have settled perhaps better than any other people; they seem to have very accurate information and receive it very quickly too. Those who have obtained a high reputation are extremely tenacious of it, and they are very punctual in their dealings. I do not think they are exceeded by the natives of any country as a commercial people, including European countries ...[31]

John Crawfurd, who governed Singapore, wrote a similar opinion in the form of a questionnaire:

> From your intercourse with the Chinese do you conceive them to be intelligent, active and commercial people? – Eminently so. They are very industrious people in every way, they are a business-like people; their manners more resemble Europeans in that part of their character than they do those of other Asiatic nations. In their industry and intelligence do you conceive them to be superior to other Asiatic nations? – For all useful and practical purposes I think they are. There are perhaps a few points in which they are inferior to other Asiatic nations but these points are of very little moment.[32]

Of Chinese diligence, English orientalist Thomas J. Newbold offered a somewhat different interpretation:

> Wherever money is to be acquired by the peaceful exercise of agriculture, by handicrafts, by the opening of mines of tin, iron or gold amidst savage hordes of wild forests, there will be found the greedy Chinese. The *auri sacra fames*[33] is with them a ruling passion: the certainty of encountering robbery and even death have scarcely any influence in deterring them from the eager pursuit of gain.[34]

Over time, Singapore eclipsed Malacca and Penang to become the most successful of the Straits Settlements. By 1864 Singapore had a population of over 80,000, including more than 50,000 Chinese, and its trade volume of over £13 million was three times as much as that of Penang. Merchants of many nations jostled in Singapore's streets but the most important were the Chinese. Having lost its monopoly in 1813, the British East India Company did little trade itself except with China. The Chinese did not confine themselves to the port settlements, but moved into the hinterland where they became the pioneer miners and cash crop farmers. From the 1820s, Chinese immigrants flocked to the tin mines of Perak, Selangor and Negri Sembilan, well before the British ventured into those states. Before British encroachment into the Malay States starting in 1874, Malaya was thinly populated with an estimated population of 300,000, but once the British established law and order in the interior, more Chinese moved in. Soon there were more Chinese men than Malay men but more Malay women than Chinese women because of a Chinese government ban on emigration by women. If there had been as many Chinese women as Chinese men, the Chinese would have outnumbered the Malays even more. Up until the 1930s, there was a constant turnover of the growing numbers of Chinese as thousands who had made their money left each year to rejoin their families. In 1911, the gender ratio stood at one female to four males in Malaya. In the 1930s, the Chinese government lifted the ban on emigration by women. At about the same time, new Malayan laws restricted entry of Chinese men but not women, many of whom came as workers in their own right, and by 1933 the gender ratio rose to 833 females to 1,000 males.[35] As the proportion of Chinese women grew, more Chinese children were born in the country and the number of Chinese who settled permanently increased steadily. Residing mainly in urban areas, the Chinese enjoyed better healthcare and lived longer than the Malays. War soon contributed to the growth of permanent Chinese settlement in Malaya. First, the Japanese invasion of China from 1937 made it difficult to return to China; then the Japanese occupation of Malaya from 1942–1945 made it impossible to leave.

The Chinese were not the only immigrants. In the beginning, there were a few thousand Indian merchants and shopkeepers in the Straits Settlements, but with the development of large European plantations growing sugar, coffee and rubber, the demand for labourers led to the entry of thousands of workers from southern India.[36] The governments of the Straits Settlements and the Federated Malay States employed large numbers of Indian labourers on the construction and maintenance of railways and roads.[37] They also recruited clerks and teachers from India and Ceylon before there were sufficient English schools in Malaya to produce them. The first policemen were largely Sikhs, and the turbaned, bearded men in khaki shorts became the Malayan equivalent of the London bobby.[38]

SECRET SOCIETIES

For mutual aid and protection in a frontier land, the Chinese established kinship organizations along dialect and place-of-origin lines. There was overlapping membership and leadership in the social organizations, including what came to be described in Western literature as 'secret societies' 会党. Originally formed to overthrow the Manchu government and restore Han rule in China, secret societies were created in Southeast Asia to provide protection where indigenous law and order was lacking. Some were little more than *ad hoc* survival strategies while others facilitated cooperation and organization on an impressive scale. Although some took part in the opium trade, gambling and prostitution, quite a few evolved into joint-stock companies that invested in mining, plantation and other legitimate businesses. In 19th century Malaya, secret societies were accepted as social institutions that provided leadership before the advent of the British who saw them as a political threat and banned them in 1889.[39] It was in the midst of fierce contest between two bands, the Hai San 海山 and Ghee Hin 義興, each allied with rival Malay factions, that Yap Ah Loy emerged.

KAPITAN YAP AH LOY

The most important Chinese figure of 19th century Malaya, Yap Ah Loy 葉亞來 (1837–1885) came from Guangdong as a 17-year-old *hakka* 客家 youth with little or no schooling. In Malacca, he went to work in a tin mine for four months before finding employment in a shop owned by a relative. After a year, arrangements were made for him to return to China, but he gambled away his money while waiting for the boat in Singapore. Ashamed to face his relative, he made his way on foot, a journey of several weeks, to Lukut, near the modern Port Dickson halfway up the peninsula, where he worked as a tin miner and petty trader. His fortunes improved when his friend Liu Ngim Kong 劉王光 became the second *kapitan* of Kuala Lumpur, the *de facto* leader of the Chinese community with authority to deal with Malay rulers and later, British officials. Yap became Liu's trusted lieutenant and succeeded Liu when he passed away in 1869. At the age of 32, Yap built a strong administration and credible constabulary but his succession was challenged by Liu's 'relatives', a group which emerged under the leadership of another *hakka* headman.[40] Civil war broke out in Selangor in 1870 between combined Chinese and Malay forces vying for control of the tin mining revenue. Kuala Lumpur changed hands repeatedly, but Yap emerged victorious in 1873 and set about rehabilitating the flooded mines and rebuilding the settlement which was burnt to the ground during the fighting.[41] Enjoying wide powers on par with Malay leaders, he built Kuala Lumpur's first school, undertook legal reform, upheld law and order with a police force of six, improved road links to mining areas and other settlements and launched a brick-making venture to produce materials for shop-houses to replace the flammable *attap* dwellings. Unlike many of his compatriots who devoted themselves to narrow commercial interests, Yap was determined to develop the settlement into a viable if not prosperous economic centre. Through his control of the tin mines, Yap amassed a considerable fortune, but his authority was curtailed by the first British resident (colonial adviser) of Kuala Lumpur who arrived in 1879. As he was preparing for his long overdue trip home, Yap fell ill and died of bronchitis at the age of 47. The attending doctor noted the exceptional brightness of his eyes.[42] British colonial administrator Sir Frank Swettenham (1850–1946) described Yap as 'remarkable', 'redoubtable' and 'doughty'[43], but despite his work in establishing Kuala Lumpur, a short street named after him in the capital is the sole reminder of the man who is mentioned only in passing in school textbooks today.

ECONOMIC PROGRESS

It was only a matter of time before the Chinese controlled the lion's share of the economy. In the early days, they contributed in the form of labour. Industrious and diligent, they quickly adapted themselves to the living conditions and hardships of early Malaya. They exhibited imagination and initiative, and small trading, shopkeeping, open-cast tin mining and transportation rapidly became their economic preserve. In the interwar period, they expanded into rubber growing and processing, banking, tin dredging and newly developing manufacturing. Chinese investments in European companies operating in Southeast Asia made it difficult to distinguish between Chinese and European capital. The Chinese often made their way into emerging sectors of the economy, and the rise of the rubber industry had a profound effect on the Chinese community. At the turn of the century, rubber became an indispensable raw material for the electrical, bicycle, and automobile industries, and its price rose from $2.36 per kilogram in 1900 to $5.55 per kilogram in 1906, boosting the industry and transforming the Malayan economy.[44] The Chinese became linked to a major world commodity, and many Chinese planters became wealthy, but no large scale commercial enterprise was possible without banking and credit.

BANKING

The period from 1901 and 1941 saw the rise of Chinese commercial banking. From the middle of the 19th century, European banks started opening branches in Malaya and Singapore. The best known was the Hongkong and Shanghai Banking Corporation (HSBS). Formed in Hong Kong by British merchants in the wake of the First Opium War (1839–1842) to finance the opium trade, it opened a branch in Singapore in 1877, and another one in Penang in 1884.[45] But many Chinese businesses shied away from the European banks because of culture and class barriers; European bank managers spoke neither Chinese nor Malay, and made little effort to cultivate local Malayan clientele. The first Chinese bank, the Kwong Yik Bank 廣益銀行, which catered to Cantonese businesses, was founded in Singapore in 1903 by Wong Ah Fook 黃亞福 (1837–1918), who came at the age of 17 to Malaya indentured to a carpenter. A peasant with little schooling, Wong managed to learn to read, write and use the abacus, and typified the Chinese rags-to-riches story. Four years later, the Teochews, another dialect group, formed the Sze Hai Tong Bank 四海通银行 in Singapore. In Malaya, a group of Cantonese businessmen led by the businessman and philanthropist Cheong Yeok Choy 張郁才 established the Kwong Yik Bank of Selangor in 1913. Like Wong, Cheong came from an impoverished family and migrated to Malaya at the age of 16 where he found employment as an office boy for a local council. This was followed by the Bank of Malaya of Ipoh in 1920. Another Singapore bank with direct influence on the Chinese communities in Malaya was the Ho Hong Bank 和丰银行 founded by a wealthy Hokkien businessman, Lim Peng Siang 林秉祥 (1872–1944) in 1917. It became the first Chinese Malayan bank to engage in international banking. Lim was an outstanding industrialist, shipowner and banker, but the bank suffered during the Great Depression and the collapse of rubber prices in the early 1930s. Between 1903 and 1941, at least seven Chinese banks came into existence in Malaya and Singapore to serve particular dialectal groups but as time passed, the dialectal lines blurred and their customers became more diversified.

MANUFACTURING

Until the First World War, the Chinese were engaged mainly in trading and retail businesses. The First World War, however, disrupted the import of manufactured goods opening up opportunities for local industry to develop. The Chinese ventured into manufacturing and related industries such as rubber and food processing followed by tin smelting and pineapple canning. The first Chinese-owned pineapple canning factory was established in Singapore by Tan Kee Pek 陳杞柏, father of the famous entrepreneur Tan Kah Kee 陳嘉庚. By the end of the first decade of the 20th century, there were 10 Chinese-owned pineapple canning factories in Singapore, but the First World War cut off access to markets in India and Europe, resulting in the closure of many canneries. By contrast, the war created a huge demand for processed rubber, and by 1918 there were an estimated 72 rubber processing mills in Malaya and Singapore. Chinese businessmen subsequently ventured into the manufacturing of rubber products such as raincoats, tennis balls, umbrellas, sports shoes, slippers, and toys, as well tires and tubes for the growing motor car industry. Others went into coconut oil refining and the manufacture of biscuits and soap.

EUROPEANS AND ASIANS

For the most part, neither Europeans nor Asians sought extensive social contacts with each other, and it was unusual for members of either community to try to eliminate the barriers to social relations between them.[46] A small number of Asian men married European women whom they met while studying in Britain. Such marriages did not encourage closer social relations between Europeans and Asians. Once an Asian and his European wife returned to Malaya, they found it difficult to fit into either European social life or the social life of the husband's community. The European wives were almost always excluded from European society, not because they had married an Asian but because most of them came from low social backgrounds in England. Only when the woman married an Asian of very high position (such as the wife of the Raja Musa of Selangor), could she be confident of being accepted in European society. Marriages between Asian men and European women were rare, and seldom lasted more than a few years. Union between European men and Asian women were even less common.[47]

POLITICAL AWAKENING

The early Chinese immigrants to Malaya showed little interest in politics. In the villages of southern China where the gentry dominated the social and political spheres, ordinary villagers played little or no part in the political process. But the immigrants' thinking changed with the rise of Chinese nationalism in Southeast Asia spurred by events in China. China's defeat in the First Sino-Japanese War (1894–1895), and the subsequent Japanese advance into Manchuria caused deep concern about China's future and aroused intense patriotic sentiments. The Treaty of Versailles, which transferred German 'concessions' in Shandong to Japan, triggered sharp indignation and large scale protests in China. The weakness of the Qing government in the face of foreign encroachment alarmed and infuriated the whole nation. These concerns about the fate of the nation quickly spread to the Chinese overseas. Reformists like Kang Youwei 康有为 and Liang Qichao 梁启超 urged reforms to save the tottering empire. The reforms failed, and Kang and Liang fled first to Japan and then to the United States. In 1900 Kang visited Malaya to raise financial support for a revolt in China. His visit and the speeches he made roused the political consciousness of the Chinese in Malaya and Singapore.

Following the reformists' footsteps, Chinese republican revolutionaries appeared soon after on the Malayan political scene. Unlike the reformists, who sought to change the existing political system from within, the republicans wanted nothing less than the complete overthrow of the Manchu political order and to replace it with a republic. Their leader was a Christian physician and thinker named Sun Yat-sen. Sun visited Malaya five months after Kang. After the failed uprising in Guangdong in 1900, many Chinese revolutionaries sought refuge in Malaya. Among them was You Lie 尤列 (1864–1936), a Cantonese leader, who laid a strong foundation for revolutionary activities in the region. More refugees fled to Malaya after the First Sino-Japanese War (1894–1895). In 1906 Sun Yat-sen arrived in Singapore to found a chapter of his party, the Tong Meng Hui 同盟会, and raise funds for another uprising in China. The republicans set up newspapers, reading clubs, and drama troupes to inform and to persuade. They attacked the Manchu government and engaged in heated debate with the reformists. Rivalry between the two camps often erupted in violence. Their activities greatly politicized the Chinese in Malaya and Singapore, and helped to coalesce the fragmented Chinese dialectal communities along ideological lines. Mirroring the socio-political ferment taking place in China, traditional norms of loyalty to the emperor, filial duty, and inequality between sexes were replaced by ideas of altruism, equality, and democracy.

With these modern ideals, came a push for universal education from all sides. In the interwar years, Chinese education in Malaya and Singapore saw great progress but the schooling provided only primary education which combined traditional subjects like the Confucian classics and moral self-cultivation with history, geography and English. This education produced students oriented toward China and the Confucian tradition. The Chinese grew more aware of the importance of secondary education following the May Fourth Movement of 1919, and millionaire businessman Tan Kah Kee soon founded the first Chinese secondary school in the region. The introduction of secondary education put Chinese schools on par with English schools, and parents no longer needed to send their children back to China for secondary education. Political developments and the rise of feminism in China in the 1920s inspired women's education, and the spread of literacy broke down traditional attitudes and improved the status of women. The change in social and political thinking would not have been possible, however, without community leadership.

TAN KAH KEE

Successful entrepreneurs, many of whom rose from the ranks of the poor, became natural leaders of the community. Perhaps the most iconic overseas Chinese figure of the first half of the twentieth century was the businessman-philanthropist Tan Kah Kee 陳嘉庚 (1874–1961). Born in Fujian province in 1874, Tan travelled to Singapore at the age of 16 to help in his father's rice trading business. In 1903, when his father's business failed, Tan started his own company and succeeded in building a commercial empire that included rubber plantations, factories, sawmills, canneries, real estate, import and export brokerage, shipping and rice trading. He earned himself the moniker 'Henry Ford of Malaya', and by the time of his death in 1961, had become a folk hero across Southeast Asia and China as a pioneer industrialist, philanthropist, social reformer, patriarch and visionary.[48] Selfless and public spirited, he used his enormous wealth to make important social and educational contributions in Singapore and in his home province of Fujian, where he founded a private university in 1921 entirely from his own resources.[49]

Tan was the most important link between the overseas Chinese and developments in China, and became the rallying point of Chinese resistance to the Japanese invasion of China and Southeast Asia. On 3 May 1928, Japanese troops occupied Jinan, the capital of Shandong, and slaughtered over 5,000 Chinese soldiers and civilians. When the news reached Singapore, Tan Kah Kee organized the Shandong Relief Fund 山東籌賑會 to raise money for the victims and heighten awareness of the Japanese aggression. When Japan launched a full scale invasion of China in 1937, Tan set up the Singapore China Relief Fund 星華籌賑會 and raised 10 million Singapore dollars (an impressive sum by 1930's terms) to support the resistance. Tan organized rallies to denounce Japanese aggression, and urged the boycott of Japanese goods. Widely respected, he dealt on equal terms with British colonial officers as well as Chinese leaders such as Chiang Kai-shek and Mao Zedong. In 1940, he left for a ten-month tour of Yan'an and Chongqing, the headquarters of the communists and the Kuomintang respectively. Returning to Singapore, he reported on the austerity he saw at Yan'an compared to the corruption in Chongqing. Tan did not hide his admiration for Mao, Zhou Enlai and Zhu De, and his disappointment with Chiang and his regime. Not surprisingly, he predicted that the communists would defeat the Kuomintang.

When Singapore fell to the Japanese in February 1942, Tan fled to Java to evade capture. There he witnessed the harsh treatment of the Chinese by the Dutch. After the war, he returned to Singapore and continued to lead public opinion. Tan became a member of the Chinese People's Political Consultative Conference (CPCC), and returned to China permanently in 1950.[50] He endorsed China's support for the independence movements in Asia, Latin America and Africa and the struggle against colonial rule and political dictatorship. He disapproved of US policy in Asia and condemned it for propping up the Chiang regime in Taiwan. He supported China's intervention to resist the Americans in the Korean War. In 1957, Tan relinquished British citizenship and was given a state funeral when he died in Beijing in 1961.

JAPANESE OCCUPATION

The capture of Malaya and Singapore was among the Japanese Army's greatest wartime achievements. The invasion began just after midnight on 8 December 1941, 70 minutes before the attack on Pearl Harbor. It was the first major battle of the

Pacific War. Elements of General Tomoyuki Yamashita's 山下
奉文 25th Army landed in southern Thailand and the north-
east coast of the Malay Peninsula. Hardened veterans of the
China war, they quickly captured the strategic Kota Baru
airfield. The next day, the British dispatched their two biggest
warships in the Pacific, the Prince of Wales and the Repulse,
up to the Gulf of Siam to halt the seaborne invasion, but
these were sunk by Japanese aircraft the following day, crip-
pling British sea power in the region. The Kota Baru airfield
gave the Japanese control over the skies, where obsolete allied
aircraft were hopelessly outclassed by the modern Japanese
Zero fighter.[51] The campaign pitted 70,000 Japanese troops
against 140,000 British, Australian and Indian defenders.
Advancing on bicycles along plantation roads, Japanese
infantry outflanked Commonwealth positions. By 11 January
1942, they had reached Kuala Lumpur. Commonwealth
troops completed their hasty retreat to Singapore on the
night of 30 January, but were unable to stop the Japanese from
crossing over to the island. The Japanese quickly overran the
defenders, and British commander General Arthur Percival
surrendered on 15 February 1942. The campaign was over
in a mere 70 days. The resounding defeat stunned the Allies
and the peoples of Malaya. The Japanese suffered 9,700 casualties against 17,500 dead and wounded Allied soldiers with
another 130,000 captured.[52] Winston Churchill called the fall
of Singapore the 'worst disaster' and 'largest capitulation' in

British military history. 'How came 100,000 men (half of them of our own race) to hold up their hands to inferior numbers of Japanese?', he asked in utter dismay.[53]

After the Allied surrender, the Japanese Army moved against Chinese residents. The Japanese regarded the Chinese, especially the communists, as implacable enemies; it was the Chinese communist armies that had inflicted the greatest casualties on the Japanese in China. Yamashita ordered the extermination of Chinese likely to resist the Japanese occupation. Supporters of the China Relief Fund, members of secret societies, communists, and politicians were rounded up. Called the *Daikensho* 大検証 or 'Great Inspection' by the Japanese, the purge soon expanded to cover almost all Chinese men, many of whom had nothing to do with the anti-Japanese groups. During the purge from 18 February to 4 March, Chinese men were sent to remote beaches and drowned or machine gunned. In Penang, entire villages were wiped out. It was the Southeast Asian equivalent of the Nanjing Massacre. Historians estimate that between 25,000 and 50,000 Chinese lost their lives. The Sook Ching Massacre 肅清大屠杀, as it came to be called, deprived the Japanese of any cooperation from the local population. As a result, significant numbers of troops were required to maintain order. Singapore politician and lawyer David Marshall (1908–1995), who fought in the Battle of Singapore, was captured and sent to a forced labour camp in Hokkaido. He wrote of his captors:

Three and a half years as a prisoner taught me humility…I realized [as a Japanese prisoner-of-war] that mankind is capable of cold-hearted cruelty. I can be angry, and I have no doubt I can be cruel for five, ten minutes. But the Japanese cruelty was cold-blooded, permanent and eternal. Man's inhumanity to man in fact, in real life, made its presence really known to me when I became a prisoner and saw it in action. Of course, I have known cruelty before. But widespread, long-term, cold-blooded, permanent cruelty, I've never experienced before, not even from the British imperialists no matter how arrogant they were. That was a major shock, the feeling that here were human beings who were not on the same wavelength as me at all, who were not even human from my point of view.[54]

The bulk of the population was powerless against the ruthless enemy.[55] Among the most tragic victims of the occupation were the so-called 'comfort women' 慰安婦, the hundreds of thousands of women and girls abducted, tricked or coerced into sexual slavery. Mostly from occupied territories especially Korea and China, and numbering as many as 410,000, they were forced to serve Japanese soldiers across the Pacific theatre.[56] Many older Singaporeans and Malaysians still remember the locations of comfort stations established throughout the peninsula. One Chinese survivor testified how at 3 am one night in 1943, Japanese soldiers raided her town, going from house to house and dragging women away. She resisted, but her two children were snatched from her arms and she was loaded onto a truck with other women. Taken to a big house and locked in, she was given a Japanese name, Hanako, and raped daily and continuously by Japanese soldiers. From 8 am the soldiers would begin coming in; at night officers came and stayed all night. On a busy day, she would be raped by about 30 soldiers. She would just lie on the bed naked as there was no time to get dressed. The soldiers were often drunk and would hit her about the face and pull her by the hair.[57]

During the occupation, the Chinese did everything they could to aid the British cause.[58] Chinese squatters and coolies rendered assistance to British troops at the risk of their own lives, and there was never a case of a European seeking refuge being turned away. The wealthier Chinese were forced to give large sums to the Japanese, and thousands suspected of pro-British sentiments were massacred. Many Chinese men fled to the jungles to join the Malayan People's Anti-Japanese Army (MPAJA), the guerrilla arm of the Communist Party of Malaya (CPM), which offered the only resistance against the Japanese occupation forces.[59] Its leader was an earnest young man named Chin Peng.

CHIN PENG

Chin Peng (1924–2013) was born Ong Boon Hua in 1924 in Sitiawan, a township 50 miles southwest of Ipoh where his father owned a motorcar and bicycle spare parts shop. He attended Chinese school where he became an avid reader of Chinese history, strategy and socialist thought. At 15, he joined the CPM and taking the *nom de guerre* Chin Peng 陳平 rose swiftly in the ranks. By 18, he had become the key liaison officer between the guerrillas and the clandestine British Force 136 operating behind enemy lines. Reporting to London about Chin Peng, Major John Davis wrote: he has an 'Unusual ability, and commanded the natural respect of men without fuss or formality. Quiet character with incisive brain and unusual ability. Frank and reliable'.[60] F. Spencer Chapman, a British unconventional warfare expert, who had lived with the communist fighters during the war, called him 'Britain's most trusted guerrilla'.[61] For his leadership and courage, the British awarded him two medals and the Order of the British Empire (OBE). Following the Japanese surrender, Chin Peng was appointed to the Central Committee, and at 23, became the party leader. When the British returned to re-colonize the country, Chin Peng began a 12-year struggle to expel them. The insurgency, euphemistically called the 'Emergency', pitted 70,000 British, Australian, New Zealand, Fijian, Gurkha and other Commonwealth troops against 10,000 guerrillas. In his memoirs, Chin Peng recalled: 'Colonial exploitation, irrespective of who were the masters, Japanese or British, was morally wrong. If you saw how the returning British functioned the way I did, you would know why I chose arms'. The war claimed over 10,000 lives and undermined British confidence in the colony. Her majesty's government rescinded Chin Peng's OBE and granted independence (or *Merdeka,* the Malay word for independent or free) in 1957 by putting in a place a government sympathetic to British interests. Britain continued to control huge swaths of the economy, garrison troops in the country, and lead the police force well after Merdeka (Sir Claude Fenner served as Inspector General of Police until 1966).[62] When Chin Peng chose at 16 to leave home and join the resistance, his mother tried hard to dissuade him with safer options, but to no avail:

> When war came, I had to be with the guerrilla force fighting the Japanese. It seemed to be the natural progression of my childhood and teenage orientation. As a young man, I saw no other route that would have sat well with me for the rest of my life. Just as I was appalled by the British colonial days before the war, I was outraged by the Japanese invasion. I had to help actively undermine the invaders. To compromise would have been more harrowing than the formidable hills and jungles we had to trudge through.[63]

The MCP signed a peace accord in 1989 and disbanded, but the Malaysian government reneged on the agreement and refused to allow Chin Peng to return from exile (on the grounds that he could not produce his birth certificate to prove his citizenship) whereas former Malay comrades such as Abdullah C.D.,

Rashid Maidin, Suriani Abdullah were warmly welcomed and fêted by royalty. Chin Peng died in Thailand and his remains are still barred.[64]

POSTWAR MALAYA

The Japanese Occupation came to an abrupt end after the atomic bomb attacks on Hiroshima and Nagasaki in August 1945 destroyed Japanese resolve to fight to the last man. The hardships and privations of the occupation had been severe. The economy was devastated, food shortages and malnutrition widespread and harsh laws brutally implemented. When the British returned, 'the people, especially the Chinese, literally wept with joy to see the Englishmen again' wrote Chapman.[65] But having been roundly beaten by the Japanese, the white man no longer commanded the same respect and the interim British Military Administration (BMA) which took charge in 1945 was made up largely of soldiers with no administrative experience. It was inept and corrupt, and protests which broke out were promptly put down. European plantation owners, many of whom were demobilized servicemen, cowed their workers with hired thugs and threats of deportation to India or China.

To put the peninsula under a single administration, the colonial government proposed a union to replace the patchwork of prewar political jurisdictions – the Straits Settlements, the

Federated Malay States, and the Unfederated Malay States.[66] Singapore would be kept as a crown colony, while Penang and Malacca would be combined with the Malay States to form the Malayan Union. The union would also confer a common citizenship and equal political rights on Malays and non-Malays alike.[67] Although few Chinese were ready to relinquish ties with their homeland, return to China was difficult and they saw they had no choice but to become Malayan citizens even as they clung to their cultural identity. Before the war, the Malay states were bound by treaty to follow the advice of the British Resident, but the union would further strengthen British control by requiring the sultans to surrender power over all matters except religion. Stripping the sultans of their powers was completely unacceptable to the Malays who rejected the plan including the idea of citizenship for non-Malays.[68]

ONN JAAFAR

Leading the protests was a charismatic Malay named Onn Jaafar (1895–1965), the son of the chief minister of Johor. His family enjoyed close ties to the Johor palace and he was treated like a son by the sultan. Sent at the age of ten to boarding school in England, Onn excelled in sports and captained the school's cricket and soccer teams. He returned five years later and enrolled at the Malay College Kuala Kangsar, a boarding school created by the British for sons of the Malay nobility.

Upon graduation from the 'Eton of the East', he entered the civil service, but later became a journalist reporting on the welfare of the Malays. Convinced that giving the economically stronger Chinese and Indians a part in government would lead to the 'extinction' of the Malay race, Onn founded the United Malay National Organization (UMNO) in 1946 to resist the planned union.[69] Among his supporters was a young student named Mahathir Mohamad. The Colonial Office relented, and adopted a revised constitution which protected Malay special rights. The Sultan of Johor rewarded Onn for the victory by appointing him chief minister. Onn, however, soon became alarmed at UMNO's communalist policies and left the party in disgust in 1951 when it refused to open membership to all races. Malaya became independent in 1957 with Tunku Abdul Rahman, a Cambridge-trained lawyer from the Kedah royal household, as its first prime minister. The constitution of the Federation of Malaya enshrined special privileges for Malays, such as through the provision of scholarships and government jobs.[70] The constitution and electoral arrangements ensured that the political influence of Malays would far exceed their slight demographic majority. By the mid 1960s, the civil service was dominated by Malays, which limited prospects for further advancement, and Malay civil servants and politicians began to turn their attention to the business sector.

13 MAY

In the first decade after independence, the population consisted of 46 per cent Malays, 36 per cent Chinese, and 10 per cent Indians, 6 per cent non-Muslim natives and 2 per cent others. Political parties were formed along racial lines, but to gain broad-based support, they depended on key leaders from each community to compromise on critical issues. Three political parties – the United Malays National Organization (UMNO), the Malayan Chinese Association (MCA), and the Malayan Indian Congress (MIC) – representing Malays, Chinese and Indians respectively, formed a coalition called the Alliance. The coalition built consensus, but underlying tensions remained. The bone of contention was special rights for the Malays which dated back to colonial times.[71] Another issue was the status of the Malay language; the Malays wanted it as the official language and the language of instruction in schools, while the others wanted the right to use English, Chinese and Tamil. In the 1969 election, the coalition retained its parliamentary majority with 66 out of 104 seats, but won less than half the votes and 10 per cent less than the previous showing. The opposition organized a parade to celebrate its 'victory', where threats were exchange with Malay bystanders. Malay politicians organized a demonstration on 13 May to show support for the government and to 'teach the Chinese a lesson'.[72] Armed Malays started looting and burning Chinese property. The police were outnumbered, and the army, composed mainly of Malays, sided with the rioters. The pillage continued for two days, despite curfews and heavy military presence. The London *Times* reported that 'in street after street were overturned and burnt-out cars, motorcycles and scooters, with no evidence of the fate that befell their passengers'.[73] Prime Minister Tunku Abdul Rahman recalled:

> Kuala Lumpur was a city on fire. I could clearly see the conflagration from my residence at the top of the hill and it was a sight that I never thought I would see in my lifetime. In fact all my work to make Malaysia a happy and peaceful country through these years, and also my dream of being the happiest prime minister in the world, were also going up in flames.[74]

Some 6,000 residents of Kuala Lumpur, about 90 per cent of whom were Chinese, lost their homes. The government reported 178 fatalities, but newspaper correspondents who were at the scene put the toll much higher.[75] On June 28, Malays organized another round of riots, this time targeting the Indians in the Sentul district. Emergency was declared and parliament suspended. When parliament was reconvened on 23 February 1971, Abdul Razak became the new prime minister and constitutional amendments were passed making it an offense to question citizenship rights, Malay special rights, the status of Islam, and the standing of Malay as the sole national language.

Acts, speeches and publications which had a 'tendency to produce feelings of ill will and enmity between different races' were outlawed.[76] The riots gave birth to the New Economic Policy (NEP).

NEW ECONOMIC POLICY

The government at first blamed political and psychological factors for the riots, but later pointed to economic causes and called for 'restructuring' to ensure interethnic peace and social justice. It announced the goal of achieving 30 per cent Malay ownership and participation in all business sectors by1990. Inequality was not measured in terms of the distribution of wealth across the society as a whole but in terms of the aggregate distribution of wealth, jobs, and economic power between communities.[77] Ostensibly designed to reduce poverty and inequality between races, the NEP benefited Malays through various forms of state intervention. Seeking to restructure society 'to eliminate the identification of race with economic function', it put key sectors such as banking, telecoms, power generation and transportation into Malay hands.[78] These Malay-controlled firms enjoyed state protection from competition, easy access to finance and unconditional subsidies. To create a Malay capitalist class, the government gave Malays licences, contracts, concessions, soft loans and share allotments which created instant millionaires but many sold the advantages to Chinese businessmen for a quick profit, and it has been argued that the NEP bred nepotism, corruption and systemic inefficiency rather than nurture able Malay entrepreneurs.[79]

CHINESE UNDER THE NEP

With the NEP, Malaysia has the most hostile policies toward Chinese businesses anywhere, and yet it produced many successes. In the words of Nietzsche, 'That which does not kill us makes us stronger' and the Chinese have adapted.[80] Many compared them favourably with the Jews in Europe. Even in places where they are a tiny minority such as the Philippines and Indonesia, they play a disproportionate role in every industry level from small rural shops to large multinational corporations.[81] Emblematic of the success is Robert Kuok Hock Nien 郭鹤年, Malaysia's wealthiest tycoon. Born in 1923, Kuok was a teenager when the Japanese invaded. During the Occupation, he worked as a clerk for Mitsubishi Corporation, Japan's largest trading company, where he rose to head the rice trading division. After the war, he built his family's business while his brother, William, joined the guerrillas battling against the British. Robert went into partnership with Japanese businessmen and cultivated Malay patronage well before the NEP. He was classmates with Hussein Onn, the son of Onn Jaafar and their families became close friends. Seeing 'the train moving in the wrong direction', he told Hussein shortly before the latter became prime minister in 1975:

> You're going to be the leader of a nation, and you have three sons, Hussein. The first-born is Malay, the second-born is Chinese, the third-born is Indian. What we have been witnessing is that the first-born is more favored than the second or third. Hussein, if you do that in a family, your eldest son will grow up very spoiled. As soon as he attains manhood, he will be in the nightclubs every night because Papa is doting on him. The second and third sons, feeling the discrimination, will grow up hard as nails. Year by year, they will become harder and harder, like steel, so that in the end they are going to succeed even more and the eldest will fail even more.[82]

He urged his friend to use 'the best brains, the people with their hearts in the right place ... regardless of race, color or creed'. When it became clear that Hussein was not going to take his advice, Kuok moved to Hong Kong where he felt duty-bound to help a backward China. He invested in hotels, real estate and bottling plants on the mainland and credits his success to his mother's guiding hand.[83] At 94, he advised the young to:

> ... *distinguish between the real and the fanciful ... [and] learn to live simply. ...Learn to be humble. Genuine humility*

*must be inner humility, guided by compassion towards your
fellow beings*

SINO-MALAYSIAN RELATIONS

In the postwar period, Sino-Malaysian relations got off to a
rocky start. A staunch anti-communist, Tunku supported
the British campaign against communist insurgents during
the 1948–1960 Emergency, but his successor, Abdul Razak,
normalized relations with China in 1974. Razak was seen
as a Malay nationalist, and recognizing Beijing was his way
of wooing Chinese voters in the general elections.[84] Beijing
had ceased to support insurgency movements, and relations
improved further after Deng Xiaoping's market reforms
and, importantly, the resolution of the status of the Chinese
in the country. Like other Southeast Asian governments,
Kuala Lumpur could not be sure of the loyalty of its Chinese
subjects, but Beijing passed a citizenship law in 1989 effectively closing the door on the overseas Chinese and Kuala
Lumpur reciprocated by lifting a longstanding travel ban to
China the following year. Mahathir Mohamad continued to
build trade ties and quietly explored for oil with China in the
South China Sea, while Najib Razak welcomed a slew of infrastructure projects under China's Belt and Road Initiative.[85]

MAHATHIR MOHAMMAD

More than any other figure, Mahathir Mohamad shaped Malaysian politics.[86] A bright student, he graduated from the King Edward VII College of Medicine in Singapore, and practised in his home town of Alor Star. In the postwar period, Mahathir championed Malay entitlement, opposed citizenship rights for non-Malays, and criticized Prime Minister Tunku Abdul Rahman for accommodating the Chinese. In *Malay Dilemma* which he wrote to explain the root causes of the May 1969 unrest, he declared that the Malays were the indigenous people of the country and deserved special rights. He argued passionately that the Malays were disadvantaged by genes and geography. Hereditary factors, he wrote, played an important part in the development of a race.[87] Among the Malays, marriage between first cousins and close relatives led to inbreeding, and even the weak in body and mind were expected to marry, thereby passing on deficient qualities, he lamented. At the same time, the favourable climate and soil of the peninsula meant that 'no great exertion or ingenuity was required to obtain food ... and even the weakest and the least diligent were able to live in comparable comfort, to marry and procreate'. By contrast, the history of China is littered with natural and man-made disasters. For the Chinese, life was a continuous struggle for survival which produced a hardy race. The Chinese proscription of marriage within the clan ensured cross-breeding and the reproduction of strong attributes.[88] Mahathir's views evoke the observation of early British colonial officers such as John Crawfurd, Stamford Raffles and Francis Light, and he went on to explain the inevitable outcome of the disparity:

The Malays whose own hereditary and environmental influence had been so debilitating could do nothing but retreat before the onslaught of the Chinese immigrants. Whatever the Malays could do, the Chinese could do better and cheaper. Before long the industrious and determined immigrants had displaced the Malays in petty trading and all branches of skilled work. As their wealth increased, so did their circle of contacts. Calling on their previous experience with officialdom in their own homeland, the Chinese immigrants were soon establishing the type of relationship between officials and traders which existed in China. The organized open gratification of the ruling class soon firmly entrenched the Chinese in the towns and helped them establish complete control of the economy.[89]

To redress the imbalance, he said the Malays must first take charge. Even while conceding British administrative competence, Mahathir enjoined self-determination:

Before independence the British ruled this country well. They may not have given the non-British inhabitants the best of everything, but certainly they were expert administrators. They got the job done efficiently. ... But we were not satisfied just because jobs were well done by the people best able to do them. We had our pride to think of. We wanted to rule this country ourselves. We may not do it as efficiently but that is irrelevant.[90]

Mahathir called for affirmative action to close the gap, but he was not blind to the risks of political power:

The question that arises now is how will heredity and this new environment affect the Malays? We can expect that the new environment will not be good for the Malays. They will become softer and less able to overcome difficulties on their own. Because of this, political power might ultimately prove their complete downfall.

But the alternative is equally without promise. Removal of all protection would subject the Malays to the primitive laws that enable only the fittest to survive. If this is done, it would perhaps be possible to breed a hardy and resourceful race capable of competing against all comers. Unfortunately, we do not have four thousand years to play around with.

The answer seems to lie somewhere ... in a sort of 'constructive protection' worked out after a careful study of the effects of heredity and environment. Until this is done, the deleterious effect of heredity and environment on the Malays is likely to continue.[91]

Mahathir became prime minister in 1981 and directed the race-based measures called for in the *Malay Dilemma*. He tried to groom Malay role models such as Halim Saad, Tajuddin Ramli and Rahim Tamby Chik, while enlisting the help of Chinese businessmen to propel Malaysia into the ranks of developed countries by 2020. To achieve *Wawasan 2020*, he initiated important projects such as car manufacturing and the construction of the North-South Highway, a brand new international airport, the Petronas Twin Towers and the Putrajaya administrative capital.[92] He famously rejected IMF prescriptions during the 1997 Asian Currency Crisis and saved the country from financial meltdown but also curbed press freedom, undermined the judiciary and curtailed the powers of the sultans – the hereditary rulers. Mahathir was critical of the West and wanted the former British colony to look East and learn from Japan.

Mahathir retired after 22 years in power but remained influential in UMNO until the clash with Prime Minister Najib Razak over the 1MDB corruption scandal. He resigned from the party and joined the opposition to contest in the 2018 general elections. The opposition won a shock landslide victory ending 61 years of Barisan rule, and at 93, Mahathir became prime minister once more, but his views on affirmative action had evolved: 'I spent 22 years trying to change the Malays. I must admit I have failed'.[93] He chided them for being 'lazy and untrustworthy', reminding them that 'We have a duty to ourselves and to our people. If we fail, it is not because of somebody else. If we fail, it is because we fail to do what is right'.[94] To his cabinet, he appointed Lim Guan Eng as finance minister who when asked how it felt to be the first ethnic Chinese finance minister in 44 years, replied: 'I am sorry but I don't consider myself Chinese; I am Malaysian' reflecting a desire among many Chinese to transcend racial barriers and take full part in nation-building. When the new government cancelled several China-funded infrastructure projects signed off by Najib, there were fears it would hurt relations with Beijing, but Mahathir's perspectives are well known:

> We have been trading with China for almost two thousand years. China was very big … they could have conquered us but they didn't. … The Europeans by contrast came in 1509 to Malacca and two years later they came with a fleet and conquered us. So I am more worried about European attitudes than about Chinese attitudes. I don't want to be involved in any confrontation with China. China is a good trading nation – 1.4 billion people, and I used to say that if 1.4 billion people take one teaspoonful of palm oil a day, we will become very rich.[95]

Palm oil is one of the country's chief exports and Sino-Malaysian relations have come a long way since the Emergency. Beijing has no reason to alienate Kuala Lumpur which thanks to its vista over the Straits of Malacca could become China's most important Southeast Asian ally.

CHAPTER 7

TERRITORIAL DISPUTES

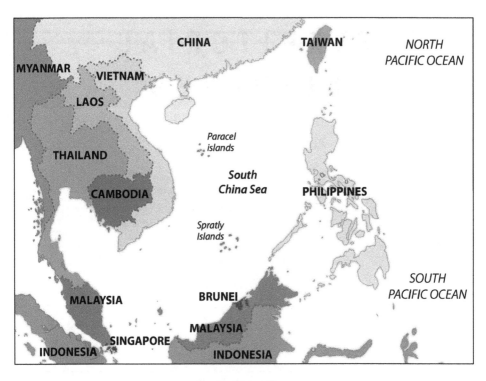

South China Sea

SOUTH CHINA SEA

In the early hours of 19 January 1974, South Vietnamese marines landed on Duncan Island in the Paracel archipelago to confront People's Liberation Army (PLA) troops, who had occupied the island. They came under fire. Outnumbered, the Vietnamese withdrew but their small fleet of four warships drew close to a number of Chinese naval vessels in a tense standoff. At mid-morning, the Vietnamese opened fire on the Chinese, and in a 40-minute sea battle, both sides took damage. The smaller Chinese craft manoeuvred to the blind spots of the Vietnamese guns, and inflicted damage on all four Vietnamese ships. One Vietnamese ship suffered engine damage and went down with its captain. The next day, Chinese aircraft bombed Vietnamese positions on Drummond, Duncan and Robert Islands followed by amphibious assault. The Vietnamese requested support from the US Seventh Fleet but the Americans did not intervene. The Vietnamese garrison surrendered, and the Chinese have controlled the Paracels since.

The islands of the South China Sea are small and none have indigenous inhabitants. The largest island is Pratas Island which measures a mere 6 km by 2 km. The islands are grouped into three archipelagos called the Paracels, the Spratlys and the Pratas. In addition, there are two submerged sandbanks called the Macclesfield Bank and the Scarborough Shoal. The Paracels consist of fifteen islets and twelve reefs and shoals, the most important being Woody Island or Yongxing 永兴 岛 which measures 2 km by 1 km. They are divided into the Crescent Group in the west and the Amphitrite Group in the east. The Spratlys are a widely scattered collection of shoals, reefs and islets stretching more than 1,000 km from southeast to northwest. Taiping Island 太平岛 is the largest in this group. The Pratas consist of only three islets of which Pratas Island is the biggest. Located in a semi-tropical zone, most of the islands are covered with brush, grass, coconut palms and mangrove swamps. Importantly, they straddle the main shipping lanes of the South China Sea.

Known traditionally to the Chinese as Nanhai 南海 or Southern Sea, the South China Sea was seen as a single, uninterrupted sea linking China with the West. While the overland routes via Central Asia were important,[1] the waters have been China's principal gateway to the world for some two thousand years.[2] Archaeological finds confirm Chinese contact with the Paracels as early as first decades of the first century AD. The earliest mention of the islands of the South China Sea

occurred in the *Record of Strange Things of the South* 南州
異物志 written during the period of the Three Kingdoms
(220 AD–280 AD):

> Over the rough Zhang Hai 涨海 the water is shallow and
> the magnetic rocks are many. Men who sail great vessels
> beyond the frontiers must rely on the iron needle to reach
> this place, [but] having arrived at this passage, [they] are
> unable to proceed because of the magnetic rocks.

General Ma Yuan 馬援 (14 BC–49 AD) sailed through these
waters with a fleet of two thousand ships to quell an uprising in
Vietnam. The *New History of the Tang Dynasty* 新唐書 includes
sailing directions from Canton to Sumatra from the period
785–805 AD. For five hundred years, from the late 10th to the
mid-15th centuries, the South China Sea saw a steady expansion in Chinese maritime presence.[3] Driven by trade, the South
China Sea became a zone of Chinese influence and power – a
veritable Chinese lake.

As a continental power, the Chinese traditionally focused
attention on the northern frontier – the source of their main
security threat. But in 1127, the Song rulers lost control of
northern China to the Jurchens, a Tungusic people from
Manchuria, and fled south of the Yangzi River to rule from
the coastal city of Hangzhou. During their 152-year rule, the
Southern Song (1127–1279) rose to become the predominant

maritime force in the region. From the late 12th to mid 15th centuries, Chinese and foreign fleets sailed the Southern Sea in a vast trading network that bought and sold Indonesian spices and aromatic woods, Arabian frankincense, and Chinese silk, porcelain and other commodities. *Record of Foreign Peoples* 諸番志, written between 1225 and 1242, provides a detailed commentary on the routes across the South China Sea with description of the Paracel Islands and Macclesfield Bank. In 1275, some thirty years later, another text, *Dreaming about the Capital* 夢梁錄 offered glimpses of the lives of sailors on those waters. The passage across the South China Sea was fraught with danger with vessels running aground or shipwrecked on the reefs and rocks lying beneath the waves. 'Going out one dreads Qizhou, coming back one fears Kunlun' 去怕七洲、回怕崑崙 became a common refrain among mariners. Nevertheless, Chinese naval presence continued to grow, and by the Yuan period (1271–1368), Chinese naval and merchant fleets dominated the shipping lanes of the South China Sea. The fleets of Kublai Khan attacked Champa (South Vietnam) in 1282, and ten years later, an armada of a thousand ships invaded Java. During the Ming period, the celebrated admiral Zheng He sailed through the Southern Sea all the way to Africa with 62 ships and some 37,000 men.[4] The Ming voyages testified to Chinese power but by the end of the 15th century, Chinese maritime exploits ceased. Chinese naval power declined just as a new force appeared on the horizon.[5]

Chinese maritime power waned on the eve of the advent of the Europeans. Fierce rivalry for control of the South China Sea began with the arrival of the Portuguese and Spaniards in the 16th century. In the 17th century, the Dutch occupied Malacca, Java and Taiwan, and were followed in the 19th century by the British in Malaya, Borneo and Hong Kong, the French in Indochina, the Japanese in Taiwan and the Americans in the Philippines. The Chinese lake became the doorway to foreign invasion, and China itself reduced to a semi-colony. Whereas they regarded the islands only as navigational hazards before, the Chinese now saw them as potential defence outposts.

SCRAMBLE FOR ROCKS

The question of sovereignty over the South China Sea and its islands now became a matter of strategic importance. Before the 19th century, the Chinese paid little attention to control of the sea. Qing maritime policy was limited to regulating coastal shipping and building shore defences against pirates. There were no jurisdictional limits, but with the rise of the Treaty Port System after 1842, the Chinese learned Western maritime rules and began to assert legal title to ocean space. China first claimed sovereignty over the South China Sea islands when it protested French attempts to incorporate them into French Indochina during the 1884–1885 Sino-French war. France formally claimed both the Paracels and the Spratlys in 1932, and annexed them the following year, ignoring Chinese and Japanese protests. In 1938, Japan took the islands from France, garrisoned them, and built a submarine base on Taiping Island. Three years later, in 1941, Japan made the Paracels and Spratlys part of Taiwan, a Japanese colony since 1895.

In 1945, in accordance with the Cairo and Potsdam Declarations, the Chinese Kuomintang government accepted the surrender of the Japanese garrisons on Taiwan, the Paracel and the Spratly Islands. The following year, the Chinese established garrisons on Woody Island or Yongxing Island in the Paracels and Taiping Island in the Spratlys. The French tried, but failed, to dislodge Kuomintang troops from Woody Island. Nevertheless, they managed to build a small camp on Pattle Island (now called Shanhu 珊瑚). In 1950, after their defeat in the Chinese civil war, the Kuomintang withdrew their garrisons from the Paracels and the Spratlys. In 1954 France, following its defeat at Dien Bien Phu, withdrew completely from East Asia and made no further territorial claims in the region. In 1956 Hanoi (North Vietnam) acknowledged the Paracel and Spratly islands as belonging to China. At around the same time, Beijing reestablished a garrison on Woody Island, while Taipei put troops back on Taiping Island. That same year, however, Saigon (South Vietnam) reopened the French camp on Shanhu Island and declared it had annexed both the Paracels and the Spratlys. Nevertheless, to focus on its war with the North, Saigon by 1966 had reduced its presence on the Paracels to a single garrison on Shanhu Island. Beijing made no attempt to remove it.[6] In 1974 Saigon attempted to enforce its claims by placing settlers in the Spratlys and expelling Chinese fishermen from the Paracels. In the ensuing naval battle in the Paracels, China defeated the Vietnamese forces, and extended control over the entire Paracel archipelago, where it has not been effectively challenged since. Five years later, Hanoi (now the government of a united Vietnam), reversing its earlier stance, claimed all the islands in the South China Sea and garrisoned the Spratlys in the early 1980s.

The Philippines too staked claims to islands in the Spratlys, although neither Spain nor the United States, her colonial masters for four centuries (1543–1946), staked claims. In 1956, Filipino businessman Tomás Cloma proclaimed the establishment of a new country called 'Freedomland' in the Spratlys, which prompted both Beijing and Taipei to reiterate claims to the Spratlys. Taipei dispatched troops to drive Cloma off Taiping Island and has kept a presence there since. At first, the Philippine government itself made no territorial claims but joined the contest in 1972. In 1974, President Ferdinand Marcos ordered Cloma to surrender his rights (whatever, if anything, these were) to the Philippine government for one peso. The same year the Philippines occupied five islets in the Spratlys, and two more islets and two reefs by 1978. Manila argued that, with the exception of Taiping Island, the maritime features were *terra nullius* (nobody's land), and that they moreover lay within the Philippines' 200-nautical-mile Exclusive Economic Zone (EEZ) which Manila declared in 1978. Kuala Lumpur followed suit by claiming the southernmost Spratlys located within its EEZ declared in 1979, seized and garrisoned troops on Pulau Layang-Layang (Swallow Reef) in 1983, and has since reclaimed enough land to build an airstrip and a resort hotel.

China was the last to act in the Spratlys, the largest group of islands in the South China Sea. After a bloody skirmish with Vietnamese forces at Johnson South Reef (Chigua 赤瓜) in March 1988, she seized seven islets and followed other claimants in reclaiming land and building structures on top of reefs and rocks. Woody Island and Taiping Island, the only two islands in the South China Sea thought to be naturally habitable, have been claimed by China for at least 130 years and held for more than a half century by Beijing and Taipei respectively. But there is now human encampment on every maritime feature in the South China Sea. A total of forty-four in the Spratlys are now occupied: twenty-five by Hanoi, eight by Manila, seven by Beijing, three by Kuala Lumpur, and one by Taipei. The countries which entered the fray earliest gained the most, and accepting the status quo would give Hanoi by far the largest share, with Manila second. This outcome is the result of policies of strategic forbearance inspired by Deng Xiaoping. Accepting that China has permanently lost territory would undermine the Party's credibility in the eyes of its citizens but rejecting the status quo risks continued friction with her neighbours.[7]

Although a non-claimant, the US sees the territorial dispute as a test of wills between Washington and Beijing. At the ASEAN Regional Forum (ARF) in Hanoi in 2010, Secretary of State Hilary Clinton declared that the US was ready to step in and facilitate multilateral talks.[8] The announcement was a victory for Hanoi, which sought to internationalize the disputes. Secretary Clinton asserted that the disputes had a bearing on US national interest, and that the US was determined to preserve free shipping in the area. She stressed that the US remained neutral on who had stronger claims to the islands although this is historically inaccurate. After World War II, Washington supported China's claims to the Paracels and Spratlys. The US Navy transported Chinese troops to disarm the Japanese on the islands because it considered them to be 'territories Japan [had] stolen from the Chinese' and which were to 'be restored to the Republic of China'.[9] From 1969 to 1971, the United States even operated a radar station on Taiping Island, under the flag of the Republic of China. The islands did not matter to the United States until they became symbols of Washington's determination to check the rise of China. In fact, none of the claimants interferes with shipping or peacetime naval transit in the South China Sea. The South China Sea is a crucial lifeline for the surrounding nations which have a much greater stake in freedom of navigation in those waters than the United States.

THE SENAKAKU/DIAOYU ISLANDS

Another potential flashpoint is the East China Sea between China and Japan. The Diaoyu or Senkaku Islands are a group of nine uninhabited islands located 190 km (120 miles) north-east of Taiwan and 400 km (250 miles) east of mainland China. They occupy and area of 6.3 km² in the East China Sea but only two are over one square kilometre; the largest is 4.3 km²; five are completely barren, and none are inhabited. Neither China nor Japan said much about the islands until a 1968 United Nations report of potential oil and gas resources in the waters around the islands.[10] Despite being an outside party, Washington, has kept matters unresolved. It went from a pro-China position during the 1943 Cairo Conference to diplomatic ambiguity as the Cold War got underway, and then to the current pro-Japan stance.[11] The policy shifts render the situation potentially explosive.

The Chinese claim to be the first to discover the islands. Chinese ships sailed across the East China Sea to Japan from as early as the Qin period (221–207 BC). According to the *Records of the Grand Historian* 史记, a monumental history of ancient China, the first Qin emperor, in his quest for immortality, sent the courtier Xu Fu 徐福 to the 'Eastern Seas' 東海in search of the elixir of life in 219 BC. He returned empty handed and was dispatched on a second expedition in 210 BC from which he never returned and is said to have settled in Japan. A golden seal bestowed on a Japanese envoy in 57 AD by the Han emperor Guangwu 光武帝 (5 BC–57 AD) represents the earliest extant record of contact with Japan.[12] The earliest extant record of the Diaoyu Islands, on the other hand, dates some five centuries later to the Sui dynasty (581–618) when the emperor Yang 隋煬帝 sent an envoy Zhu Kuan 朱宽 to the Ryukyu Kingdom to solicit allegiance to his court.[13] Compelling evidence of Chinese knowledge of the Diaoyu Islands comes from Ming imperial archives and popular literature of the period (1368–1644). The Diaoyu Islands lie just to the north of Taiwan, along the route from the port of Fuzhou 福州 to the Ryukyuan capital of Naha. From 1373 to 1633, the Ming court sent a total of 17 investiture missions to the Ryukyu Kingdom.[14] The 1534 mission led by Chen Kan 陳侃 set sail from the Fujian coast escorted by Ryukyuan boats. The envoy noted in his log:

On the fifth of the fifth month, vessels left Fujian … On the ninth, we spotted a small mountain,[15] which must be Xiaoliuqiu [Taiwan].[16] A brisk southerly wind on the tenth day carried the ship forward. We sailed past Pingjia Shan [Pengjia Mountain], the Diaoyu Yu 釣魚嶼 [Diaoyu Island], Huangmao Yu 黄毛嶼 [Huangwei Island], and Chi Yu 赤嶼 [Chiwei Island], covering in a day a distance which normally takes three. The Ryukyuan boats lagged behind due to their smaller sails.

Chen's report was carried by Shō Shōken 向象賢, a Ryukyuan official, in the kingdom's chronicles.[17] Chinese and Ryukyuans ships used the Diaoyu Islands as navigation markers much like modern-day lighthouses. Before Chen's trip, there were eleven investiture missions to the Ryukyu Kingdom and more than a hundred tribute missions in the opposite direction using the same route. The islands were known to the Chinese and the Ryukyuans as Diaoyu. In his *Illustrated Description of Three Countries* published in 1785, renowned Japanese military scholar Hayashi Shihei referred to the islands by their Chinese name.[18] From the notes of the Chinese envoy Guo Rulin's 郭 汝霖 mission to the Ryukyus in 1561, Japanese historian Inoue Kiyoshi inferred that the islands did not belong to the Ryukyu Kingdom.[19] Taking the route used by Chen Kan, Guo reported:

We left Meihua[20] for Ryukyu … . After seeing Xiaoliuqiu [Taiwan], we passed Huangmao [Huangwei Island]. On the first of the fifth month, our vessels passed Diaoyu Yu [Diaoyu Island]. On the third, we passed Chi Yu [Chiwei Island], which marks the boundary with the Ryukyu Kingdom. One more day with the wind, and we can reach Gumi Shan.[21]

Once past the islands, the envoys knew they had entered Ryukyuan waters. Ming archives show Chinese as well as Ryukyuan officials calling the islands Diaoyu; the name Senkaku was never used. Japanese scholar Suganuma Unryu points out that since the Diaoyu Islands lie south of the Ryukyus, it is unlikely that Japan, situated north of the Ryukyus, owned the islands.[22]

Another mention of the early name of the islands is found in *Voyage with a Tail Wind* 順風相送.[23] Published as early as 1403, it is one of the oldest navigation guides extant, and an important source of information about the Fuzhou-Naha route (a copy survives in the Oxford Bodleian Library). *Voyage* explains the use of a mariner's compass and navigation by stars, but also provides details such as harbour depth, presence of submerged reefs, and places to shelter from a bad storm. According to the guide, 'with berths 15 *tuo* deep [a *tuo* = 6 inches], the Diaoyu Islands are a good place to take on wood and drinking water.

During the Ming period, the authorities built coastal defenses against frequent pirate attacks.[24] Further evidence of Ming knowledge of the islands comes from the 13-volume *Illustrated Compendium on Maritime Security* completed by the geographer Zheng Ruozeng 鄭若曾 in 1561, which catalogues islands along the coast; the first volume titled *Map of Fujian Coastal Mountains and Isles*[25] lists Diaoyu, Huangwei and Chiwei.[26] Later, Qing archives point to Chinese possession of the islands. One oft cited document is the 1893 edict by the Empress Dowager Cixi permitting a doctor in the imperial household to harvest medicinal herbs from the islands. From textual evidence, Suganuma concludes that:

There is no doubt that the Chinese discovered the Diaoyu Islands first, named them, developed their own practice of marine space, and delimited marine boundaries between China and the Liuqiu [Ryukyu] Kingdom as early as the sixteenth century. There is little room for pro-Japan irredentist scholars to contend with pro-China irredentist claims of sovereignty over the Diaoyu Islands.[27]

Geographer Yoshiwara Shigeyasu noted that few Japanese visited the uninhabited Diaoyu Islands, and most doubted their existence.[28] It was not until the late 19th century, when the governor of Okinawa asked to build a national landmark there, that the Japanese government came to know of the islands.

TOKYO'S CLAIM

Japan first laid formal claim to the Diaoyu Islands in 1895, following its spectacular victory in the first Sino-Japanese War. Tokyo then incorporated the islands into Taiwan, which had been ceded to Japan under the Treaty of Shimonoseki.[29] Although Japanese civilians have harvested guano there, Japan has never established a permanent military or civilian presence on the islands. Tokyo bases its current claim on two arguments. First, the islands were *terra nullius* in the 19th century:

From 1885 on, surveys of the Senkaku Islands had been thoroughly made by the Government of Japan through agencies of the Okinawa Prefecture and by way of other methods. Through these surveys, it was confirmed that the Senkaku Islands had been uninhabited and showed no trace of having been under the control of China. Based on this confirmation, the Government of Japan made a Cabinet decision on 14 January 1895 to erect a marker on the Islands to formally incorporate the Senkaku Islands into the territory of Japan.[30]

Secondly, Tokyo maintains that under the San Francisco Peace Treaty of 1951, Japan renounced Taiwan but kept the Senkaku Islands because neither Beijing nor Taipei objected at the time.[31] The assertions, however, do not stand up to scrutiny. At the first Cairo Conference in November 1943, President Franklin Roosevelt, Prime Minister Winston Churchill and Generalissimo Chiang Kai-shek were unequivocal in their stand against Japan:

Japan shall be stripped of all the islands of the Pacific which she has seized or occupied since the beginning of the First World War in 1914, and that all the territories Japan has stolen from the Chinese, such as a Manchuria [Northeast China], Formosa [Taiwan], and the Pescadores [Penghu Archipelago], shall be restored to the Republic of China.

Japan will also be expelled from all other territories which she has taken by violence and greed.[32]

Subsequently, on 26 July 1945, the three powers, demanding Japanese surrender, issued the Potsdam Proclamation, which stressed that 'the terms of Cairo Declaration shall be carried out and Japanese sovereignty shall be limited to the islands of Honshū, Hokkaidō, Kyūshū, and Shikoku and such minor island as we determine'.[33] On 15 August 1945, Japan surrendered according to the Potsdam terms.[34] Four years later, however, the Chinese communists defeated the US-backed Kuomintang, and swept to power in 1949. The following year, the Korean War broke out pitting Chinese against US troops. The war changed Washington's geopolitical calculus in the region.

In 1951, infringing the United Nations Declaration of 1 January 1942 which forbade signatory powers from making a separate peace with Japan and Germany, the US government summoned a conference in San Francisco to work out a peace treaty with Japan. Neither Taipei nor Beijing were invited, despite the fact that China bore the brunt of Japanese aggression. Drafted by Washington and London, the *Treaty of San Francisco* stipulated that Japan renounce all rights to Taiwan and the Pescadores without stating that the territories be restored to China. Beijing declared the treaty null and void:

The ... Government of the People's Republic of China considers that the Draft Peace Treaty with Japan as proposed by the United States and British Governments is a draft which violates international agreements and is therefore basically unacceptable and that the conference which has been scheduled to meet on September 4 at San Francisco, under the compulsion of the United States Government, and which audaciously excludes the People's Republic of China is a conference which repudiates international commitments and therefore basically cannot be recognized.

Whether considered from the procedure through which it was prepared or from its contents, the United States-British Draft Peace Treaty with Japan flagrantly violates these important international agreements to which the United States and British Governments were signatories, viz, the United Nations Declaration of January 1, 1942, the Cairo Declaration, the Yalta Agreement, the Potsdam Declaration and Agreement, and the Basic Post-Surrender Policy for Japan which was adopted by the Far Eastern Commission on June 19, 1947. The United Nations Declaration provides that no separate peace should be made. The Potsdam Agreement states that the 'preparatory work of the peace settlements' should be undertaken by those states which were signatories to the terms of surrender imposed upon the enemy state concerned ....

The United States has monopolized the task of preparing the Draft Peace Treaty with Japan as now proposed, excluding most of the states that had fought against Japan and particularly the two principal Powers in the war, China and the Soviet Union, from the preparatory work for the peace treaty … .[35]

In 1952, US forces withdrew from mainland Japan (comprising the islands of Hokkaidō, Honshū, Shikoku and Kyūshū) but continued to occupy Okinawa (the Ryukyu Islands), and declared that the treaty gave the US administrative powers over the Senkaku Islands as well.[36] These assumed powers were then transferred to Japan in 1971 by the Okinawa Reversion Agreement restoring Okinawa to Japanese rule. Around this time, Washington, mired in the Vietnam War, sought to improve ties with China, and secret diplomatic overtures culminated in President Richard Nixon's historic visit to Beijing in 1972. The visit took Tokyo by surprise; Prime Minister Eisaku Satō was informed of the visit just three minutes before it was made public.[37] Tokyo, which since 1945 had taken its cue from Washington and refrained from building closer ties with Beijing, felt betrayed.[38] Once it recovered from the shock, Tokyo normalized relations with China. Neither Beijing nor Tokyo wanted the islands to get in the way of warming ties, as Deng Xiaoping explained:

Our two sides agreed not to touch upon this (Diaoyu Islands) question when diplomatic relations were normalized between China and Japan. This time when we are negotiating the Treaty of Peace and Friendship, the two sides again agreed not to touch on it … . It does not matter if this question is shelved for some time, say, ten years. Our generation is not wise enough to find common language on this question. Our next generation will certainly be wiser. They will surely find a solution acceptable to all.[39]

In an atmosphere of rapprochement, Washington too adopted a neutral stance with respect to the sovereignty of the islands. Commenting on the Okinawa Reversion Agreement in 1971, the US Senate Foreign Relations Committee stated:

The Republic of China, the People's Republic of China and Japan claim sovereignty over these islands. The Department of State has taken the position that the sole source of rights of the United States in this regard derives from the Peace Treaty under which the United States action in transferring its rights of administration, not sovereignty. Thus, United States action in transferring its rights of administration to Japan does not constitute a transfer of underlying sovereignty nor can it affect the underlying claims of any of the disputants. The Committee reaffirms that the provisions of the Agreement do not affect any claims of sovereignty with respect to the Senkaku or Tiao-Yu Tai Islands by any state.[40]

As recently as 24 March 2004, the US State Department reaffirmed that 'the US does not take a position on the question of the ultimate sovereignty of the Senkaku/Diaoyu Islands. This has been our longstanding view'.[41] Nevertheless, the congressional US-China Economic and Security Review Commission warned in its 2006 annual report that China might 'take advantage of a more advanced military to threaten use of force, or actually use force, to facilitate desirable resolutions…of territorial claims.'[42] China's growing economic strength had begun to worry some in Washington, and angst deepened following the 2008 Global Financial Crisis, which weakened the American economy while allowing China to gain even more ground. In 2010, China became the world's second biggest economy, and was now perceived as a dangerous threat.[43] Washington abandoned its neutrality on the island dispute, and declared that it was obliged to come to Japan's aid in the event of armed conflict over the islands.[44]

Territory is a delicate matter for any nation. In China's case, sensitivity is heightened by a history of deep humiliation. In an address at the US Army War College in 1997, PLA General Li Jijun 李际均 told his audience:

Before 1949, when the People's Republic of China was established, more than 1,000 treaties and agreements, most of which were unequal in their terms, were forced upon China by Western powers. As many as 1.8 million square kilometers were also taken away from Chinese territory. This was a period of humiliation that the Chinese can never forget. This is why the people of China show such strong emotions in matters concerning our national independence, unity, integrity of territory and sovereignty. This is also why the Chinese are so determined to safeguard them under any circumstances and at all costs.[45]

Despite the powerful memories, however, the Chinese have been willing to compromise. Since 1949, Beijing has been involved in twenty-three territorial disputes with its neighbours on land and at sea. Yet it has compromised in seventeen of these conflicts and usually accepted less than half of the territory contested. Through these concessions, China abandoned claims to more than 3.4 million square kilometres of land belonging to the Qing empire at its height in the early 19th century. In total the PRC has contested roughly 238,000 square kilometres or just 7 per cent of the territory once part of the Qing.[46] Political scientist M. Fravel Taylor observes that:

China has not been highly prone to using force in its territorial disputes ... China has been more likely to compromise in its territorial conflicts and less likely to use force than many policy analysts assert, theories of international relations predict, or scholars of China expect. China has not become more aggressive in pursuit of many of its claims as it has accumulated economic and military power over the past two decades. Instead it has compromised frequently and, in some cases, substantially. China has used force in a minority of its disputes, not to pursue broad expansion but to defend the claims it has maintained since 1949.[47]

Former US diplomat Douglas Paal points out that the tensions over the islands originate outside China, but people notice the strong reactions in China more than they notice what Japan or Vietnam or the Philippines did to provoke those reactions in the first place.[48]

The disputes can also be considered in a wider context.[49] The UN Convention of the Law of the Sea (UNCLOS) enacted in 1983 allows countries to claim an economic exclusion zone (EEZ) of 200 nautical miles from their coastline. China is a signatory of the convention, and the South China Sea dispute centres on the extent of the EEZ that China claims compared to those of rival claimants. Importantly, the UNCLOS entitles islands to the same 200-nautical mile rule as land territory. Although most Western colonies were dismantled after the World War II, numerous islands remain as colonies or under the control of high-income countries. The EEZ of the US, France and the UK vastly exceed their home territories. Many of these territories consist of groups of small islands such as British Indian Ocean Territory, the French Kerguelan Islands and the US North Mariana Islands which allow these countries to claim sole access to the resources within their vast economic exclusion zones. The US, France, the UK, Australia, New Zealand and Russia boast the largest economic exclusion zones. They have a combined population of 604 million, less than half of China's 1.3 billion, but an EEZ of 54 million km², three-quarters of which is separate from their home territories; China's undisputed EEZ is 0.9 million km², or about the size of one of the smaller overseas EEZ areas of the US, France or the UK. If it succeeds in all its disputed claims, its EEZ would not exceed 3 million km². Apart from its claims in the South China Sea, China has no overseas island territories.

Unlike the West, China did not build an overseas empire, and this has profoundly affected the distribution of property rights over the oceans' resources. The US has by far the largest EEZ of 12.236 million km², eighty per cent of which consists of overseas territory. The disparity is even more stark when one considers that much of the territory, home and overseas, was acquired through violence against the indigenous population, the conquest of North America by white settlers being only one example.[50] Hawaii was a sovereign kingdom before being annexed by a coup in 1893. The Chinese can perhaps be forgiven for detecting a note of hypocrisy when the Western media criticizes them for making indignant claims in the sea. Cambridge scholar Peter Nolan observes:

> The West's preoccupation with Beijing's involvement in the South China Sea contrasts sharply with the complete absence of discussion of the West's vast exclusive economic zones in the region, deriving from colonial conquest .... It is as though the Western media have succeeded in focusing the minds of their populations on a mouse, when a mighty elephant stands behind them unnoticed.[51]

CHAPTER 8

CHINA AND THE WORLD ORDER

For centuries, China dealt with the outside world through the tribute system, a hierarchical framework which assumed Chinese primacy. Tribute states acknowledged Chinese cultural superiority in exchange for diplomatic recognition and trade opportunity. Vassal states sought prestige and legitimacy through the investiture of their rulers by the Chinese court. At the same time, trade with China was a highly profitable privilege.[1] China was self-sufficient and preferred to keep foreigners at arm's length, but her world changed rapidly from the 16th century onward. Within 260 years of the arrival of the first European traders and missionaries, China had become a semi-colony.[2] Just as they scrambled to colonize Africa, foreign powers carved China up into competing spheres of influence called concessions. Concessions were territory ceded by a weaker power to a stronger one which enforced its own laws within the enclaves. Some were city districts where the Chinese were either barred or treated as second class citizens. Others could be several hundred square miles of territory including ports, islands and entire stretches of important railway lines. In 1924, Sun Yat-sen

(1866–1925), father of republican China, summed up the nation's pitiful state:

> Compared to the other peoples of the world we have the greatest population and our civilization is four thousand years old; we should therefore be advancing in the front rank with the nations of Europe and America. ... in reality [we] are just a heap of loose sand. Today we are the poorest and weakest nation in the world, and occupy the lowest position in international affairs. Other men are the carving knife and serving dish; we are the fish and the meat. Our position at this time is most perilous.[3]

The story of China's modern encounters with foreign powers is a grim one, starting with the Portuguese and the Dutch and then the English, French, Americans and Japanese. The sorry history illustrates a number of common themes, such as the opportunistic use of force against and disregard for the sovereignty of the weak. This chapter describes Chinese thinking about the world order in each succeeding period.

THE PORTUGUESE

The Portuguese conquest of Malacca in 1511, a Chinese tributary state, did nothing for Sino-Portuguese relations, especially when the Malaccans reported Portuguese duplicity (how they

disguised plans for conquest as commercial overtures) and atrocities.[4] Two years later, Portuguese explorer Jorge Álvares, the
first European to arrive in China by sea, landed on an island near
the southern port city of Canton (Guangzhou). The Portuguese
began trading locally and gradually expanded into Macau. Relations with the Chinese soured when a Portuguese fleet arrived
in 1519 and, disregarding Chinese law, proceeded to build a fort
on a Tamão Island in the Pearl River delta. The Portuguese soon
demanded priority in trade over ships from other countries.
When news spread that they were kidnapping and trafficking
Chinese children, the Chinese authorities executed several
Portuguese envoys.[5] All the same, the Portuguese managed,
through bribery, to establish trading posts in Ningbo and
Quanzhou. By 1542, the Portuguese in Ningbo had grown into a
sizable community and began pillaging neighbouring ports and
abducting local inhabitants for the slave trade. The provincial
governor ordered the settlement destroyed in 1548, but relations
improved gradually when the Portuguese helped to suppress
Japanese *wokou* pirates. The Ming government leased Macau to
the Portuguese in 1557, and to improve ties, Lisbon banned the
enslavement and trafficking of Chinese citizens in 1624.

THE DUTCH

Coming on the heels of the Portuguese, the Dutch first
requested to trade with China in 1601, but were refused as

the Chinese had already granted exclusive trading rights to the Portuguese. At war with Portugal at the time, the Dutch demanded the Chinese open up a port in Fujian and expel the Portuguese from Macau. They harassed Chinese shipping to force the Chinese to meet their demands.[6] In 1622, after an unsuccessful assault on Macau, the Dutch set up a base on Penghu (the Pescadores) and built a fort at Magong with forced local labour.[7] Some 1,300 Chinese died building the fort.[8] The Dutch threatened to disrupt Chinese shipping unless the authorities allowed them to trade from the Pescadores. Wanting to keep the Dutch at a safe distance, the governor of Fujian demanded that they leave the Pescadores and trade from Taiwan instead. The Dutch continued raiding the Fujian coast until the governor finally sent a fleet to expel them from the Pescadores in 1624. The Dutch then moved to Taiwan where they built another fort. The Dutch East India Company colonized the island (1624–1662) to trade with China and Japan but also to disrupt Portuguese and Spanish shipping. The Dutch were hated on the island, but revolts by the aborigines and Han settlers were promptly crushed by Company troops. They attempted to levy taxes on ships in the Taiwan Straits, and war broke out in 1633. The Ming loyalist Zheng Chenggong 鄭成功 eventually defeated the Dutch and drove them off the island in 1661.

THE BRITISH

On 27 June 1637, four heavily armed ships sponsored by London merchants arrived at Macau to open up trade between England and China. The Portuguese, invoking their exclusive agreement with the Chinese, refused to allow the British to do business in Macau, but the English would not take no for an answer. They captured a fort and spent several weeks engaged in smuggling and skirmishes along the coast before leaving on 27 December. By the 18th century, foreigners were allowed to trade at Guangzhou (Canton) through a guild of Chinese merchants called the Cohong 公行. British merchants paid for Chinese goods with silver and the rapidly expanding trade quickly led to a shortage of silver with which to pay for goods. The British wanted to reduce the trade deficit by introducing other British products to China. They also desired access to other ports and lobbied for a mission to be sent to the Qing court to address these matters. In 1793, Lord Earl George Macartney led a mission to the court of Emperor Qianlong to showcase British products and press for access to more ports. Bearing gifts of elaborate clocks, globes and porcelain, the earl was taken on a tour of pavilions 'furnished in the richest manner … that our presents must shrink from the comparison and hide their diminished heads'.[9] To his requests, the emperor replied:

… our empire possesses all things in abundance and lacks no product within its borders. There was therefore no need to import manufactures of barbarians in exchange for our own produce. But as the tea, silk and porcelain which the empire produces are absolute necessities to European nations and to yourselves, we have permitted, as a mark of favor, foreign trading houses to be established at Guangzhou so that your wants may be supplied …[10]

The balance of trade was so decidedly in China's favour that it was emptying England of silver. The British then came upon a solution. Starting from the mid 1700s, they began trading opium grown in India for silver. British exports of opium to China grew from an estimated 15 tons in 1730 to 75 tons in 1773. By 1804, the trade deficit with China had turned into a surplus, leading to 7 million silver dollars going to India between 1806 and 1809. Americans joined the trade with Turkish opium, and by 1810 commanded 10 per cent of the trade in Canton.[11] In addition to the drain of silver, the number of Chinese opium addicts shot up to between 4 and 12 million by 1838, causing enormous economic and social ravages. To stem the tide, the Daoguang Emperor sent the scholar-official Lin Zexu 林則徐 to Guangzhou, where he arrested Chinese opium dealers and demanded foreign firms turn over their opium stocks with no compensation. When they refused, Lin placed them under virtual siege in their warehouses. Forcing them to surrender their stocks, Lin destroyed more than 20,000 chests of opium (some 1,400 tons), a process which took 23 days. The aggrieved traders demanded compensation from their home government, but Lin appealed in an impassioned letter to Queen Victoria to intervene and bring an end to the odious trade. Pointing to flagrant double standards, Lin beseeched:

> I have heard that the smoking of opium is very strictly forbidden by your country; that is because the harm caused by opium is clearly understood. Since it is not permitted to do harm to your own country, then even less should you let it be passed on to the harm of other countries – how much less to China!

The queen did not reply. Instead her Majesty's government dispatched an expeditionary force from India, which in a series of battles ravaged the China coast. Outgunned, the Chinese sued for peace in 1842 by the Treaty of Nanjing which granted Britain extraterritoriality, opened five treaty ports, and ceded the island of Hong Kong. In addition, 6 million dollars (equivalent to $170 million today) in compensation were paid to the British government for the destroyed opium and a further 12 million dollars ($340 million today) in war reparations.[12] Britain's imports from China grew swiftly and reached nine times its exports to the country by 1854. Since the Chinese had little need for British manufactures, only opium could balance the deficit. The British soon had an excuse to renew hostilities and extract further concessions. In 1856, the Chinese authorities seized a vessel, the Arrow, for smuggling opium and harbouring Chinese pirates. The Chinese crew members arrested were wanted criminals. With an expired British registration, the ship had no right to fly the Union Jack, but the captain told the British authorities that Chinese officials had taken down the flag of a British ship. All the same, when the English protested, the Chinese apologized and released the ship and crew, but not before three of the Chinese crew members with long records of opium smuggling were executed. The English demanded a guarantee that such seizures would not be repeated even though such an assurance would have been an open invitation to every opium smuggler along the coast to raise the Union Jack when pursued by Chinese authorities. When the Chinese refused, the Royal Navy bombarded Guangzhou and landed marines to take the city.[13] Liberals under William Gladstone, opposed fighting a war for the sake of the opium but lost seats in parliament to the Conservatives led by Lord Palmerston, who secured support to wage war. Gladstone saw it as 'a war more unjust in its origin, a war more calculated in its progress to cover this country with permanent disgrace', and felt 'in dread of the judgments of God upon England for our national iniquity towards China'.[14] The legalization of opium by the Treaty of Tianjin in 1858 appalled the medical missionary J.G. Kerr who called it 'a disgrace not only to the nation that had brought it about but to all of Christendom', and yet rationalized that '… God can make the calamities of war and all the evils growing out of it to work together for the accomplishment of His own gracious purposes of mercy to our fallen race'.[15]

THE FRENCH

The earliest Chinese contacts with the French came in the form of Jesuit missions during the 17th century. At first, the attraction was mutual. The Chinese were impressed with the Jesuit knowledge of science while Chinese culture and style became *de rigueur* in France. In the 18th century, the Jesuit Michel Benoist helped the Emperor Qianlong build a European-style summer palace, and Jean-Joseph-Marie Amiot became the official translator of Western languages in the Qing court. But relations deteriorated as the Europeans scrambled for colonies. In 1844 China and France concluded the Treaty of Whampoa, which gave France the same trade and legal privileges earlier extended to Britain. Citing the execution of a French missionary as excuse, the French joined forces with the British during the Second Opium War.[16] Anglo-French troops captured Guangzhou in 1857 and controlled it for nearly four years. In April 1858, allied troops in British warships reached Tianjin and forced the Chinese to negotiate. The Treaty of Tianjin provided for residence in the capital Beijing for foreign envoys, opened up more ports to Western trade and residence, allowed foreigners to travel in the interior of China, and freedom of movement for Christian missionaries. In further talks in Shanghai, the importation of opium was legalized, and in 1860, to celebrate their military victory, French and British soldiers looted the emperor's summer palace of precious objects – porcelain, silks and ancient books – before burning the complex to the ground in a fire that raged for three days.[17] France carved out its own concessions in Shanghai and seized Guangzhouwan 廣州灣 on the southern coast as a treaty port. The port was 'leased' to France for 99 years and placed under the authority of the French governor in Hanoi.

THE AMERICANS

In the absence of large economic and strategic interests, American policymakers saw their relations with China as benevolent and principled. Interests groups consisting of businessmen, missionaries and diplomats propagated at home a paternalistic vision of defending and reforming China. Americans in China carried with them what Harvard scholar John K. Fairbank called 'the missionary and cowboy attitudes that informed America's transcontinental and trans-Pacific expansion'. At first, Britain did the fighting, while the Americans enjoyed the opportunities to trade and to proselytize secured by the British. But China was never considered an equal in its relations by America. Although American missionaries in China sometimes suffered mob action, none died whereas scores of Chinese labourers hired to build railways in America were lynched by American workers. Missionary and sinologist Samuel Wells Williams noted in 1868: 'If the Americans in China suffered one tithe of the wrongs that the Chinese have endured within the United States since 1855, there would certainly have been a war on account of it'.[18] Sino-American treaties provided for reciprocal trade and residence rights, but the American labour movement denied such rights to Chinese labourers.[19] Chinese statesmen who sought American help against the British, Japanese and Russians were consistently disappointed. When Li Hongzhang 李鸿章 (1823–1901) tried to enlist US support, American naval officers and diplomats were more quick with words than action, and Zhang Zhidong 張之洞 (1837–1909) appealed in vain for US support against Russo-Japanese encroachment in Manchuria. Meanwhile, US immigration officers harassed and humiliated Chinese students, scholars, and officials seeking to enter America. Blaming the Chinese for declining wages and economic ills even though the Chinese comprised a mere 0.002 percent of the US population, Congress passed the Chinese Exclusion Act of 1882 which barred Chinese immigration into the United States.[20] The racism finally triggered a Chinese boycott against American goods in 1905.[21]

THE MISSIONARIES

No account of Western encroachment on China is complete without mention of the role of missionaries. At a time of intellectual and social ferment, Christian missionaries made important contributions to education, healthcare and science in China. They built churches, schools, colleges and hospitals, and engaged in service and philanthropy of all kinds. Missionaries founded Yenching University, the forerunner of Peking University, in 1916 and its first president, John Leighton Stuart (1876–1962), was born in China to Presbyterian missionaries.[22] Raised in Hangzhou until the age of 11, Stuart considered himself more Chinese than American. Later as US ambassador to China, he mediated between Chiang Kai-shek and communist leaders, some of whom were Yenching graduates. Wu Leichuan 吳雷川 (1870–1944), the first Chinese vice-chancellor of Yenching, was a member of the Hanlin Academy, the most prestigious position attainable under the Confucian examination system.[23] From an early age, he was drilled in the Confucian classics, but was baptized into the Anglican faith in 1915. Wu tried to fuse Christian theology with Confucian concepts and devoted his spare time to spreading Christianity among Peking intellectuals.[24] Christianity found resonance among students and intellectuals, and many saw it as the answer to the spiritual vacuum left by the disenchantment with Confucian tradition. Chen Duxiu 陳獨秀, co-founder of the Chinese Communist Party in 1921, urged readers of his influential monthly *New Youth* 新青年 to study Christianity seriously and 'knock at [Jesus'] door and ask that his lofty character and warm spirit be united with us'.[25] By the mid 1910s, the Young Men's Christian Association had become one of the most popular organizations among students. In 1913, 100 of the 300 students of Tsinghua College were enrolled in YMCA Bible study groups, while scholars and reformists such as Tang Shaoyi, Yan Fu, Liang Qichao, and Cai Yuanpei served on YMCA boards.[26] The number of converts to Protestant Christianity between 1911 and 1922 rose to 100,000, almost equal to the number converted over the previous hundred years. But what were missionary perceptions of the Chinese?

For a whole century beginning in the 1840s, people-to-people contact between Westerners and Chinese took place under a system of unequal treaties, whereby Westerners enjoyed 'extraterritoriality' or immunity from Chinese law.[27] Missionaries came into close contact with the common folk, and there were moving examples of hardship, sacrifice and love for the Chinese.[28] Hudson Taylor (1832–1905), the son of a Methodist lay preacher, founded the China Inland Mission to work in the interior of China. In his 51 years in China, Taylor was responsible for bringing over 800 missionaries, who won some 18,000 converts. Like the 16th century Jesuit Matteo Ricci (1552–1610), he was sensitive to Chinese culture; the Yorkshireman dyed his hair black, wore it in a pigtail, and preached in Mandarin as well as the Chaozhou and Wu dialects. He famously declared: 'If I had a thousand pounds, China should have it. If I had a thousand lives, China should have them'. Another remarkable figure, Gladys Aylward

(1902–1970), a petite London working-class woman, went without knowing a word of Chinese but soon became a fluent speaker and a naturalized Chinese citizen. She won reverence through her work among orphaned children during the desperate war years. In 1938, Alyward led nearly a hundred young children, four to eight years old, on a hundred-mile trek to safety before advancing Japanese troops.[29]

But some missionaries took a harsher view of the Chinese. Young J. Allen (1836–1907), a Southern Methodist from Georgia, and editor of the weekly *Church News* 教會新報 concluded that the Chinese were 'ignorant beyond measure of the simplest laws of natural philosophy, chemistry, and astronomy as their vague notions, senseless superstitions, and the ceremonies and rites … fully attest'.[30] Missionaries in 19th century China faced restrictions, and many believed that normal diplomacy could not obtain the right to seek converts freely. Some were convinced that negotiations should be backed by the 'thunder of British batteries'. Jacob Gould Schurman, president of Cornell University, advised President William McKinley that 'all Asiatic peoples have no trust in mere words without force behind them'.[31] *The Chinese Repository*, edited by the American missionaries Elijah Coleman Bridgman and Samuel Wells Williams, offered similar advice: the 'imbecilic' Chinese 'will insult so long as they meet no resistance, but when force is opposed to force, their courage fails'. They considered an assault on Peking as the only honorable response to Lord

Napier's humiliation.[32] 'The more forbearance and indulgence' shown to the Chinese, the 'more proud and overbearing they become', warned the editors. Force alone would 'break down their minds' and 'compel China to a course more consistent with her rights and obligations', abandoning her 'haughty isolation', which was 'in open violation of the law – thou shalt love thy neighbor as thyself'.[33] 'The British flag has been insulted and British blood has been spilt. These hostile acts should be complained of, and reparation demanded and *obtained*'. They urged in no uncertain terms that:

> The Government of Great Britain could alone, were it necessary, dictate to the Chinese, and enforce any terms it pleased; and could by the exercise of its naval power effect the removal of all grievances which it is in the province of the government to remove. This power we hope, will be speedily exerted and this effect produced. Recent injuries demand this. Humanity demands it. And justice will approve of it.[34]

For David Abeel of the American Reformed Mission, nothing short of an armed invasion would sweep away the hateful barriers to the gospel.[35] When war was slow to break out, missionary teacher Samuel Brown demanded: 'How long will England continue to wear the lion on her crest and yet play the part of the hare?'. When the English guns began firing, American missionary Henrietta Shuck confessed: 'How these difficulties do rejoice my heart because I think the English government may be enraged, and God, in His power may break down the barriers which prevent the gospel of Christ from entering China'.[36] Once negotiations collapsed, England had every moral right to make war on China as T.L. McBryde explained to the Presbyterian flock at home:

> After many months had been occupied in vain attempt to negotiate, it became clear to every observer that in order to lay the foundation for free and friendly intercourse with this nation on safe and honorable terms, such as are recognized by all civilized states, recourse must be had to restraint and coercion.[37]

THE TREATY OF VERSAILLES

China's encounter of the international system of governance inspired little confidence. The Chinese saw yawning gaps between the theory and practice of international law. In 1898, Germany obtained the use of Jiaozhou Bay on the Shandong peninsula, and the right to construct a naval base at Qingdao. In 1915, forced by a Japanese ultimatum, a weak Chinese government caved in to Japan's Twenty-One Demands which included the giving of railway and mining rights in Shandong, special privileges in Manchuria, and access to harbours, bays and islands along the Chinese coast. Having supported the Allies during World War I, China expected German concessions in Shandong to be returned to China. At the 1919 Versailles Peace Conference ending World War I, the question arose of whether to transfer to Japan the German privileges in Shandong. In a backroom deal struck with the Allies, Japan agreed to back British and French claims to German possessions in other parts of the world in return for support on the Shandong question. Before the conference, US President Woodrow Wilson had made bold statements championing self-determination and world democracy, raising expectations of a just peace. When the Allies handed Shandong to the Japanese, mass protests broke out across China. This was the last straw after decades of 'open door' policies, which saw Europe and Japan carve up huge territories within China using treaties as legal cover.[38] China refused to sign the treaty. Another conference convened in Washington in 1922 only succeeded in awarding China sham sovereignty in Shandong by giving Japan the railways and thereby *de facto* control of the province's economy.

China's problems were far from over. Emboldened by the complicity of the West, Japan pressed on. Officers of the powerful Kwantung Army 関東軍 in Manchuria detonated a small explosive charge close to the Japanese-owned South Manchurian Railway in September 1931. Blaming the Chinese for the attack, the Japanese army launched a full-scale invasion of Manchuria and created the puppet state of Manchukuo six months later. Then in July 1937, the Japanese army invaded China beginning a bitter 8-year struggle, which drew in the Allies when Japan attacked Pearl Harbour, the Philippines and Malaya in 1941. Chiang Kai-shek fielded 4 million troops, and among the Allies, China suffered the heaviest casualties.[39] Had she capitulated, Japan's capacity to fight the US in the Pacific would have been multiplied by the strength of the Kwantung Army which by 1945 still consisted of 30 infantry divisions totalling some 700,000 men. After the war, however, she became a forgotten ally.[40]

FROM ISOLATION TO INTEGRATION

In 1949 the Chinese communists defeated the US-backed Kuomintang and founded the People's Republic of China. The fledgling republic tried to establish ties with the US but was rebuffed, leaving it no alternative but to ally with the Soviet Union despite its hazards. Chinese leaders saw how Soviet armies withdrawing from Manchuria in 1946 looted factories leaving Mukden (modern day Shenyang), which once boasted more than 5,000 factories, looking like a dead city.[41] China became the victim of a trade embargo directed, in the words of Washington, at thwarting 'the aggressive designs of a nation bent on world conquest'.[42] It was excluded from postwar reconstruction plans and shut out of the United Nations. The Korean War, a US-led intervention backed by the UN, and the creation of the SEATO security alliance deepened Chinese mistrust of multilateral institutions.[43] Mao called for the violent overthrow of the international system:

> Experience in class struggle in the era of imperialism teaches us that it is by the power of the gun that the working class and the laboring masses can defeat the armed bourgeoisie and landlords; in this sense we may say that only with guns can the whole world be transformed.[44]

Reports of Beijing's support for armed insurrection across the developing world in the 1960s featured regularly in the party organ:

> A police patrol had marched to None Hi Village in Nakhon Phanom Province, northeast Thailand. As usual, these butchers were riding roughshod over the peasants and massacring patriots. But they got what they least expected – a surprise attack from the people's forces. A police corporal was killed and the colonel who led the patrol seriously wounded. The rest ran for their lives. When the government heard what had happened and helicoptered hundreds of police to the scene, the people's forces had long since disappeared. This took place on August 7 two years ago. It was the first shot fired by the Thai people's armed struggle. Since then, led by the Communist Party of

Thailand, the people's forces ... have dealt US imperialism and its lackeys heavy blows and have grown in strength. In the two years, they have fought over 500 battles and wiped out more than 1,000 enemies. Of these, 977 were killed or wounded and 26 captured.[45]

And when the Association of Southeast Asian Nations (ASEAN) was formed in 1967, Beijing reacted with scorn:

Bangkok was during August 5–8 a meeting place for the reactionaries of Indonesia, Thailand, the Philippines, Singapore and 'Malaysia', that is, the handful of US imperialism's running dogs in Southeast Asia. There, with Washington pulling the wires, they conspired and formally knocked together a so-called 'Association of Southeast Asian Nations' (ASEAN). This set-up is an out-and-out counter-revolutionary alliance rigged up to oppose China, communism and the people, another instrument fashioned by US imperialism for pursuing neocolonialist ends in Asia. In its Joint Declaration issued on August 8, this alliance of US stooges openly supported the existence of US military bases in Southeast Asia, not even bothering to make any excuses for them. All this proves that this reactionary association formed in the name of 'economic cooperation' is a military alliance directed specifically against China.[46]

Mao saw a link between capitalism, imperialism and racism, and understood racial injustice in terms of class struggle:

> US capitalism and imperialism have grown up in the ruthless exploitation of the Afro-Americans. And racial discrimination in the United States has always been a form of class oppression. The US rulers have pushed racial discrimination to the most vicious lengths for the sole purpose of strengthening class exploitation and oppression. This barbarous institution not only yields them several billion dollars in super-profits annually, but provides them with a great labor reserve and also a weapon against the oppressed white people to force them to put up with the monopoly capitalists' exploitation and enslavement. To maintain the reactionary rule of monopoly capital, the US rulers use racial discrimination to spread racial prejudice and hatred among the working people of different colors, to practice divide and rule, and to undermine the unity and struggle of the American working class and other laboring people.[47]

Soviet schemes were not to be trusted either. In 1968, Soviet leader Leonid Brezhnev affirmed the right of the Soviet Union to intervene in the affairs of communist states in order to strengthen world communism. As Moscow tightened its grip on East European states through this doctrine, Beijing viewed

Soviet-backed institutions as little better than Western ones and urged solidarity among Third World countries in the struggle against the two superpowers.[48] Things only began to change when America sought rapprochement with Beijing. In June 1971, President Richard Nixon lifted the 21-year embargo on trade with China, ending her isolation and opening the way for economic reforms. China's imports at that time totalled a mere $2 billion – little more than two weeks' worth of total US exports in 1971.[49] Mao, who presided over the Cultural Revolution, a 10-year long socio-political movement marked by anarchy and terror, died in 1976 and Deng Xiaoping soon assumed leadership. In a sharp course correction at the 1978 Party Congress, China's leaders renounced class struggle and took up economic development as their central focus.[50] Deng announced China's opening up to the outside world, beginning the steady process of integration into the international order.[51]

China's journey from isolation to full participation in the global order has been an unqualified success. It is now a full member of major international organizations and signatory to all important international treaties. It had to carry out wide ranging reforms in order to comply with international trade and investment regimes. After fifteen years of tariff cuts, market liberalization and scaling back of industrial policies, it became a member of the WTO in 2001. The transition from a command economy to a market economy was fraught with risks (as seen from Russia's disastrous restructuring).

Like the Russians, the Chinese had no road map; only Deng Xiaoping's guidance to 'cross the stream by feeling the stones [on the riverbed]'.[52] The Chinese took experimental steps and learned by doing. New policy measures were tried out in a special economic zone, city or province before applying them across the country. Along the way, Chinese policy-makers faced intense pressure from Western economists, business leaders and the World Bank to open up key sectors, such as banking, energy, and telecommunications to foreign investors. The Chinese held on to the family jewels (or what Marx called 'the commanding heights') but transformation in other sectors proceeded apace, and China soon became a vital part of the global supply chain, producing a vast array of products from shoes to computers and solar panels at low cost. According to the World Bank, she has since 1978 lifted 800 million people (the equivalent of six Japans) out of poverty – an unprecedented accomplishment in the history of economic development. China reached all Millennium Development Goals[53] by 2015 and has been the largest contributor to world economic growth since the global financial crisis of 2008.[54] In the face of enormous political, economic and strategic change, however, there is now vigorous debate in China about the future shape of the global order. The discussions steer foreign policy and are influenced by domestic priorities.[55] The government seeks to continue domestic reforms while managing the country's rise in the international system.[56] It wants to protect its own national interests but also shape the way the world is run. Deng spelled out the bottom line at the 12th National Congress in 1982:

> Independence and self-reliance have always been and will forever be out basic stand. We Chinese people value our friendship and cooperation with other countries and people. We value even more our hard-won independence and sovereign rights. No foreign country can expect China to be its vassal or expect it to swallow any bitter fruit detrimental to its own interests.[57]

From Beijing's perspective, there are better ways to achieve well-being than by adopting Western policies which have produced significant social, economic and political discontent around the world.[58] Rejecting US demands for wider market liberalization, Chinese president Xi Jinping told party leaders in a speech in 2018 commemorating the 40th anniversary of Deng Xiaoping's 'reform and opening up' policy that:

> To promote reform and development in China – a large country with a more than 5,000 year history of civilization and more than 1.3 billion people – there is no textbook that can be regarded as a golden rule, and there is no great master who can dictate to the Chinese people. … What should be and can be reformed, we will resolutely reform.

What should not or cannot be reformed, we will resolutely not reform. … China's development does not pose a threat to any country. No matter how far China develops, it will never seek hegemony.[59]

Observers such as US diplomat Charles Freeman Jr. believe China is not interested in dominating Asia, much less the world.[60] Freeman warns that analogies to other rising powers with shorter histories such as France, the United States, Germany, Japan, and the USSR are not helpful in predicting the consequences of China's rise.[61] He points out that:

China has no messianic ideology to export; no doctrine of 'manifest destiny' to advance; no belief in social Darwinism or imperative of territorial expansion to act upon; no cult of the warrior to animate militarism or glorify war; no exclusion from contemporary global governance to overcome; no satellite states to garrison; no overseas colonies or ideological dependencies.[62]

Lord Charles Powell, trusted foreign policy advisor to Margaret Thatcher and John Major, believes that:

Any intention on the part of China to rule the world would be completely contrary to its history. China has generally in the past disdained the rest of the world. It has felt self-sufficient. It hasn't needed the rest of the world and has had no great ambition to lead it.[63]

China's rise does not threaten the West[64] but China will be China, not an honorary member of the West.[65] It wants to share this century as co-equals with the United States, but will rely on economic rather than military power to do so. China will take its place alongside the US and others at the head of a multilateral system of global governance where it will enjoy prestige but no monopoly of power. The US will remain the only military power with global reach for years to come. Few nations endured as harsh a history as did China in the 20th century and none has accomplished what she did in the past two generations. Those achievements, the Chinese believe, deserve the world's respect and its expressed desire to share a peaceful, wealthy world with its trading partners should be accepted.

NOTES

Chapter 1

1   John C.G. Rohl, *The Kaiser and His Court: Wilhelm II and the Government of Germany* (Cambridge: Cambridge University Press, 1996), 203.

2   David G. Myers, *Social Psychology*, 11th ed. (New York: McGraw-Hill, 2013), 6.

3   Raymond Stanley Dawson, *The Legacy of China*, The Legacy Series (Oxford: Clarendon Press, 1964), 2.

4   John K. Fairbank, *The United States and China* (Cambridge, MA: Harvard University Press, 1948), 310.

5   Errol Morris, *The Fog Of War: Eleven Lessons from the Life of Robert McNamara* [DVD] [2004], DVD (Sony Pictures Home Entertainment, 2004).

6   Tim Weiner, 'Robert S. McNamara, Architect of a Futile War, Dies at 93', *The New York Times*, July 7, 2009, sec. US, http://www.nytimes.com/2009/07/07/us/07mcnamara.html?pagewanted=6&_r=1&th&emc=th.

7   Judith F. Kornberg and John R. Faust, *China in World Politics*, 2nd ed. (Boulder, CO: Lynne Rienner Publishers, 2005).

8   David Shambaugh, 'China Engages Asia: Reshaping the Regional Order', *International Security* 29, no. 3 (1 January, 2005): 64-99, http://www.mitpressjournals.org/doi/abs/10.1162/0162288043467496.

Chapter 2

1   角田 柳作 Tsunoda Ryūsaku and L. Carrington Goodrich, *Japan in the Chinese Dynastic Histories: Later Han through Ming Dynasties*, Vol. no. 2, Perkins Asiatic Monographs, (South Pasadena [Calif.]: P.D. and I. Perkins, 1951).

2　王貞平 Wang Zhenping, *Ambassadors from the Islands of Immortals: China-Japan Relations in the Han-Tang Period*, Asian Interactions and Comparisons (Honolulu, HI: Association for Asian Studies; University of Hawaii Press, 2005).

3　Ibid., 8.

4　Tsunoda Ryūsaku and Goodrich, *Japan in the Chinese Dynastic Histories.*

5　Wang Zhenping, *Ambassadors from the Islands of Immortals*, 216.

6　David Kang, *East Asia before the West: Five Centuries of Trade and Tribute* (New York: Columbia University Press, 2010), 140.

7　George H. Kerr, *Okinawa: The History of an Island People*, Rev. (Rutland, Vt ; Tokyo: Tuttle Publishing, 2000), 67–68.

8　平野邦雄 Hirano Kunio, '日、朝、中三國関係論についての覚書 Memorandum on Theory of Sino-Korean-Japanese Relations', 東京女子大学付属比較文化研究所紀要 41 (1980): 101–30.

9　Kang, *East Asia before the West: Five Centuries of Trade and Tribute*, 145.

10　聯谊以夷制夷 The strategy of allying with one barbarian against another.

11　Wang Zhenping, *Ambassadors from the Islands of Immortals*, 219.

12　The jimi system is described in *Border Defence* 邊防典, volume 185 of the 8th century encyclopedic *Comprehensive Institutions* or *Tongdian* 通典.

13　Wang Zhenping, *Ambassadors from the Islands of Immortals*, 225.

14　日本書紀 Vol. 10

15　Wiebke Denecke, Wai-Yee Li, and Xiaofei Tian, *The Oxford Handbook of Classical Chinese Literature (1000 BCE–900 CE)* (Oxford: Oxford University Press, 2017), 300.

16　Wang Zhenping, *Ambassadors from the Islands of Immortals*, 202.

17　Joshua A. Fogel, *Articulating the Sinosphere: Sino-Japanese Relations in Space and Time* (Harvard University Press, 2009), 17.

18　Ibid., 18.

19　Ibid., 23.

20　Tsunoda and Goodrich, *Japan in the Chinese Dynastic Histories*, no. 2, 60–61.

21 Fogel, *Articulating the Sinosphere*, 24.

22 Ibid., 27.

23 Mary Elizabeth Berry, *Hideyoshi* (Cambridge, MA: Harvard University Press, 1982), 9.

24 Walter Dening, *The Life of Toyotomi Hideyoshi*, 3rd ed. (J.L. Thompson & Co. Ltd., 1930), 9.

25 Stephen R. Turnbull, *Samurai Invasion: Japan's Korean War*, 1592–98 (London: Cassell & Co, 2002).

26 Joshua A. Fogel, *Maiden Voyage: The Senzaimaru and the Creation of Modern Sino-Japanese Relations* (Oakland, CA: University of California Press, 2014).

27 Sir Adolphus William Ward et al., *The Cambridge Modern History* (London: Macmillan, 1910), 573.

28 Thomas David Dubois, 'Rule of Law in a Brave New Empire: Legal Rhetoric and Practice in Manchukuo', *Law and History Review* 26, no. 2 (2008): 285–318.

29 Paul H. Kratoska, *Asian Labor in the Wartime Japanese Empire: Unknown Histories* (Abingdon: Routledge, 2014); Zhifen Ju, 'Japan's Atrocities of Conscripting and Abusing North China Draftees after the Outbreak of the Pacific War', *Joint Study of the Sino-Japanese War*, 2002.

30 John K. Fairbank, Edwin Oldfather Reischauer, and Albert Morton Craig, *East Asia : Tradition & Transformation*, Rev. (Boston, Mass.: Houghton Mifflin, 1989), 714.

31 Iris Chang, *The Rape of Nanking: The Forgotten Holocaust of World War II* (London: Penguin, 1998).

32 Herbert P. Bix, *Hirohito and the Making of Modern Japan*, 1st Perennial Ed. (New York: HarperCollins, 2001).

33 Ibid., 326–27.

34 Michael Yahuda, *Sino-Japanese Relations After the Cold War: Two Tigers Sharing a Mountain* (Routledge, 2013), 14, http://www.routledge.com/books/details/9780415843089/.

35 'The Number of Japanese Nationals Studying Overseas and the Annual Survey of International Students in Japan', *MEXT*, February 27, 2015, http://www.mext.go.jp/english/topics/1357495.htm.

36 John W. Dower, 'The San Francisco System: Past, Present, Future in U.S.-Japan-China Relations', *The Asia-Pacific Journal: Japan Focus*, February 23, 2014, http://apjjf.org/2014/12/8/John-W.-Dower/4079/article.html.

37 'The Unquiet Past', *The Economist*, August 12, 2015, http://www.economist.com/news/essays/en/asia-second-world-war-ghosts.

38 趙全勝 Zhao Quansheng, *Japanese Policymaking: The Politics behind Politics: Informal Mechanisms and the Making of China Policy* (Westport, Conn.: Praeger, 1993), 15.

39 Al Kamen, 'Among Leaders at Summit, Hu's First', *The Washington Post*, April 14, 2010, sec. Politics, http://www.washingtonpost.com/wp-dyn/content/article/2010/04/13/AR2010041304461.html.

40 Gavan McCormack, 'Obama vs Okinawa', *New Left Review*, II, no. 64 (2010): 5–26.

41 Urs Matthias Zachmann, *China and Japan in the Late Meiji Period: China Policy and the Japanese Discourse on National Identity*, 1895–1904 (London; New York: Routledge, 2009).

42 鈴木章悟 Suzuki Shogo, *Civilization and Empire: China and Japan's Encounter with European International Society*, The New International Relations (London: Routledge, 2009), 114–39.

43 川島真 Kawashima Shin, 'Historical Dialog and Documentary Research', in *Toward a History beyond Borders* (Cambridge, MA: Harvard University Asia Center, 2012), 413.

44 The flying geese paradigm of economic development was advanced by Japanese economist Kaname Akamatsu 赤松要 (1896–1974) who saw Japan lead the way in Asia.

45 In 2017, China and the US accounted for 19.0% and 19.3% of Japan's export respectively.

46 In 2017, Chinese and US economy grew by 6.9% and 2.3% respectively.

47 Between 1991 and 2017, China's GDP per capita increased from $1,526 to $15,308 while US GDP per capita went from $36,543 to $54,225.

Chapter 3

1   George H. Kerr, *Okinawa: The History of an Island People*, Rev. (Tokyo: Tuttle Publishing, 2000), 22.

2   Shunzō Sakamaki, 'Ryukyu and Southeast Asia', *The Journal of Asian Studies* 23, no. 3 (1964): 383–89.

3   Kerr, *Okinawa*, 65.

4   They settled in the Kumemura 久米村 district of the capital Naha.

5   Kerr, *Okinawa*, 146.

6   Ibid., 126.

7   Gregory Smits, *Visions of Ryukyu: Identity and Ideology in Early-Modern Thought and Politics* (Honolulu: University of Hawai'i Press, 1999), 16.

8   Prasenjit Duara, *Rescuing History from the Nation: Questioning Narratives of Modern China* (Chicago; London: University of Chicago Press, 1995).

9   Satsuma annexed the islands of Kikai, Amami-ōshima, Tokunoshima, Okinoerabu, and Yoron.

10 Barry D. Steben, 'The Transmission of Neo-Confucianism to the Ryukyu Islands and Its Geopolitical Significance: Ritual and Rectification of Names in a Bipolar Authority Field', in *Crossing the Yellow Sea* (Norwalk, CT: EastBridge, 2007), 79.

11 台灣の生藩が日本国属民に対し、妄りに害を加えた。

12 Steben, 'The Transmission of Neo-Confucianism to the Ryukyu Islands and Its Geopolitical Significance: Ritual and Rectification of Names in a Bipolar Authority Field', 91.

13 Steve Rabson, 'Memories of Okinawa : Life and Times in the Greater Osaka Diaspora," in *Islands of Discontent* (Lanham, Md.: Rowman & Littlefield Publishers, 2003), 110.

14 Ibid., 113.

15 Ibid., 114.

16 Steve Rabson, *The Okinawan Diaspora in Japan: Crossing the Borders Within* (Hawaii: University of Hawai'i Press, 2012).

17 Kerr, *Okinawa*, 305.

18 Ibid., 300.

19 Ibid., 312.

20 John W. Dower, *War without Mercy: Race and Power in the Pacific War* (London: Faber, 1986).

21 Matthew Allen, 'Wolves at the Back Door : Remembering the Kume-jima Massacres', in *Islands of Discontent* (Rowman & Littlefield Publishers, 2003), 46–49.

22 Gavan McCormack and Satoko Oka Norimatsu, *Resistant Islands: Okinawa Confronts Japan and the United States* (Lanham, Md.: Rowman & Littlefield Publishers, 2012), 23.

23 Asato Eiko, 'Okinawan Identity and Resistance to Militarization and Maldevelopment', in *Islands of Discontent* (Lanham, Md.: Rowman & Littlefield Publishers, 2003), 228.

24 Ibid., 229.

25 Julia Yonetani, 'Future "Assets", but at What Price? The Okinawa Initiative Debate', in *Islands of Discontent* (Lanham, Md.: Rowman & Littlefield Publishers, 2003), 244.

26 Jesse Johnson, 'In First, U.S. Admits Nuclear Weapons Were Stored in Okinawa during Cold War', *The Japan Times Online*, February 20, 2016, http://www.japantimes.co.jp/news/2016/02/20/national/history/first-u-s-admits-nuclear-weapons-stored-okinawa-cold-war/?utm_source=Daily+News+Updates&utm_campaign=f547f22477-Sunday_email_updates21_02_2016&utm_medium=email&utm_term=0_c5a6080d40-f547f22477-332789745.

27 Linda Isako Angst, 'The Rape of a Schoolgirl', in *Islands of Discontent* (Lanham, Md.: Rowman & Littlefield Publishers, 2003), 141.

Chapter 4

1 Brantly Womack, *China and Vietnam: The Politics of Asymmetry* (Cambridge: Cambridge University Press, 2006).

2 William J. Duiker, *China and Vietnam: The Roots of Conflict*, Indochina Research Monograph 1 (Berkeley: Institute of East Asian Studies, University of California, 1986), 3.

3 The water buffalo was domesticated in China about 4,000 years ago.

4   Keith Weller Taylor, *The Birth of Vietnam* (Oakland, CA: University of California Press, 1976), 70.

5   Jay Taylor, *China and Southeast Asia: Peking's Relations with Revolutionary Movements* (New York: Praeger Publishers, 1976), 48–54.

6   Hock-Lam Chan, 'The Chien-Wen, Yung-Lo, Hung-Hsi, and Hsüan-Te Reigns, 1399–1435', in *The Cambridge History of China. Volume 7: The Ming Dynasty, 1368–1644, Part I*, ed. Pierre-Etienne Will (Cambridge: Cambridge University Press, 1990), 229.

7   David Joel Steinberg, ed., *In Search of Southeast Asia : A Modern History* (Honolulu: University of Hawaii Press, 1985), 73–74.

8   Ben Kiernan, *Blood and Soil: A World History of Genocide and Extermination from Sparta to Dafur* (New Haven, CT: Yale University Press, 2007), 110.

9   Oscar Chapuis, *A History of Vietnam: From Hong Bang to Tu Duc* (Westport, CT: Greenwood Press, 1995), 46.

10 Steinberg, *In Search of Southeast Asia : A Modern History*, 74.

11 Frédéric Mantienne, *Monseigneur Pigneau de Béhaine* (Monsignor Pigneau de Béhaine), Paris : Editions Eglises d'Asie, 1999), 78.

12 Mark W. McLeod, *The Vietnamese Response to French Intervention, 1862–1874* (Westport, CT: Greenwood Publishing Group, 1991).

13 Jean-Pascal Bassino, 'Public Finance in Vietnam under French Rule, 1895–1954', *Quantitative Economic History of Vietnam* 1990 (1900): 269–92.

14 Ibid.

15 Lauriston Sharp, 'Colonial Regimes in Southeast Asia', *Far Eastern Survey* 15, no. 4 (1946): 49–53.

16 Kim Khánh Huỳnh, *Vietnamese Communism, 1925–1945* (Ithaca, NY: Cornell University Press, 1986).

17 William J. Duiker, *Ho Chi Minh: A Life* (Paris: Hachette Books, 2012).

18 Zeng Xueming became pregnant but her mother persuaded her to abort the child because of Ho's uncertain existence.

19 Long-Hsuen Hsu, Ming-Kai Chang, and Ha-Hsing Wen, *History of the Sino-Japanese War*, 2nd ed. (Taipei: Chung Wu Publishing Company, 1972).

20 George Kilpatrick Tanham, *Communist Revolutionary Warfare: The Vietminh in Indochina*, 96 (New York: Praeger Publishers, 1967).

21 Duiker, *Ho Chi Minh: A Life*.

22 Martin Windrow, *The Last Valley: Dien Bien Phu and the French Defeat in Vietnam* (London: Hachette UK, 2011), 412.

23 John Prados, *The Sky Would Fall: Operation Vulture: The US Bombing Mission in Indochina, 1954* (New York: Dial Press, 1983).

24 Thomas J. Christensen, *Worse than a Monolith: Alliance Politics and Problems of Coercive Diplomacy in Asia*, Princeton Studies in International History and Politics (Princeton, N.J: Princeton University Press, 2011), Chap. 6.

25 翟强 Zhai Qiang, *China and the Vietnam Wars, 1950–1975*, The New Cold War History (Chapel Hill: University of North Carolina Press, 2000).

26 陈兼 Chen Jian, 'China's Involvement in Vietnam, 1964–1969', *China Quarterly*, no. 142 (June 1995): 356–87.

27 Duiker, *China and Vietnam*, 44.

28 Duiker, 50.

29 Lewis Sorley, *Westmoreland: The General Who Lost Vietnam* (Boston, MA: Houghton Mifflin Harcourt, 2011).

30 Carl Berger et al., 'The United States Air Force in Southeast Asia, 1961–1973' (DTIC Document, 1977), 366.

31 C. Michael Hiam, *Who the Hell Are We Fighting: The Story of Sam Adams and the Vietnam Intelligence Wars* (Hanover: Steerforth Press, 2006).

32 John A. Farrell, 'Nixon's Vietnam Treachery', *The New York Times*, 31 December, 2016, https://www.nytimes.com/2016/12/31/opinion/sunday/nixons-vietnam-treachery.html.

33 David Model, *Lying for Empire: How to Commit War Crimes with a Straight Face* (Monroe, ME: Common Courage Press, 2005), 140.

34 Draft memorandum from Defense Secretary Robert McNamara to President Johnson, 3 November 1965.

35 Ellesberg, as quoted in Oliver Stone and Peter Kuznick, *The Untold History of the United States* (New York: Simon and Schuster, 2012), 385.

36 Wilfred G. Burchett, *The China-Cambodia-Vietnam Triangle* (Lahore, Pakistan: Vanguard books, 1981).

37 Jacob Bercovitch, 'Superpowers and Client States: Analysing Relations and Patterns of Influence,' in *Superpowers and Client States in the Middle East: The Imbalance of Influence* (New York: Routledge, Chapman & Hall, 1991), 9–32.

38 Bruce Grant, *The Boat People: An Age Investigation* (Harmondsworth: Penguin Books, 1979).

39 Guy Faure and Laurent Schwab, *Japan-Vietnam: A Relation under Influences* (Singapore: NUS Press, 2008), 56.

40 Joseph Y.S. Cheng, 'Sino-Vietnamese Relations in the Early Twenty-First Century: Economics in Command?', *Asian Survey* 51, no. 2 (1 March, 2011): 379–405, https://doi.org/10.1525/AS.2011.51.2.379.

41 明确方向，逐步推进，大局为重，要好协商. Clarify the direction, proceed step-by-step, keep in mind the big picture, and consult in a cordial spirit.

42 Conceived by Jawaharlal Nehru and Zhou Enlai in 1954, the Five Principles are: mutual respect for each other's territorial integrity and sovereignty, mutual non-aggression, mutual non-interference in each other's internal affairs, equality and cooperation for mutual benefit, and peaceful coexistence 独立自主、完全平等、互相尊重、互不干涉内部事务.

43 林明华 Lin Minghua, '中越关系正常化十周年回顾与展望 Tenth Anniversary of the Normalization of Sino-Viet Relations: Retrospect and Prospect', 当代亚太 *Contemporary Asia-Pacific*, no. 12 (2001): 49.

Chapter 5

1 See Volumes 5 and 6 of the 12-volume Ming dynasty work by Zhang Xie 张燮 called the *Research on Eastern and Western Oceans* 东西洋考 published in 1617.

2 Maria Christine Halili, *Philippine History* (Manila: Rex Bookstore, Inc., 2004), 49.

3 Teodoro A. Agoncillo and Oscar M. Alfonso, *History of the Filipino People*, Revised ed. (Quezon City, 1971), 58.

4 Ibid., 27–28.

5 Berthold Laufer, 'The Relations of the Chinese to the Philippine islands', in *European Entry into the Pacific : Spain and the Acapulco and Manila Galleons,* (Abingdon: Routledge, 2017), 55-92.

6 William Lytle Schurz, *The Manila Galleon* (New York: E.P. Dutton, 1939).

7 Agoncillo and Alfonso, *History of the Filipino People*, 647.

8 Ibid., 420.

9 David P. Barrows, *History of the Philippines*, Rev. ed. (Yonkers-on-Hudson, N.Y., Chicago: World Book Company, 1924), 154–55.

10 Edgar Wickberg, *Chinese in Philippine Life, 1850–98* (New Haven: Yale University Press, 1965), 4–6.

11 Sangley probably comes from the Chinese *shanglü* 商旅, or merchant, but it soon became a term of derogation.

12 Margaret Wyant Horsley, *Sangley: The Formation of Anti-Chinese Feeling in the Philippines, a Cultural Study of the Stereotypes of Prejudice* (New York: Columbia University Press, 1950).

13 Wickberg, *Chinese in Philippine Life, 1850–98*, 10–11.

14 Sir John Bowring, *A Visit to the Philippine Islands* (Manila: Filipiniana Book Guild, 1859), 70.

15 David Joel Steinberg, ed., *In Search of Southeast Asia : A Modern History* (Honolulu: University of Hawaii Press, 1985), 93.

16 Antonio S. Tan, 'The Chinese Mestizos and the Formation of the Filipino Nationality', *Archipel* 32, no. 1 (1986): 141–62.

17 Kwok-Chu Wong, *The Chinese in the Philippine Economy, 1898–1941* (Manila, Philippines: Ateneo de Manila University Press, 1999), 21.

18 Antonio S. Tan, 'The Chinese Mestizos and the Formation of the Filipino Nationality', *Archipel* 32, no. 1 (1986): 141–62, https://doi.org/10.3406/arch.1986.2316.

19 Wickberg, *Chinese in Philippine Life, 1850–98*, 144.

20 Gregorio Sancianco, *The Progress of the Philippines: Economic, Administrative and Political Studies: Economic Part*, trans. Encarnacion Alzona (Manila: National Historical Institute, 1975).

21 Esteban de Ocampo, 'Chinese Greatest Contribution to the

Philippines – The Birth of Dr. Jose Rizal', in *Chinese Participation in Philippine Culture and Economy* (Manila: Bookman, 1964), p. 89–95.

22 Steinberg, *In Search of Southeast Asia: A Modern History*, 160.

23 Raymond Nelson, *The Philippines* (London: Thames and Hudson, 1968), 101.

24 Renato Constantino, *The Philippines: A Past Revisited* (Detroit, MI: Tala Publishing Services, 1975).

25 Agoncillo and Alfonso, *History of the Filipino People*, 136.

26 Antonio S. Tan, *The Chinese in the Philippines, 1898–1935: A Study of Their National Awakening* (Manila: RP Garcia Pub. Co., 1972).

27 *Katungkulang Gagawin ng mga* Z.Ll.B. where Z.Ll.B was Katipunan code for A.B.N. – *anak ng bayan* or sons of the people.

28 Agoncillo and Alfonso, *History of the Filipino People*, 193.

29 Ibid., 234.

30 Teodoro A. Agoncillo, *Introduction to Filipino History* (Manila: Radiant Star Pub., 1974).

31 The US Senate approved the treaty by a vote of 57 to 27, only one vote more than the two-thirds majority required.

32 Paolo E. Coletta, 'McKinley, the Peace Negotiations, and the Acquisition of the Philippines', *Pacific Historical Review* 30, no. 4 (1961): 341–50.

33 Leon Wolff, *Little Brown Brother: America's Forgotten Bid for Empire Which Cost 250,000 Lives* (White Plains, NY: Kraus Reprint Co., 1970).

34 Agoncillo and Alfonso, *History of the Filipino People*, 256–57.

35 William H. Blanchard, *Neocolonialism American Style, 1960–2000*, 372 (Westport, CT: Greenwood Publishing Group, 1996), 130.

36 John R.M. Taylor, *The Philippine Insurrection against the United States: A Compilation of Documents with Notes and Introduction*, vol. 2 (Eugenio Lopez Foundation, 1971).

37 Teresita Ang See and Bon Juan Go, The Ethnic Chinese in the Philippine Revolution (Manila: Kaisa Para Sa Kaunlaran, 1996).

38 The British occupied the city of Manila and the port of Cavite for 20 months; the occupation ended as part of the settlement of the Seven Years' War.

39 John R.M. Taylor, *The Philippine Insurrection against the United States: A Compilation of Documents with Notes and Introduction*, vol. 2 (Pasig City, Philippines: Eugenio Lopez Foundation, 1971).

40 Arnaldo Dumindin, 'Philippine-American War, 1899–1902', 2009.

41 Ibid.

42 Howard Zinn, *A People's History of the United States: From 1492 to the Present*, 2nd ed. (London: Longman, 1996), 230.

43 James Bradley, *The Imperial Cruise: A Secret History of Empire and War* (London: Hachette UK, 2009).

44 Zedong Mao, 'Problems of War and Strategy (6 November 1938)', in Selected Works of Mao Zedong, Vol. II (Beijing: Foreign Languages Press, 1961), 225..

45 Mark Twain, 'To the Person Sitting in Darkness', *The North American Review* 172, no. 531 (1901): 161–76.

46 Michael H. Hunt and Steven I. Levine, *Arc of Empire: America's Wars in Asia from the Philippines to Vietnam* (Chapel Hill, NC: University of North Carolina Press, 2012), 55.

47 Wong, *The Chinese in the Philippine Economy, 1898–1941*, 27.

48 Ibid., 28.

49 Ibid., 56.

50 Ibid., chap. 2.

51 Ibid., 74.

52 國民革命軍北伐 The Northern Expedition was a military campaign launched by the Kuomintang army in 1926 to reunify the country.

53 Agoncillo and Alfonso, *History of the Filipino People*, 470–80.

54 Antonio S. Tan, *The Chinese in the Philippines during the Japanese Occupation, 1942–1945* (Quezon City, Philippines: University of the Philippines Press, 1981), 37–39.

55 Theresa C. Cariño, *Chinese Big Business in the Philippines: Political Leadership and Change* (Singapore: Time Academic Press, 1998), 22.

56 Caroline S. Hau, *The Chinese Question: Ethnicity, Region and Nation in and beyond the Philippines* (Singapore: NUS Press, 2014), 174–75.

57 The Philippine Anti-Japanese Guerrilla Force 菲律宾抗日支队 or *Huazhi* for short.

58 Yuk-Wai Li, *The Huaqiao Warriors: Chinese Resistance Movements in the Philippines, 1942–1945* (Quezon City: Ateneo de Manila University Press, 1996), 107–8.

59 Tan, *The Chinese in the Philippines during the Japanese Occupation, 1942–1945*, 80.

60 Ibid., 114.

61 *Daily News*, Manila, September 25, 1945.

62 Quoted in Yuk-Wai, *The Huaqiao Warriors: Chinese Resistance Movements in the Philippines, 1942–1945*, 170.

63 Ibid., 6.

64 Da Chen, *Emigrant Communities in South China: A Study of Overseas Migration and Its Influence on Standards of Living and Social Change* (New York: Secretariat, Institute of Pacific Relations, 1940).

65 Wong, *The Chinese in the Philippine Economy, 1898–1941*, 79–80.

66 Cariño, *Chinese Big Business in the Philippines: Political Leadership and Change*, 137.

67 Excerpts from Senator Claro M. Recto's commencement address at the University of the Philippines on 17 April 1951 regarding the foreign policy of the republic.

68 Oliver Holmes, 'Philippines Cannot Be "the Little Brown Brothers of America", Says Minister', *The Guardian*, September 16, 2016, sec. World news, https://www.theguardian.com/world/2016/sep/16/philippines-we-cannot-be-the-little-brown-brothers-of-america.

Chapter 6

1 The Neolithic in China ended with the introduction of metallurgy around 2,000 BC. In India, the Hindu civilization began to develop about 1,000 BC.

2 Many fragments of china of the Han dynasty have been found in Malaya.

3 Gerald Percy Dartford, *A Short History of Malaya* (Kuala Lumpur: Longmans of Malaysia, 1963), 9.

4 Paul Michel Munoz, *Early Kingdoms of the Indonesian Archipelago and the Malay Peninsula*, Reprint edition (Paris: Editions Didier Millet, 2016).

5   Ma Huan's *Yingyai Shenglan* 赢涯胜览、Fei Xin's *Xingcha Shenglan* 星槎胜览 and the *Ming Shi* 明史.

6   Gungwu Wang, 'The Opening of Relations between China and Malacca, 1403–5', in *Admiral Zheng He and Southeast Asia* (Singapore: Institute of Southeast Asian Studies, 2005).

7   Zainal Abidin bin Abdul Wahid, 'Glimpses of the Malacca Empire – 1', in *Glimpses of Malaysian History* (Kuala Lumpur: Dewan Bahasa dan Pustaka, 1980), 19.

8   Like many old weight systems, the tael was not an absolute standard but the Chinese tael was 37.5 grams or 1.2 troy ounces.

9   Victor Purcell, *The Chinese in Malaya* (Singapore: Oxford University Press, 1948), 17.

10 Jerome Ch'ên and Nicholas Tarling, eds., *Studies in the Social History of China and Southeast Asia: Essays in Memory of Victor Purcell* (Cambridge: Cambridge University Press, 1970), 397.

11 Mansel Longworth Dames, *The Book of Duarte Barbosa: An Account of the Countries Bordering on the Indian Ocean*, Vol. 2 (Abingdon: Routledge, 2016), sec. 110.

12 Anthony Reid, *Southeast Asia in the Age of Commerce, 1450–1680* (New Haven; London: Yale University Press, 1988), 271.

13 Brian Harrison, *South-East Asia: A Short History* (New York: St. Martin's Press, 1966).

14 Reid, *Southeast Asia in the Age of Commerce, 1450–1680*, 208.

15 David Joel Steinberg, ed., *In Search of Southeast Asia: A Modern History*, Rev. ed (Honolulu: University of Hawaii Press, 1987), 80.

16 Purcell, *The Chinese in Malaya*, 28.

17 Dartford, *A Short History of Malaya*, 52.

18 Purcell, *The Chinese in Malaya*, 36.

19 Constance Mary Turnbull, *The Straits Settlements, 1826–67: Indian Presidency to Crown Colony* (Atlantic Highlands, NJ: Athlone Press, 1972).

20 Singapore left the federation 9 August 1965.

21 颜清湟 Yen Ching-hwang, 'Historical Background', in *The Chinese in Malaysia* (New York: Oxford University Press, 2000), 2.

22 Purcell, *The Chinese in Malaya*, 29.

23 Ibid., 34.

24 Thomas Stamford Raffles, *The History of Java*, Vol. 2 (J. Murray, 1830), 224.

25 T.M. Ward and J.P. Grant, *Official Papers on the Medical Statistics and Topography of Malacca and Prince of Wales Island and on the Prevailing Diseases of the Tenasserim Coast* (Penang: Government Press, 1830), 2–3.

26 Purcell, *The Chinese in Malaya*, 62.

27 John Crawfurd, *History of the Indian Archipelago: Containing an Account of the Manners, Arts, Languages, Religions, Institutions, and Commerce of Its Inhabitants* (London: Cass, 1967).

28 Dartford, *A Short History of Malaya*, 118.

29 Ibid., 88–89.

30 Yen Ching-hwang, 'Historical Background', 6–7; Carl A. Trocki, 'The Rise and Fall of the Ngee Heng Kongsi in Singapore', in *'Secret Societies' Reconsidered* (Armonk, N.Y: M. E. Sharpe, 1993), 100.

31 Purcell, *The Chinese in Malaya*, 52.

32 Crawfurd, *History of the Indian Archipelago: Containing an Account of the Manners, Arts, Languages, Religions, Institutions, and Commerce of Its Inhabitants*.

33 Cursed hunger for gold

34 Thomas John Newbold, *Political and Statistical Account of the British Settlements in the Straits of Malacca* (2), Vol. 1 (London: J. Murray, 1839), 10.

35 Yen Ching-hwang, 'Historical Background', 28.

36 The workers were mainly Tamils.

37 Established by the British in 1895, the Federated Malay States (FMS) consisted of Selangor, Perak, Pahang and Negri Sembilan whose rulers gave up political power to the British. They were protectorates which shared common institutions. The first Resident General (governor) was Frank Swettenham.

38 Dartford, *A Short History of Malaya*, 146–47.

39 David Ownby, 'Secret Societies Reconsidered', in *'Secret Societies'*

Reconsidered: Perspectives on the Social History of Modern South China and Southeast Asia (Armonk, N.Y.: M. E. Sharpe, 1993).

40 Sharon A. Carstens, 'From Myth to History: Yap Ah Loy and the Heroic Past of Chinese Malaysians', *Journal of Southeast Asian Studies* 19, no. 2 (1988): 185–208.

41 John Michael Gullick, *The Story of Kuala Lumpur, 1857–1939* (Kuala Lumpur: Eastern Universities Press (M), 1983), chapter 4.

42 John Michael Gullick, *The Story of Early Kuala Lumpur* (Singapore: Donald Moore, 1956), chapter 15.

43 Ernest Chew, 'Frank Swettenham and Yap Ah Loy: The Increase of British Political "influence" in Kuala Lumpur, 1871–1885', *Journal of the Malaysian Branch of the Royal Asiatic Society* 57, no. 1 (246) (1984): 70–87.

44 Colin Barlow, *The Natural Rubber Industry. Its Development, Technology, and Economy in Malaysia.* (Singapore: Oxford University Press, 1978), 25.

45 Liew Seong Chee, 'The History and Development of the Hong Kong and Shanghai Banking Corporation in Peninsula Malaysia', in *Eastern Banking* (Atlantic Heights, NJ: Athlone Press, 1983), 352.

46 John G. Butcher, *The British in Malaya, 1880–1941: The Social History of a European Community in Colonial South-East Asia* (Singapore: Oxford University Press, 1979), 188.

47 Ibid., 185–86.

48 Ching Fatt Yong, *Tan Kah-Kee: The Making of an Overseas Chinese Legend* (Singapore: Oxford University Press, 1987).

49 陈嘉庚 Tan Kah-kee, 南桥回忆录 *Memoir of a Southeast Asian Chinese* (Singapore: Nanyang Publishing 南洋印刷社, 1946).

50 The Chinese People's Political Consultative Conference is a political advisory body in the People's Republic of China.

51 Raymond Callahan, *The Worst Disaster: The Fall of Singapore* (Newark, DE: Associated University Press, 1977), 196.

52 Lionel Wigmore, *The Japanese Thrust*, Vol. 4 (Canberra: Australian War Memorial, 1957).

53 Lord Moran of Manton, *Churchill: Taken from the Diaries of Lord*

Moran: The Struggle for Survival, 1940–1965 (London: Norman Berg, 1976).

54 Kevin Tan, *Marshall of Singapore: A Biography* (Singapore: Institute of Southeast Asian Studies, 2008).

55 Dartford, *A Short History of Malaya*, 187.

56 Hua-Lun Huang, *The Missing Girls and Women of China, Hong Kong and Taiwan: A Sociological Study of Infanticide, Forced Prostitution, Political Imprisonment,'Ghost Brides', Runaways and Thrownaways, 1900–2000s* (Jefferson, NC: McFarland, 2012), 206.

57 中原道子 Nakahara Michiko, 'Comfort Women in Malaysia', *Critical Asian Studies* 33, no. 4 (2001): 581–89.

58 Purcell, *The Chinese in Malaya*, 245.

59 Richard Stubbs, *Hearts and Minds in Guerrilla Warfare: The Malayan Emergency 1948–1960* (Singapore: Oxford University Press, 1989), 42.

60 Peng Chin, *Alias Chin Peng: My Side of History* (Singapore: Media Masters, 2003), 30.

61 F. Spencer Chapman, *The Jungle Is Neutral* (London: Chatto and Windus, 1949).

62 Nicholas J. White, *British Business in Post-Colonial Malaysia, 1957–70: Neo-Colonialism Or Disengagement?* (Abingdon: Routledge, 2004), 9.

63 Chin, *Alias Chin Peng*, 510.

64 KiniTV, *'Chin Peng Did Apply to Return Home'* 亲友力证陈平曾经申请回国, 2013, https://www.youtube.com/watch?v=dQOClJ76stQ.

65 F. Spencer Chapman, *The Jungle Is Neutral* (London: Chatto and Windus, 1949), 419.

66 The Unfederated Malay states were Johor, Kedah, Kelantan, Perlis, and Terengganu. Unlike the Federated Malay States, the Unfederated Malay States were standalone British protectorates without common institutions and did not form a single state under international law.

67 Anthony John Stockwell, *British Policy and Malay Politics during the Malayan Union Experiment, 1945–1948*, 8 (Kuala Lumpur: Art Printing Works, 1979).

68 Mohamed Noordin Sopiee, *From Malayan Union to Singapore Separation: Political Unification in the Malaysia Region 1945–1965* (Kuala Lumpur: Penerbit University Malaya, 1974), chapter 2.

69 Christopher Bayly and Tim Harper, *Forgotten Wars: The End of Britain's Asian Empire* (London: Penguin, 2008), chapter 3.

70 Article 153 of the Constitution safeguards the special position of the Malays.

71 Gordon P. Means, '"Special Rights" as a Strategy for Development: The Case of Malaysia', *Comparative Politics* 5, no. 1 (October 1972): 29, https://doi.org/10.2307/421353.

72 Gordon P. Means, *Malaysian Politics: The Second Generation* (Singapore: Oxford University Press, 1991), 7.

73 Leon Comber, *13 May 1969: The Darkest Day in Malaysian History* (Singapore: Marshall Cavendish, 2009), 70.

74 Tunku Abdul Rahman, *May 13 Before and After* (Kuala Lumpur: Utusan Melayu Press, 1969), 93–94.

75 John Slimming, *Malaysia: Death of a Democracy* (London: J. Murray, 1969), 29–48.

76 Government of Malaysia, *Emergency Ordinance No. 45 of 1970*.

77 Means, *Malaysian Politics: The Second Generation*, 23–27.

78 Jomo K. Sundaram, 'A Specific Idiom of Chinese Capitalism in Southeast Asia: Sino-Malaysian Capital Accumulation in the Face of State Hostility', in *Essential Outsiders* (Seattle, WA: University of Washington Press, 1997), 238.

79 Jeff Tan, 'Rent-Seeking and Money Politics in Malaysia', in *Routledge Handbook of Contemporary Malaysia* (Abingdon: Routledge, 2015); Syed Husin Ali, *The Malays: Their Problems and Future* (New York: The Other Press, 2008), 182.

80 Sundaram, 'A Specific Idiom of Chinese Capitalism in Southeast Asia: Sino-Malaysian Capital Accumulation in the Face of State Hostility', 252.

81 Daniel Chirot, 'Conflicting Identities', in *Essential Outsiders* (Seattle, WA: University of Washington Press, 1997), 26.

82 Robert Kuok and Andrew Tanzer, *Robert Kuok: A Memoir* (Singapore: Landmark Books, 2018).

83 Pek Koon Heng and Mei Ling Sieh Lee, 'The Chinese Business Community in Peninsular Malaysia, 1957–1999', in *The Chinese in Malaysia* (Singapore: Oxford University Press, 2000), 133–34.

84 Abdul Razak Baginda, *China-Malaysia Relations and Foreign Policy* (Abingdon: Routledge, 2016), chapter 6.

85 Ibid.

86 Mohamad is not a surname but a patronymic.

87 Mahathir Mohamad, *The Malay Dilemma* (Singapore: Donald Moore for Asia Pacific Press, 1970), 16.

88 Ibid., 24.

89 Ibid., 35.

90 Ibid., 76–77.

91 Ibid, 31.

92 Wawasan 2020 or Vision 2020 aimed to propel the country into the ranks of developed nations by 2020.

93 Barisan Nasional is the ruling coalition in power since independence.

94 'Dr M: I Failed to Change the Malays', *The Edge Markets*, 12 September, 2014, http://www.theedgemarkets.com/article/dr-m-i-failed-change-malays; Mahathir Mohamad, *Malays Are Lazy, Dishonest*, 2014, https://www.youtube.com/watch?v=fSlPGgQAtk8.

95 Mahathir Mohamad, I don't have any problems with China but I don't like American policies, September 17, 2013, https://www.youtube.com/watch?v=pCiFhnhXsd8; Mahathir Mohamad, *Mahathir on China*, June 25, 2015, https://www.youtube.com/watch?v=LAWmq0JIViA.

Chapter 7

1 Edward H. Schafer, *The Golden Peaches of Samarkand: A Study of T'ang Exotics* (Oakland, CA: University of California Press, 1963).

2 Friedrich Hirth, *China and the Roman Orient: Researches into Their Ancient and Mediaeval Relations as Represented in Old Chinese Records* (G. Hirth, 1885); Geoffrey Francis Hudson, *Europe and China: A Survey of Their Relations from the Earliest Times to 1800* (London: G. Hirth, 1931); Gungwu Wang, *The Nanhai Trade: Early Chinese Trade in*

the South China Sea, Ethnic Studies (Singapore: Eastern Universities Press, 2003).

3   Marwyn Samuels, *Contest for the South China Sea* (London: Methuen, 1982), 22–25.

4   *History of the Ming Dynasty* 明史

5   C.P. Fitzgerald, *The Southern Expansion of the Chinese People: Southern Fields and Southern Ocean* (London: Barrie and Jenkins, 1972), 100–16.

6   M. Taylor Fravel, *Strong Borders, Secure Nation: Cooperation and Conflict in China's Territorial Disputes*, Princeton Studies in International History and Politics (Princeton, N.J.: Princeton University Press, 2008), 267–99.

7   Chas Freeman, 'Diplomacy on the Rocks: China and Other Claimants in the South China Sea', *Chas W. Freeman Jr* (blog), 10 April, 2015, http://chasfreeman.net/diplomacy-on-the-rocks-china-and-other-claimants-in-the-south-china-sea/.

8   Mark Landler, 'Offering to Aid Talks, U.S. Challenges China on Disputed Islands', *The New York Times*, 23 July, 2010, sec. Asia Pacific, https://www.nytimes.com/2010/07/24/world/asia/24diplo.html.

9   According to the Cairo Declaration of 1943.

10 A survey on coastal mineral resources commissioned by the UN Economic Commission for Asia and the Far East (ECAFE) in 1968 indicated the presence of hydrocarbon reserves potentially rivalling the Persian Gulf.

11 The Cairo Conference of 22–26 November 1943 outlined Allied position against Japan during World War II and made decisions about postwar Asia.

12 The King of Na gold seal was discovered in 1784 on Shikanoshima Island 志賀島 in Fukuoka Prefecture, Japan.

13 琉球國 Liuqiu Kingdom (Chinese reading) or Ryūkyū Kingdom (Japanese reading) was an independent island kingdom stretching north to south from the Japanese island of Kyūshū to Taiwan until it was invaded by the Japanese in 1609.

14 菅沼雲龍 Suganuma Unryu, *Sovereign Rights and Territorial Space in*

Sino-Japanese Relations: Irredentism and the Diaoyu/Senkaku Islands (Honolulu: University of Hawaii Press, 2000), 46.

15 Ancient Chinese texts often refer to islands as 'mountains' 山.

16 小琉球 Xiaoliuqiu or 'little Liuqiu' the old Chinese name for Taiwan.

17 琉球國中山世鑑 *The Liuqiu Chūzan Chronicles*, Vol. 5 completed in 1650.

18 林子平 Hayashi Shihei's 三国通覧図説 *An Illustrated Description of Three Countries.*

19 井上清 Inoue Kiyoshi, 尖閣列島：釣魚諸島の史的解明 *Senkaku Islands: Historical Analysis of the Diaoyu Islands* (Tokyo: Gendai Hyōronsha, 1972). A specialist in modern Japanese history, Inoue taught at Kyoto University.

20 梅花港 Meihua – a port on the Fujian coast at the mouth of the Min River 闽江.

21 郭汝霖 Guo Rulin, 重刻史琉球錄 *Record of the Mission to the Ryukyu Kingdom*, Vol. 1 (China, 1561).

22 Suganuma Unryu, *Sovereign Rights and Territorial Space in Sino-Japanese Relations: Irredentism and the Diaoyu/Senkaku Islands*, 58.

23 A copy housed in the Bodleian Library of Oxford University was completed during the reign of the Emperor Wanli (1572–1620).

24 張廷玉 Zhang Tingyu, *History of the Ming Dynasty* 明史 (Shanghai: Zhonghua Book Company 中华书局, 1991).

25 福建沿海山沙图 *Map of Fujian Coastal Mountains and Isles* drawn in 1562.

26 菅沼雲龍 Suganuma Unryu, *Sovereign Rights and Territorial Space in Sino-Japanese Relations: Irredentism and the Diaoyu/Senkaku Islands*, (Honolulu, HI: University of Hawaii Press, 2000), 63.

27 Ibid., 102–3.

28 吉原重康 Yoshiwara Shigeyasu, '琉球無人島の地理 Geography of Uninhabited Ryukyu Islands', 地理学雑誌 *Journal of Geology* 7, no. 20 (20 June, 1900): 177–82.

29 The Treaty of Shimonoseki was concluded between Japan and the Qing government of China on 17 April 1895 following China's defeat in the First Sino-Japanese War.

30 Japanese Ministry of Foreign Affairs, 'The Basic View on the Sovereignty over the Senkaku Islands'. www.mofa.go.jp/region/asia-paci/senkaku/index.html

31 'The Senkaku Islands: Japan's Basic Position on the Senkaku Islands and Facts' (Japanese Ministry of Foreign Affairs, March 2013), http://www.mofa.go.jp/region/asia-paci/senkaku/pdfs/senkaku_en.pdf.

32 Charles I. Bevans, ed., 'First Cairo Conference', in *Treaties and Other International Agreements of the United States of America 1776–1949*, Vol. 3 (Washington D.C., 1969), 858.

33 Charles I. Bevans, ed., 'Terms of Japanese Surrender', in *Treaties and Other International Agreements of the United States of America 1776–1949*, Vol. 3 (Washington D.C., 1969), 1204–5.

34 Ibid., 1251.

35 'Zhou Enlai's Statement on the Peace Treaty with Japan', *Xinhua News Agency*, 1951, http://www.straittalk88.com/uploads/5/5/8/6/55860615/appendix_13_--_prc_foreign_minister_chou_en-lais_statement_on_the_u.s._proposal_of_the_japanese_peace_treaty__1951_.pdf.

36 Article 3 of the Treaty of Peace with Japan gives the US sole powers of administration of Nansei Shoto south of 29 north latitude. In 1953 the US Civil Administration of the Ryukyus proclaimed (USCAR 27) that Nansei Shoto south of 29 latitude north included the Senkaku/Diaoyu Islands.

37 Yukinori Komine, *Negotiating the US–Japan Alliance: Japan Confidential* (Abingdon: Taylor & Francis, 2016), chapter 8.

38 Ezra F. Vogel, Gilbert Rozman, and Ming Wan, 'The US-Japan-China Triangle: Who's the Odd Man Out?', Asia Report (Wilson Center, 7 July, 2011) accessed May 21, 2016, https://www.wilsoncenter.org/sites/default/files/asia_rpt113.pdf.

39 'New Upsurge in Friendly Relations between China and Japan', *Beijing Review*, November 3, 1978, 16.

40 'Agreement with Japan Concerning the Ryukyu Islands and the Daito Islands', in *Congressional Record*, 92nd Congress, 1st session (Washington D.C., 1971).

41 Daily press briefing of Adam Ereli, Deputy Spokesman at the US State Department, Washington D.C., 24 March, 2004.

42 *2006 Report to Congress of the US-China Economic and Security Review Commission*, November 2006, p. 130.

43 Peter Navarro and Greg Autry, *Death by China: Confronting the Dragon – a Global Call to Action* (Upper Saddle River: Prentice Hall, 2011).

44 Mark E. Manyin, 'Senkaku (Diaoyu) Island Dispute: US Treaty Obligations', CRS Report for Congress (Congressional Research Service, 14 October, 2016).

45 Thomas Kane, 'China's Foundations: Guiding Principles of Chinese Foreign Policy', *Comparative Strategy* 20, no. 1 (2001): 45–55.

46 M. Fravel Taylor, *Strong Borders, Secure Nation: Cooperation and Conflict in China's Territorial Disputes*, Princeton Studies in International History and Politics (Princeton, N.J.: Princeton University Press, 2008), 1–2.

47 Ibid., 300.

48 Douglas Paal, 'Territorial Disputes in Asian Waters', *Carnegie Endowment for International Peace*, 16 October, 2012, http://carnegieendowment.org/2012/10/16/territorial-disputes-in-asian-waters/e1ex##.

49 Peter Nolan, 'Imperial Archipelagos,' *New Left Review*, II, no. 80, (April 2013): 77–95.

50 John Grenier, *The First Way of War: American War Making on the Frontier, 1607–1814*, 1st ed. (Cambridge: Cambridge University Press, 2008).

51 Peter Nolan, 'Imperial Archipelagos', *New Left Review*, no. 80, II (April 2013): 77–95.

Chapter 8

1 Angus Maddison, 'A Comparison of Levels of GDP per Capita in Developed and Developing Countries 1700-1980', *Journal of Economic History* 43, no. 1 (1983): 27–41.

2 From the arrival of Matteo Ricci *circa* 1580 to the First Opium War and the cessation of Hong Kong in 1841.

3   William Theodore de Bary, *Sources of Chinese Tradition: From 1600 through the Twentieth Century*, Vol. 2 (New York City: Columbia University Press, 1999), 321.

4   Nigel Cameron, *Barbarians and Mandarins: Thirteen Centuries of Western Travelers in China* (Chicago, IL: University of Chicago Press, 1976).

5   João de Pina-Cabral, *Between China and Europe: Person, Culture and Emotion in Macao* (London: Continuum, 2002).

6   John Phillips Cooper, 'The Decline of Spain and the Thirty Years War, 1609-59', in *New Cambridge Modern History IV* (Cambridge: Cambridge University Press, 1979).

7   Magong 馬公 the largest urban settlement in Penghu.

8   James W. Davidson, *The Island of Formosa: Past and Present* (Taipei: Southern Materials Center, 1988).

9   Frederic Wakeman, *Fall of Imperial China* (New York City: Simon and Schuster, 1977), 101.

10 Edict from the Qianlong Emperor on the occasion of Lord Macartney's mission to China, September 1793.

11 Thomas N. Layton, *The Voyage of the 'Frolic': New England Merchants and the Opium Trade* (Redwood City, CA: Stanford University Press, 1997), 28.

12 Articles IV and VI of the Treaty of Nanking.

13 Stuart Creighton Miller, 'Ends and Means: Missionary Justification of Force in Nineteenth Century China', in *The Missionary Enterprise in China and America* (Cambridge, MA: Harvard University Press, 1974), 257–58.

14 Peter Ward Fay, *The Opium War, 1840–1842: Barbarians in the Celestial Empire in the Early Part of the Nineteenth Century and the War by Which They Forced Her Gates Ajar* (Chapel Hill, NC: University of North Carolina Press, 2000).

15 Miller, 'Ends and Means: Missionary Justification of Force in Nineteenth Century China', 262.

16 French missionary Father Auguste Chapdelaine was executed on 29 February 1856 by Chinese authorities in Guangxi Province, which at the time was not opened to foreigners.

17 The Yuan Ming Gardens 圓明園, the emperor's summer palace, was a vast ensemble of lakes, gardens and palaces in Beijing covering nearly three square kilometres. An architectural wonder containing a priceless collection of artwork and historic antiques, its destruction represented an immeasurable loss of cultural heritage.

18 John K. Fairbank, 'Introduction: The Many Faces of Protestant Missions in China and the United States', in *The Missionary Enterprise in China and America* (Cambridge, MA: Harvard University Press, 1974), 20.

19 Alexander Saxton, *The Indispensable Enemy: Labor and the Anti-Chinese Movement in California* (Oakland, CA: University of California Press, 1975).

20 The act was only repealed in 1943 with the Magnuson Act which permitted an annual quota of 105 Chinese immigrants.

21 Michael H. Hunt, *The Making of a Special Relationship: The United States and China to 1914* (New York City: Columbia University Press, 1983).

22 Yenching 燕京 was an alternative name of old Beijing 北平.

23 The Hanlin Academy 翰林院, established in the 8th century by Tang Emperor Xuanzong, was an élite institution consisting of top Confucian scholars who served in the imperial court.

24 Philip West, 'Christianity and Nationalism: The Career of Wu Lei-Ch'uan at Yenching University', in *The Missionary Enterprise in China and America* (Cambridge, MA: Harvard University Press, 1974), 229.

25 陈独秀 Chen Duxiu, 'Christianity and the Chinese 基督教与中国人', *New Youth* 新青年, 1 February, 1920.

26 Tang Shaoyi 唐绍儀、Yan Fu 嚴復、Liang Qichao 梁啟超、Cai Yuanpei 蔡元培.

27 John K Fairbank, *The United States and China* (Cambridge, MA: Harvard University Press, 1948), 167–71.

28 John K. Fairbank, 'Introduction: The Many Faces of Protestant Missions in China and the United States', in *The Missionary Enterprise in China and America* (Cambridge, MA: Harvard University Press, 1974), 1.

29 Gladys Aylward and Christine Hunter, *Gladys Aylward: The Little Woman* (Chicago: Moody Press, 1970); 'Gladys Aylward, Missionary, Dies', *The New York Times*, January 4, 1970, sec. Archives, https://www.nytimes.com/1970/01/04/archives/gladys-aylward-missionary-dies-briton-who-prompted-inn-of-sixth.html.

30 Adrian A. Bennett and Kwang-ching Liu, 'Christianity in the Chinese Idiom: Young J. Allen and the Early Chiao-Hui Hsin Pao 教會新報 1868-1870', in *The Missionary Enterprise in China and America* (Cambridge, MA: Harvard University Press, 1974), 165.

31 *San Francisco Call*, 1 May 1899, p.1

32 The inexperienced Lord Napier was sent in 1834 to seek a settlement of dispute between British merchants and Chinese authorities but his mission failed in part due to the lack of understanding in Europe of the Chinese and their system of government.

33 *The Chinese Repository* 3:345, 393–405, 425–428 (1835).

34 *The Chinese Repository* 3:421, 428, 444 (1835).

35 David Abeel, *An Exhibition of the Claims of the World to the Gospel* (New York: Leopold Classic Library, 2016), 244.

36 Henrietta Shuck, *A Memoir of Mrs. Henrietta Shuck: The First American Female Missionary to China* (New York: Leopold Classic Library, 2015), 38.

37 McBryde circular, 14 January 1842, Vol. 1, no. 152, Board of Foreign Missions of the Presbyterian Church (BFMPC) archives.

38 Rana Mitter, *A Bitter Revolution: China's Struggle with the Modern World* (Oxford University Press, 2004), 3–40.

39 Western historians estimate at least 20 million deaths, comparable to losses suffered by the Soviet Union during World War II.

40 Rana Mitter, *Forgotten Ally: China's World War II, 1937–1945* (Boston, MA: Houghton Mifflin Harcourt, 2013).

41 'Soviet Says Difficulty in Manchurian Withdrawal', *The Canberra Times*, 8 May, 1946.

42 Percy Timberlake, *The 48 Group: The Story of the Icebreakers in China* (The 48 Group Club, 1994), chapter 1.

43 Southeast Asian Treaty Organization (SEATO) consisting of the US, France, Great Britain, Australia, New Zealand, the Philippines, Thailand and Pakistan was formed in September 1954 to contain the spread of communism in the region. Despite its name, the organization had only two Southeast Asian member states.

44 Zedong Mao, 'Problems of War and Strategy (6 November 1938)', in *Selected Works of Mao Zedong*, Vol. II, 1961, 225.

45 'Steeled in Battle', *Peking Review*, August 18, 1967.

46 'Puny Counter-Revolutionary Alliance', *Peking Review*, 18 August, 1967.

47 人民日报 Remin Ribao, 'Afro-Americans' Just Struggle Will Triumph', *Peking Review*, 18 August, 1967.

48 James C. Hsiung and Victor H. Li, 'Chinese Critique of the "Socialist Commonwealth": Implications for Proletarian Internationalism and Peaceful Coexistence', *The American Journal of International Law* 67, no. 5 (1973): 64–70.

49 Robert B. Semple Jr., 'President Ends 21-Year Embargo on Peking Trade', *The New York Times*, 11 June, 1971, sec. Archives, https:// www.nytimes.com/1971/06/11/archives/president-ends-21year-em-bargo-on-peking-trade-authorizes-export-of.html.

50 Yu Guangyuan, Stevine I. Levine, and Ezra F. Vogel, *Deng Xiaoping Shakes the World* (Norwalk, CT: Eastbridge, 2004).

51 Elizabeth Economy and Michel Oksenberg, eds., *China Joins the World: Progress and Prospects* (New York City: Council on Foreign Relations, 1999).

52 摸着石头过河 The phrase was originally uttered by vice-premier Chen Yun 陈云 on 7 April 1950 in a discussion about how to tackle inflation.

53 The eight Millennium Development Goals (MDG) adopted by the United Nations in 2000 to be achieved by 2015 include universal primary education, the eradication of extreme poverty and hunger, the promotion of gender equality and combatting HIV/AIDS, malaria and other diseases.

54 'The World Bank in China', World Bank, 28 March, 2017, http://www.worldbank.org/en/country/china/overview.

55 张勇进 Zhang Yongjin, 'Understanding Chinese Views of the Global Order', in *China and the New International Order* (Abingdon: Routledge, 2008), 161–62.

56 Robert D. Putnam, 'Diplomacy and Domestic Politics: The Logic of Two-Level Games', *International Organization* 42, no. 3 (1988): 427–60, https://doi.org/10.1017/S0020818300027697.

57 郑伟志 Weizhi Zheng, 'Independence Is the Basic Canon: An Analysis of the Principles of China's Foreign Policy', *Beijing Review* 28, no. 1 (7 January, 1985).

58 Judith F. Kornberg and John R. Faust, *China in World Politics*, 2nd ed. (Boulder, CO: Lynne Rienner Publishers, 2005).

59 Gabriel Wildau, Yizhen Jia, and Xinning Liu, 'Xi Says No One Can 'Dictate to the Chinese People', *Financial Times*, 18 December, 2018, https://www.ft.com/content/658e78ce-0287-11e9-99df-6183 d3002ee1.

60 Chas Freeman, *Interesting Times: China, America, and the Shifting Balance of Prestige* (Washington, DC: Just World Books, 2013).

61 With a Harvard law degree, Freeman accompanied Nixon to China as his interpreter in 1972.

62 Chas Freeman, 'China's Challenge to American Hegemony', (20 January, 2012), http://www.mepc.org/articles-commentary/speeches/chinas-challenge-american-hegemony.

63 Remarks by Lord Charles Powell at the Oxford Union in 15 November 2012.

64 Edward S. Steinfeld, *Playing Our Game: Why China's Rise Doesn't Threaten the West* (Oxford University Press, USA, 2010); Peter Nolan, *Is China Buying the World?* (Polity Press, 2012).

65 Graham Allison, Robert D. Blackwill, and Ali Wyne, *Lee Kuan Yew: The Grand Master's Insights on China, the United States, and the World* (Cambridge, Massachusetts: The MIT Press, 2013), 3, 7.

REFERENCES

Chapter 1

Dawson, Raymond Stanley. *The Legacy of China*. The Legacy Series. Oxford: Clarendon Press, 1964.

Kornberg, Judith F., and John R. Faust. *China in World Politics*. 2nd ed. Boulder, CO: Lynne Rienner Publishers, 2005.

Morris, Errol. *The Fog Of War: Eleven Lessons from the Life of Robert McNamara [DVD] [2004]*. DVD. Sony Pictures Home Entertainment, 2004.

Myers, David G. *Social Psychology*. 11th ed. New York: McGraw-Hill, 2013.

Rohl, John C.G. *The Kaiser and His Court: Wilhelm II and the Government of Germany*. Cambridge: Cambridge University Press, 1996.

Shambaugh, David. 'China Engages Asia: Reshaping the Regional Order.' *International Security* 29, no. 3 (1 January, 2005): 64–99. https://doi.org/10.1162/0162288043467496.

Weiner, Tim. 'Robert S. McNamara, Architect of a Futile War, Dies at 93.' *The New York Times*, July 7, 2009, sec. US. http://www.nytimes.com/2009/07/07/us/07mcnamara.html?pagewanted=6&r=1&th&emc=th.

Chapter 2

Berry, Mary Elizabeth. *Hideyoshi*. Cambridge, MA: Harvard University Press, 1982.

Bix, Herbert P. *Hirohito and the Making of Modern Japan*. 1st Perennial Ed. New York: HarperCollins, 2001.

Chang, Iris. *The Rape of Nanking: The Forgotten Holocaust of World War II*. London: Penguin, 1998.

Denecke, Wiebke, Wai-Yee Li, and Xiaofei Tian. *The Oxford Handbook of Classical Chinese Literature (1000 BCE–900 CE)*. Oxford: Oxford University Press, 2017.

Dening, Walter. *The Life of Toyotomi Hideyoshi*. 3rd ed. London: J.L. Thompson & Co. Ltd., 1930.

Dower, John W. 'The San Francisco System: Past, Present, Future in U.S.-Japan-China Relations.' *The Asia-Pacific Journal: Japan Focus*, February 23, 2014. http://apjjf.org/2014/12/8/John-W.-Dower/4079/article.html.

Dubois, Thomas David. 'Rule of Law in a Brave New Empire: Legal Rhetoric and Practice in Manchukuo.' *Law and History Review* 26, no. 2 (2008): 285–318.

Fairbank, John K., Edwin Oldfather Reischauer, and Albert Morton Craig. *East Asia: Tradition & Transformation*. Rev. Boston, Mass.: Houghton Mifflin, 1989.

Fogel, Joshua A. *Articulating the Sinosphere: Sino-Japanese Relations in Space and Time*. Cambridge, MA: Harvard University Press, 2009.

———. *Maiden Voyage: The Senzaimaru and the Creation of Modern Sino-Japanese Relations*. Oakland, CA: University of California Press, 2014.

Hirano Kunio, 平野邦雄. '日、朝、中三國関係論についての覚書 Memorandum on Theory of Sino-Korean-Japanese Relations.' 東京女子大学付属比較文化研究所紀要 41 (1980): 101–30.

Ju, Zhifen. 'Japan's Atrocities of Conscripting and Abusing North China Draftees after the Outbreak of the Pacific War.' *Joint Study of the Sino-Japanese War*, 2002.

Kamen, Al. 'Among Leaders at Summit, Hu's First.' *The Washington Post*, April 14, 2010, sec. Politics. http://www.washingtonpost.com/wp-dyn/content/article/2010/04/13/AR2010041304461.html.

Kang, David. *East Asia before the West: Five Centuries of Trade and Tribute*. New York: Columbia University Press, 2010.

Kawashima Shin, 川島真. 'Historical Dialog and Documentary Research.' In *Toward a History beyond Borders*. Cambridge, MA: Harvard University Asia Center, 2012.

Kerr, George H. *Okinawa: The History of an Island People*. Rev. Rutland, Vt; Tokyo: Tuttle Publishing, 2000.

Kratoska, Paul H. *Asian Labor in the Wartime Japanese Empire: Unknown Histories*. Abingdon: Routledge, 2014.

McCormack, Gavan. 'Obama vs Okinawa.' *New Left Review*, II, no. 64 (2010): 5–26.

Suzuki Shogo, 鈴木章悟. *Civilization and Empire: China and Japan's Encounter with European International Society.* The New International Relations. London: Routledge, 2009.

'The Unquiet Past.' *The Economist*, August 12, 2015. http://www.economist.com/news/essays/en/asia-second-world-war-ghosts.

Tsunoda Ryūsaku, 角田 柳作, and L. Carrington Goodrich. *Japan in the Chinese Dynastic Histories: Later Han through Ming Dynasties.* Vol. no. 2. Perkins Asiatic Monographs. South Pasadena [Calif.]: P.D. and I. Perkins, 1951.

Turnbull, Stephen R. *Samurai Invasion: Japan's Korean War, 1592–98.* London: Cassell & Co, 2002.

Wang Zhenping, 王貞平. *Ambassadors from the Islands of Immortals: China-Japan Relations in the Han-Tang Period.* Asian Interactions and Comparisons. Honolulu, HI: Association for Asian Studies; University of Hawaii Press, 2005.

Ward, Sir Adolphus William, George Walter Prothero, Sir Stanley Mordaunt Leathes, and Ernest Alfred Benians. *The Cambridge Modern History.* London: Macmillan, 1910.

Yahuda, Michael. *Sino-Japanese Relations After the Cold War: Two Tigers Sharing a Mountain.* Routledge, 2013. http://www.routledge.com/books/details/9780415843089/.

Zachmann, Urs Matthias. *China and Japan in the Late Meiji Period: China Policy and the Japanese Discourse on National Identity, 1895–1904.* London; New York: Routledge, 2009.

Zhao Quansheng, 趙全勝. *Japanese Policymaking: The Politics behind Politics: Informal Mechanisms and the Making of China Policy.* Westport, Conn.: Praeger, 1993.

Chapter 3

Allen, Matthew. 'Wolves at the Back Door : Remembering the Kumejima Massacres.' In *Islands of Discontent.* Lanham, Md,: Rowman & Littlefield Publishers, 2003.

Dower, John W. *War without Mercy: Race and Power in the Pacific War.* London: Faber, 1986.

Duara, Prasenjit. *Rescuing History from the Nation: Questioning Narratives of Modern China.* Chicago; London: University of Chicago Press, 1995.

Eiko, Asato. 'Okinawan Identity and Resistance to Militarization and Maldevelopment.' In *Islands of Discontent.* Lanham, Md.: Rowman & Littlefield Publishers, 2003.

Isako Angst, Linda. 'The Rape of a Schoolgirl.' In *Islands of Discontent.* Lanham, Md.: Rowman & Littlefield Publishers, 2003.

Johnson, Jesse. 'In First, U.S. Admits Nuclear Weapons Were Stored in Okinawa during Cold War.' *The Japan Times Online,* February 20, 2016. http://www.japantimes.co.jp/news/2016/02/20/national/history/first-u-s-admits-nuclear-weapons-stored-okinawa-cold-war/?utm_source=Daily+News+Updates&utm_campaign=f547f22477-Sunday_email_updates21_02_2016&utm_medium=email&utm_term=0_c5a6080d40-f547f22477-332789745.

Kerr, George H. *Okinawa: The History of an Island People.* Rev. Tokyo: Tuttle Publishing, 2000.

McCormack, Gavan, and Satoko Oka Norimatsu. *Resistant Islands: Okinawa Confronts Japan and the United States.* Lanham, Md.: Rowman & Littlefield Publishers, 2012.

Rabson, Steve. 'Memories of Okinawa: Life and Times in the Greater Osaka Diaspora.' In *Islands of Discontent.* Lanham, Md.: Rowman & Littlefield Publishers, 2003.

———. *The Okinawan Diaspora in Japan: Crossing the Borders Within.* University of Hawai'i Press, 2012.

Sakamaki, Shunzō. 'Ryukyu and Southeast Asia.' *The Journal of Asian Studies* 23, no. 3 (1964): 383–89.

Smits, Gregory. *Visions of Ryukyu: Identity and Ideology in Early-Modern Thought and Politics.* Honolulu: University of Hawai'i Press, 1999.

Steben, Barry D. 'The Transmission of Neo-Confucianism to the Ryukyu Islands and Its Geopolitical Significance: Ritual and Rectification of Names in a Bipolar Authority Field.' In *Crossing the Yellow Sea.* Norwalk, CT: EastBridge, 2007.

Yonetani, Julia. 'Future "Assets", but at What Price? The Okinawa Initiative Debate.' In *Islands of Discontent*. Lanham, Md.: Rowman & Littlefield Publishers, 2003.

Chapter 4

Bassino, Jean-Pascal. 'Public Finance in Vietnam under French Rule, 1895–1954.' *Quantitative Economic History of Vietnam* 1990 (1900): 269–92.

Berger, Carl, Jack S. Ballard, Ray L. Bowers, Roland W. Doty Jr, and R. Frank Futrell. 'The United States Air Force in Southeast Asia, 1961–1973.' DTIC Document, 1977.

Bercovitch, Jacob. 'Superpowers and Client States: Analysing Relations and Patterns of Influence.' In *Superpowers and Client States in the Middle East: The Imbalance of Influence* (New York: Routledge, Chapman & Hall, 1991),

Burchett, Wilfred G. *The China-Cambodia-Vietnam Triangle*. Lahore, Pakistan: Vanguard books, 1981.

Chan, Hock-Lam. 'The Chien-Wen, Yung-Lo, Hung-Hsi, and Hsüan-Te Reigns, 1399–1435.' In *The Cambridge History of China. Volume 7: The Ming Dynasty, 1368-1644, Part I*, edited by Pierre-Etienne Will. Cambridge: Cambridge University Press, 1990.

Chapuis, Oscar. *A History of Vietnam: From Hong Bang to Tu Duc*. Westport, CT: Greenwood Press, 1995.

Chen Jian, 陈兼. 'China's Involvement in Vietnam, 1964–1969.' *China Quarterly*, no. 142 (June 1995): 356–87.

Cheng, Joseph Y.S. 'Sino-Vietnamese Relations in the Early Twenty-First Century: Economics in Command?' *Asian Survey* 51, no. 2 (1 March, 2011): 379–405. https://doi.org/10.1525/AS.2011.51.2.379.

Christensen, Thomas J. *Worse than a Monolith: Alliance Politics and Problems of Coercive Diplomacy in Asia*. Princeton Studies in International History and Politics. Princeton, N.J: Princeton University Press, 2011.

Duiker, William J. *China and Vietnam: The Roots of Conflict*. Indochina Research Monograph 1. Berkeley: Institute of East Asian Studies, Oakland, CA: University of California, 1986.

Duiker, William J. *Ho Chi Minh: A Life*. Hachette Books, 2012.

Farrell, John A. 'Nixon's Vietnam Treachery.' *The New York Times*, 31 December, 2016. https://www.nytimes.com/2016/12/31/opinion/sunday/nixons-vietnam-treachery.html.

Faure, Guy, and Laurent Schwab. *Japan-Vietnam: A Relation under Influences.* Singapore: NUS Press, 2008.

Grant, Bruce. *The Boat People: An Age Investigation.* Harmondsworth: Penguin Books, 1979.

Hiam, C. Michael. *Who the Hell Are We Fighting: The Story of Sam Adams and the Vietnam Intelligence Wars.* Hanover: Steerforth Press, 2006.

Hsu, Long-Hsuen, Ming-Kai Chang, and Ha-Hsing Wen. *History of the Sino-Japanese War.* 2nd ed. Taipei: Chung Wu Publishing Company, 1972.

Huỳnh, Kim Khánh. *Vietnamese Communism, 1925–1945.* Ithace, NY: Cornell University Press, 1986.

Kiernan, Ben. *Blood and Soil: A World History of Genocide and Extermination from Sparta to Dafur.* New Haven, CT: Yale University Press, 2007.

Lin Minghua, 林明华. '中越关系正常化十周年回顾与展望 Tenth Anniversary of the Normalization of Sino-Viet Relations: Retrospect and Prospect.' 当代亚太 *Contemporary Asia-Pacific*, no. 12 (2001): 46–51.

Mantienne, Frédéric. *Monseigneur Pigneau de Béhaine.* (Monsignor Pigneau de Béhaine), Paris: Editions Eglises d'Asie, 1999.

McLeod, Mark W. *The Vietnamese Response to French Intervention, 1862–1874.* Westport, CT: Greenwood Publishing Group, 1991.

Model, David. *Lying for Empire: How to Commit War Crimes with a Straight Face.* Monroe, ME: Common Courage Press, 2005.

Nguyen, Khac Giang. 'Vietnam's China Challenge.' *East Asia Forum*, 18 February, 2016. http://www.eastasiaforum.org/2016/02/18/vietnams-china-challenge-2/.

Prados, John. *The Sky Would Fall: Operation Vulture: The US Bombing Mission in Indochina, 1954.* New York: Dial Press, 1983.

Sharp, Lauriston. 'Colonial Regimes in Southeast Asia.' *Far Eastern Survey* 15, no. 4 (1946): 49–53.

Sorley, Lewis. *Westmoreland: The General Who Lost Vietnam.* Boston, MA: Houghton Mifflin Harcourt, 2011.

Steinberg, David Joel, ed. *In Search of Southeast Asia: A Modern History.* Honolulu: University of Hawaii Press, 1985.

Stone, Oliver, and Peter Kuznick. *The Untold History of the United States.* New York: Simon and Schuster, 2012.

Tanham, George Kilpatrick. *Communist Revolutionary Warfare: The Vietminh in Indochina.* 96. New York: Praeger Publishers, 1967.

Taylor, Jay. *China and Southeast Asia: Peking's Relations with Revolutionary Movements.* New York: Praeger Publishers, 1976.

Taylor, Keith Weller. *The Birth of Vietnam.* Oakland, CA: University of California Press, 1976.

'Viet-China Trade Likely to Reach $100 Billion.' vietnamnews.vn, 21 January, 2018. http://vietnamnews.vn/economy/421539/vn-china-trade-likely-to-reach-100-billion.html.

Vietnam. 'Chinese FDI in Vietnam: Growing Economic Ties, Despite Strains.' *Vietnam Briefing News,* 25 September, 2017. https://www.vietnam-briefing.com/news/vietnam-and-china-growing-economic-ties-despite-strains.html/.

Windrow, Martin. *The Last Valley: Dien Bien Phu and the French Defeat in Vietnam.* London: Hachette UK, 2011.

Womack, Brantly. *China and Vietnam: The Politics of Asymmetry.* Cambridge: Cambridge University Press, 2006.

Zhai Qiang, 翟强. *China and the Vietnam Wars, 1950–1975.* The New Cold War History. Chapel Hill: University of North Carolina Press, 2000.

Chapter 5

Agoncillo, Teodoro A. *Introduction to Filipino History.* Manila: Radiant Star Pub., 1974.

Agoncillo, Teodoro A., and Oscar M. Alfonso. *History of the Filipino People.* Revised ed. Quezon City, 1971.

Alvarez, Santiago V. *The Katipunan and the Revolution: Memoirs of a General.* Quezon City: Ateneo University Press, 1992.

Barrows, David P. *History of the Philippines*. Rev. ed. Yonkers-on-Hudson, N.Y., Chicago: World Book Company, 1924.

Blanchard, William H. *Neocolonialism American Style, 1960–2000*. 372. Westport, CT: Greenwood Publishing Group, 1996.

Bowring, Sir John. *A Visit to the Philippine Islands*. Manila: Filipiniana Book Guild, 1859.

Bradley, James. *The Imperial Cruise: A Secret History of Empire and War*. Hachette UK, 2009.

Cariño, Theresa C. *Chinese Big Business in the Philippines: Political Leadership and Change*. Singapore: Time Academic Press, 1998.

Chen, Da. *Emigrant Communities in South China: A Study of Overseas Migration and Its Influence on Standards of Living and Social Change*. Secretariat, Institute of Pacific Relations, 1940.

Coletta, Paolo E. 'McKinley, the Peace Negotiations, and the Acquisition of the Philippines.' *Pacific Historical Review* 30, no. 4 (1961): 341–350.

Constantino, Renato. *The Philippines: A Past Revisited*. Detroit, MI: Tala Publishing Services, 1975.

Dumindin, Arnaldo. 'Philippine-American War, 1899–1902', 2009.

Halili, Maria Christine. *Philippine History*. Manila: Rex Bookstore, Inc., 2004.

Hau, Caroline S. *The Chinese Question: Ethnicity, Region and Nation in and beyond the Philippines*. Singapore: NUS Press, 2014.

Holmes, Oliver. 'Philippines Cannot Be "the Little Brown Brothers of America", Says Minister.' *The Guardian*, September 16, 2016, sec. World news. https://www.theguardian.com/world/2016/sep/16/philippines-we-cannot-be-the-little-brown-brothers-of-america.

Horsley, Margaret Wyant. *Sangley: The Formation of Anti-Chinese Feeling in the Philippines, a Cultural Study of the Stereotypes of Prejudice*. New York: Columbia University Press, 1950.

Hunt, Michael H., and Steven I. Levine. *Arc of Empire: America's Wars in Asia from the Philippines to Vietnam*. Chapel Hill, NC: University of North Carolina Press, 2012.

Nelson, Raymond. *The Philippines*. London: Thames and Hudson, 1968.

Laufer, Bertauld. 'The relations of the Chinese to the Philippine Islands', in *European Entry into the Pacific*, 1st ed., London: Routledge.

Ocampo, Esteban de. 'Chinese Greatest Contribution to the Philippines – The Birth of Dr. Jose Rizal.' In *Chinese Participation in Philippine Culture and Economy*. Manila: Bookman, 1964.

Sancianco, Gregorio. *The Progress of the Philippines: Economic, Administrative and Political Studies: Economic Part*. Translated by Encarnacion Alzona. Manila: National Historical Institute, 1975.

Schurz, William Lytle. *The Manila Galleon*. Historical Conservation Society, 1985.

Steinberg, David Joel, ed. *In Search of Southeast Asia: A Modern History*. Honolulu: University of Hawaii Press, 1985.

Tan, Antonio S. *The Chinese in the Philippines, 1898–1935: A Study of Their National Awakening*. Manila: RP Garcia Pub. Co., 1972.

———. *The Chinese in the Philippines during the Japanese Occupation, 1942–1945*. Quezon City: University of the Philippines Press, 1981.

Tan, Antonio S. 'The Chinese Mestizos and the Formation of the Filipino Nationality.' *Archipel* 32, no. 1 (1986): 141–62.

Tan, Antonio S. 'The Chinese Mestizos and the Formation of the Filipino Nationality.' *Archipel* 32, no. 1 (1986): 141–62. https://doi.org/10.3406/arch.1986.2316.

Taylor, John R.M. *The Philippine Insurrection against the United States: A Compilation of Documents with Notes and Introduction*. Vol. 2. Pasig City, Philippines: Eugenio Lopez Foundation, 1971.

———. *The Philippine Insurrection against the United States: A Compilation of Documents with Notes and Introduction*. Vol. 2. Pasig City, Philippines: Eugenio Lopez Foundation, 1971.

Twain, Mark. 'To the Person Sitting in Darkness.' *The North American Review* 172, no. 531 (1901): 161–76.

Wickberg, Edgar. *Chinese in Philippine Life, 1850–98*. New Haven: Yale University Press, 1965.

Wolff, Leon. *Little Brown Brother: America's Forgotten Bid for Empire Which Cost 250,000 Lives*. Kraus Reprint Co., 1970.

Wong, Kwok-Chu. *The Chinese in the Philippine Economy, 1898–1941*. Quezon City: Ateneo de Manila University Press, 1999.

Yuk-Wai, Yung Li. *The Huaqiao Warriors: Chinese Resistance Movements in the Philippines, 1942–1945.* Quezon City: Ateneo de Manila University Press, 1996.

Zinn, Howard. *A People's History of the United States: From 1492 to the Present.* 2nd ed. London: Longman, 1996.

Chapter 6

Abdul Wahid, Zainal Abidin bin. 'Glimpses of the Malacca Empire – 1'. In *Glimpses of Malaysian History*. Kuala Lumpur: Dewan Bahasa dan Pustaka, 1980.

Ali, Syed Husin. *The Malays: Their Problems and Future.* New York City: The Other Press, 2008.

Baginda, Abdul Razak. *China-Malaysia Relations and Foreign Policy.* Abingdon: Routledge, 2016.

Barlow, Colin. *The Natural Rubber Industry. Its Development, Technology, and Economy in Malaysia.* Singapore: Oxford University Press, 1978.

Bayly, Christopher, and Tim Harper. *Forgotten Wars: The End of Britain's Asian Empire.* New York: Penguin, 2008. https://www.amazon.co.uk/Forgotten-Wars-Britains-Asian-Empire-ebook/dp/B002RI94N2/ref=sr_1_1?ie=UTF8&qid=1518162385&sr=8-1&keywords=harper+forgotten+wars.

Butcher, John G. *The British in Malaya, 1880–1941: The Social History of a European Community in Colonial South-East Asia.* Singapore: Oxford University Press, 1979.

Callahan, Raymond. *The Worst Disaster: The Fall of Singapore.* Newark, DE: Associated University Press, 1977.

Carstens, Sharon A. 'From Myth to History: Yap Ah Loy and the Heroic Past of Chinese Malaysians', *Journal of Southeast Asian Studies* 19, no. 2 (1988): 185–205

Chapman, F. Spencer. *The Jungle Is Neutral.* London: Chatto and Windus, 1949.

———. *The Jungle Is Neutral.* London: Chatto and Windus, 1949.

Chee, Liew Seong. 'The History and Development of the Hongkong and Shanghai Banking Corporation in Peninsula Malaysia'. In *Eastern Banking.* London: Athlone Press, 1983.

Ch'ên, Jerome and Tarling, Nicholas eds., *Studies in the Social History of China and Southeast Asia: Essays in Memory of Victor Purcell.* Cambridge: Cambridge University Press, 1970.

Chew, Ernest. 'Frank Swettenham and Yap Ah Loy: The Increase of British Political "influence" in Kuala Lumpur, 1871–1885', *Journal of the Malaysian Branch of the Royal Asiatic Society* 57, no. 1 (246) (1984).

Chin, Peng. *Alias Chin Peng: My Side of History.* Singapore: Media Masters, 2003.

Chirot, Daniel. 'Conflicting Identities'. In *Essential Outsiders.* Seattle, WA: University of Washington Press, 1997.

Comber, Leon. *13 May 1969: The Darkest Day in Malaysian History.* Singapore: Marshall Cavendish, 2009.

Crawfurd, John. *History of the Indian Archipelago: Containing an Account of the Manners, Arts,*

Languages, Religions, Institutions, and Commerce of Its Inhabitants. London: Cass, 1967.

Dames, Mansel Longworth. *The Book of Duarte Barbosa: An Account of the Countries Bordering on the Indian Ocean.* Vol. 2. Abingdon: Routledge, 2016.

Dartford, Gerald Percy. *A Short History of Malaya.* Kuala Lumpur: Longmans of Malaysia, 1963.

'Dr M: I Failed to Change the Malays.' *The Edge Markets*, 12 September, 2014. http://www.theedgemarkets.com/article/dr-m-i-failed-change-malays.

Harrison, Brian. *South-East Asia: A Short History.* New York: St. Martin's Press, 1966.

Heng, Pek Koon, and Mei Ling Sieh Lee. 'The Chinese Business Community in Peninsular Malaysia, 1957–1999.' In *The Chinese in Malaysia.* Singapore: Oxford University Press, 2000.

Huang, Hua-Lun. *The Missing Girls and Women of China, Hong Kong and Taiwan: A Sociological Study of Infanticide, Forced Prostitution, Political Imprisonment, 'Ghost Brides', Runaways and Thrownaways, 1900–2000s.* Jefferson, NC: McFarland, 2012.

Gullick, John Michael. *The Story of Kuala Lumpur, 1857-1939.* Kuala Lumpur: Eastern Universities Press (M), 1983.

Gullick, John Michael. *The Story of Early Kuala Lumpur.* Singapore: Donald Moore, 1956.

KiniTV. *'Chin Peng Did Apply to Return Home'* 亲友力证陈平曾经申请回国, 2013. https://www.youtube.com/watch?v=dQOClJ76stQ.

Kuok, Robert, and Andrew Tanzer. *Robert Kuok: A Memoir.* Singapore: Landmark Books, 2018.

Lord Moran of Manton. *Churchill: Taken from the Diaries of Lord Moran: The Struggle for Survival, 1940–1965.* London: Norman Berg, 1976.

Mahathir Mohamad. I don't have any problems with China but I don't like American policies, 17 September, 2013. https://www.youtube.com/watch?v=pCiFhnhXsd8.

———. *Mahathir on China*, 25 June, 2015. https://www.youtube.com/watch?v=LAWmq0JIViA.

———. *Malays Are Lazy, Dishonest*, 2014. https://www.youtube.com/watch?v=fSlPGgQAtk8.

———. *The Malay Dilemma.* Singapore: Donald Moore for Asia Pacific Press, 1970. http://umplibrary.ump.edu.my.

Means, Gordon P. *Malaysian Politics: The Second Generation.* Singapore: Oxford University Press, 1991.

———. '"Special Rights" as a Strategy for Development: The Case of Malaysia.' *Comparative Politics* 5, no. 1 (October 1972): 29. https://doi.org/10.2307/421353.

Munoz, Paul Michel. *Early Kingdoms of the Indonesian Archipelago and the Malay Peninsula.* Reprint edition. Paris: Editions Didier Millet, 2016.

Nakahara Michiko, 中原道子. 'Comfort Women in Malaysia.' *Critical Asian Studies* 33, no. 4 (2001): 581–89.

Newbold, Thomas John. *Political and Statistical Account of the British Settlements in the Straits of Malacca* (2). Vol. 1. 2 vols. London: J. Murray, 1839.

Purcell, Victor. *The Chinese in Malaya.* Singapore: Oxford University Press, 1948.

Raffles, Thomas Stamford. *The History of Java.* Vol. 2. J. Murray, 1830.

Rahman, Tunku Abdul. *May 13 Before and After*. Kuala Lumpur: Utusan Melayu Press, 1969.

Reid, Anthony. *Southeast Asia in the Age of Commerce, 1450–1680*. New Haven; London: Yale University Press, 1988.

See, Teresita Ang, and Bon Juan Go. *The Ethnic Chinese in the Philippine Revolution* (Malila: Kaisa Para Sa Kaunlaran, 1966.

Slimming, John. *Malaysia: Death of a Democracy*. London: J. Murray, 1969.

Sopiee, Mohamed Noordin. *From Malayan Union to Singapore Separation: Political Unification in the Malaysia Region 1945–1965*. Kuala Lumpur: Penerbit University Malaya, 1974.

Steinberg, David Joel, ed. *In Search of Southeast Asia: A Modern History*. Revised ed. Honolulu: University of Hawaii Press, 1987.

Stockwell, Anthony John. *British Policy and Malay Politics during the Malayan Union Experiment, 1945–1948*. 8. Kuala Lumpur: Art Printing Works, 1979.

Stubbs, Richard. *Hearts and Minds in Guerrilla Warfare: The Malayan Emergency 1948–1960*. Singapore: Oxford University Press, 1989.

Sundaram, Jomo K. 'A Specific Idiom of Chinese Capitalism in Southeast Asia: Sino-Malaysian Capital Accumulation in the Face of State Hostility.' In *Essential Outsiders*. Seattle, WA: University of Washington Press, 1997.

Tan, Jeff. 'Rent-Seeking and Money Politics in Malaysia.' In *Routledge Handbook of Contemporary Malaysia*. Abingdon: Routledge, 2015.

Tan Kah-kee, 陈嘉庚. 南桥回忆录 *Memoir of a Southeast Asian Chinese*. Singapore: Nanyang Publishing 南洋印刷社, 1946.

Tan, Kevin. *Marshall of Singapore: A Biography*. Institute of Southeast Asian Studies, 2008.

Trocki, Carl A. 'The Rise and Fall of the Ngee Heng Kongsi in Singapore.' In *'Secret Societies' Reconsidered*. Armonk, N.Y: M. E. Sharpe, 1993.

Turnbull, Constance Mary. *The Straits Settlements, 1826–67: Indian Presidency to Crown Colony*. Atlantic Highlands, NJ: Athlone Press, 1972.

Wang, Gungwu. 'The Opening of Relations between China and Malacca, 1403–5.' In *Admiral*

Zheng He and Southeast Asia. Singapore: Institute of Southeast Asian Studies, 2005.

Ward, T.M., and J.P. Grant. *Official Papers on the Medical Statistics and Topography of Malacca and Prince of Wales Island and on the Prevailing Diseases of the Tenasserim Coast.* Penang, Malaysia: Government Press,1830.

White, Nicholas J. *British Business in Post-Colonial Malaysia, 1957–70: Neo-Colonialism Or Disengagement?* Abingdon: Routledge, 2004.

Wigmore, Lionel. *The Japanese Thrust.* Vol. 4. Canberra: Australian War Memorial, 1957.

Yen Ching-hwang, 颜清湟. 'Historical Background.' In *The Chinese in Malaysia.* New York: Oxford University Press, 2000.

Yong, Ching Fatt. *Tan Kah-Kee: The Making of an Overseas Chinese Legend.* Singapore: Oxford University Press, 1987.

Chapter 7

'Agreement with Japan Concerning the Ryukyu Islands and the Daito Islands.' In *Congressional Record.* 92nd Congress, 1st session. Washington D.C., 1971.

Bevans, Charles I., ed. 'First Cairo Conference.' In *Treaties and Other International Agreements of the United States of America 1776–1949*, Vol. 3. Washington D.C., 1969.

———, ed. 'Terms of Japanese Surrender.' In *Treaties and Other International Agreements of the United States of America 1776–1949*, Vol. 3. Washington D.C., 1969.

Fitzgerald, C.P. *The Southern Expansion of the Chinese People: Southern Fields and Southern Ocean.* London: Barrie and Jenkins, 1972.

Fravel, M. Taylor. *Strong Borders, Secure Nation : Cooperation and Conflict in China's Territorial Disputes.* Princeton Studies in International History and Politics. Princeton, N.J.: Princeton University Press, 2008.

Freeman, Chas. 'Diplomacy on the Rocks: China and Other Claimants in the South China Sea.' *Chas W. Freeman Jr* (blog), 10 April, 2015. http:// chasfreeman.net/diplomacy-on-the-rocks-china-and-other-claimants-in-the-south-china-sea/.

Grenier, John. *The First Way of War: American War Making on the Frontier, 1607–1814*. 1st ed. Cambridge: Cambridge University Press, 2008.

Guo Rulin, 郭汝霖. 重刻史琉球錄 *Record of the Mission to the Ryukyu Kingdom*. Vol. 1. China, 1561.

Hirth, Friedrich. *China and the Roman Orient: Researches into Their Ancient and Mediaeval Relations as Represented in Old Chinese Records*. London: G. Hirth, 1885.

Hudson, Geoffrey Francis. *Europe and China: A Survey of Their Relations from the Earliest Times to 1800*. London: Edward Arnold and Co, 1931.

Inoue Kiyoshi, 井上清. 尖閣列島：釣魚諸島の史的解明 *Senkaku Islands: Historical Analysis of the Diaoyu Islands*. Tokyo: Gendai Hyōronsha, 1972.

Kane, Thomas. 'China's Foundations: Guiding Principles of Chinese Foreign Policy.' *Comparative Strategy* 20, no. 1 (2001): 45–55.

Komine, Yukinori. *Negotiating the US–Japan Alliance: Japan Confidential*. Abingdon: Taylor & Francis, 2016.

Landler, Mark. 'Offering to Aid Talks, U.S. Challenges China on Disputed Islands.' *The New York Times*, 23 July, 2010, sec. Asia Pacific. https://www.nytimes.com/2010/07/24/world/asia/24diplo.html.

Manyin, Mark E. 'Senkaku (Diaoyu) Island Dispute: US Treaty Obligations.' CRS Report for Congress. Congressional Research Service, 14 October, 2016.

Navarro, Peter, and Greg Autry. *Death by China: Confronting the Dragon – a Global Call to Action*. Upper Saddle River, NJ: Prentice Hall, 2011.

'New Upsurge in Friendly Relations between China and Japan.' *Beijing Review*, 3 November, 1978.

Nolan, Peter. 'Imperial Archipelagos', *New Left Review*, II, No. 80 (April 2013), 77–95.

Paal, Douglas. 'Territorial Disputes in Asian Waters.' *Carnegie Endowment for International Peace*, October 16, 2012. http://carnegieendowment.org/2012/10/16/territorial-disputes-in-asian-waters/e1ex##.

Samuels, Marwyn. *Contest for the South China Sea*. London: Methuen, 1982.

Schafer, Edward H. *The Golden Peaches of Samarkand: A Study of T'ang Exotics*. Oakland, CA: University of California Press, 1963.

Suganuma Unryu, 菅沼雲龍. *Sovereign Rights and Territorial Space in Sino-Japanese Relations: Irredentism and the Diaoyu/Senkaku Islands.* Honolulu: University of Hawaii Press, 2000.

'The Senkaku Islands: Japan's Basic Position on the Senkaku Islands and Facts.' Japanese Ministry of Foreign Affairs, March 2013. http://www.mofa.go.jp/region/asia-paci/senkaku/pdfs/senkaku_en.pdf.

Vogel, Ezra F., Gilbert Rozman, and Ming Wan. 'The US-Japan-China Triangle: Who's the Odd Man Out?' Asia Report (Wilson Center, 7 July, 2011) https://www.wilsoncenter.org/sites/default/files/asia_rpt 113.pdf. Accessed May 21, 2016. https://www.wilsoncenter.org/sites/default/files/asia_rpt113.pdf.

Wang, Gungwu. *The Nanhai Trade: Early Chinese Trade in the South China Sea.* Ethnic Studies. Singapore: Eastern Universities Press, 2003.

Yoshiwara Shigeyasu, 吉原重康. '琉球無人島の地理 Geography of Uninhabited Ryukyu Islands.' 地理学雑誌 *Journal of Geology* 7, no. 20 (20 June, 1900): 177–82.

Zhang Tingyu, 張廷玉. *History of the Ming Dynasty* 明史. Shanghai: Zhonghua Book Company 中华书局, 1991.

'Zhou Enlai's Statement on the Peace Treaty with Japan.' *Xinhua News Agency*, 1951. http://www.straittalk88.com/uploads/5/5/8/6/55860615/appendix_13_--_prc_foreign_minister_chou_en-lais_statement_on_the_u.s._proposal_of_the_japanese_peace_treaty__1951_.pdf.

琉球國中山世鑑 *The Liuqiu Chūzan Chronicles.* Vol. 5, 1650.

Chapter 8

Abeel, David. *An Exhibition of the Claims of the World to the Gospel.* New York: Leopold Classic Library, 2016.

Allison, Graham, Robert D. Blackwill, and Ali Wyne. *Lee Kuan Yew: The Grand Master's Insights on China, the United States, and the World.* Cambridge, Massachusetts: The MIT Press, 2013.

Aylward, Gladys, and Christine Hunter. *Gladys Aylward: The Little Woman.* Chicago: Moody Press, 1970.

Bary, William Theodore de. *Sources of Chinese Tradition: From 1600 through the Twentieth Century*. Vol. 2. New York City: Columbia University Press, 1999.

Bennett, Adrian A., and Kwang-ching Liu. 'Christianity in the Chinese Idiom: Young J. Allen and the Early Chiao-Hui Hsin Pao 教會新報 1868–1870.' In *The Missionary Enterprise in China and America*. Cambridge, MA: Harvard University Press, 1974.

Cameron, Nigel. *Barbarians and Mandarins: Thirteen Centuries of Western Travelers in China*. Chicago, IL: University of Chicago Press, 1976.

Chen Duxiu, 陈独秀. 'Christianity and the Chinese 基督教与中国人.' *New Youth* 新青年, 1 February, 1920.

Cooper, John Phillips. 'The Decline of Spain and the Thirty Years War, 1609–59.' In *New Cambridge Modern History IV*. Cambridge: Cambridge University Press, 1979.

Davidson, James W. *The Island of Formosa: Past and Present*. Taipei: Southern Materials Center, 1988.

Economy, Elizabeth, and Michel Oksenberg, eds. *China Joins the World: Progress and Prospects*. New York: Council on Foreign Relations, 1999.

Fairbank, John K. *The United States and China*. Cambridge, MA: Harvard University Press, 1948.

———. 'Introduction: The Many Faces of Protestant Missions in China and the United States.' In *The Missionary Enterprise in China and America*. Cambridge, MA: Harvard University Press, 1974.

Fay, Peter Ward. *The Opium War, 1840–1842: Barbarians in the Celestial Empire in the Early Part of the Nineteenth Century and the War by Which They Forced Her Gates Ajar*. Chapel Hill, NC: University of North Carolina Press, 2000.

Freeman, Chas. 'China's Challenge to American Hegemony.' 20 January, 2012. http://www.mepc.org/articles-commentary/speeches/chinas-challenge-american-hegemony.

———. *Interesting Times: China, America, and the Shifting Balance of Prestige*. Just World Books, 2013.

'Gladys Aylward, Missionary, Dies.' *The New York Times*, 4 January, 1970, sec. Archives. https://www.nytimes.com/1970/01/04/archives/gladys-aylward-missionary-dies-briton-who-prompted-inn-of-sixth.html.

Hsiung, James C., and Victor H. Li. 'Chinese Critique of the "Socialist Commonwealth": Implications for Proletarian Internationalism and Peaceful Coexistence.' *The American Journal of International Law* 67, no. 5 (1973): 64–70.

Hunt, Michael H. *The Making of a Special Relationship: The United States and China to 1914.* New York City: Columbia University Press, 1983.

Kornberg, Judith F. and John R. Faust. *China in World Politics.* 2nd ed. Boulder, CO: Lynne Rienner Publishers, 2005.

Layton, Thomas N. *The Voyage of the 'Frolic': New England Merchants and the Opium Trade.* Redwood City, CA: Stanford University Press, 1997.

Maddison, Angus. 'A Comparison of Levels of GDP per Capita in Developed and Developing Countries 1700–1980.' *Journal of Economic History* 43, no. 1 (1983): 27–41.

Mao Zedong. 'Problems of War and Strategy (6 November 1938)', in *Selected Works of Mao Zedong*, Vol. II. Beijing: Foreign Languages Press, 1961.

McBryde circular, 14 January 1842, Vol. 1, no. 152, Board of Foreign Missions of the Presbyterian Church (BFMPC) archives.

Miller, Stuart Creighton. 'Ends and Means: Missionary Justification of Force in Nineteenth Century China.' In *The Missionary Enterprise in China and America.* Cambridge, MA: Harvard University Press, 1974.

Mitter, Rana. *A Bitter Revolution: China's Struggle with the Modern World.* Oxford: Oxford University Press, 2004.

Mitter, Rana. *Forgotten Ally: China's World War II, 1937–1945.* Boston, MA: Houghton Mifflin Harcourt, 2013.

Nolan, Peter. *Is China Buying the World?* Cambridge: Polity Press, 2012.

Pina-Cabral, João de. *Between China and Europe: Person, Culture and Emotion in Macao.* London: Continuum, 2002.

'Puny Counter-Revolutionary Alliance', *Peking Review*, 18 August, 1967.

Putnam, Robert D. 'Diplomacy and Domestic Politics: The Logic of Two-Level Games.' *International Organization* 42, no. 3 (1988): 427–60. https://doi.org/10.1017/S0020818300027697.

Remin Ribao, 人民日报. 'Afro-Americans' Just Struggle Will Triumph.' *Peking Review*, 18 August, 1967.

Saxton, Alexander. *The Indispensable Enemy: Labor and the Anti-Chinese*

Movement in California. Oakland, CA: University of California Press, 1975.

Semple Jr., Robert B. 'President Ends 21-Year Embargo on Peking Trade.' *The New York Times*, 11 June, 1971, sec. Archives. https://www.nytimes.com/1971/06/11/archives/president-ends-21year-embargo-on-peking-trade-authorizes-export-of.html.

Shuck, Henrietta. *A Memoir of Mrs. Henrietta Shuck: The First American Female Missionary to China.* New York: Leopold Classic Library, 2015.

Schurz, William Lytle. *The Manila Galleon.* New York: E.P. Dutton, 1939.

'Soviet Says Difficulty in Manchurian Withdrawal.' *The Canberra Times*, 8 May, 1946.

Steinfeld, Edward S. *Playing Our Game: Why China's Rise Doesn't Threaten the West.* Oxford: Oxford University Press, USA, 2010.

'The World Bank in China.' World Bank, 28 March, 2017. http://www.worldbank.org/en/country/china/overview.

Timberlake, Percy. *The 48 Group: The Story of the Icebreakers in China.* The 48 Group Club, 1994.

Wakeman, Frederic. *Fall of Imperial China.* New York City: Simon and Schuster, 1977.

West, Philip. 'Christianity and Nationalism: The Career of Wu Lei-Ch'uan at Yenching University.' In *The Missionary Enterprise in China and America.* Cambridge, MA: Harvard University Press, 1974.

Wildau, Gabriel, Yizhen Jia, and Xinning Liu. 'Xi Says No One Can "Dictate to the Chinese People".' *Financial Times*, 18 December, 2018. https://www.ft.com/content/658e78ce-0287-11e9-99df-6183d3002ee1.

Yu, Guangyuan, Stevine I. Levine, and Ezra F. Vogel. *Deng Xiaoping Shakes the World: An Eyewitness Account of China's Party Work Conference and the Third Plenum (November–December 1978).* Norwalk, CT: EastBridge, 2004.

Zhang Yongjin, 张勇进. 'Understanding Chinese Views of the Global Order.' In *China and the New International Order.* Abingdon: Routledge, 2008.

Zheng Weizhi, 郑伟志. 'Independence Is the Basic Canon: An Analysis of the Principles of China's Foreign Policy.' *Beijing Review* 28, no. 1 (7 January, 1985).

INDEX

tribute system 15–8, 23, 28, 44, 46, 62, 142, 206, 221
Trung sisters 62
Tunku Abdul Rahman 180, 181, 186, 187
Twain, Mark 122

UMNO (United Malays National Organisation) 180
Unit 731 30

Victoria, Queen 227
Viet Minh 76, 77, 78, 80, 86
Vietcong 84, 88, 89

Vo Nguyen Giap 87, 75, 76, 77, 87

Westmoreland, William 84
Wu, Emperor 16, 60

Xi Jinping 244
Xu Fu 12, 13

Yap Ah Loy 160–2
Yasukuni Shrine 35

Zen monks 24
Zheng He 100